IMAGES
of America

DAYTONA BEACH
100 YEARS OF RACING

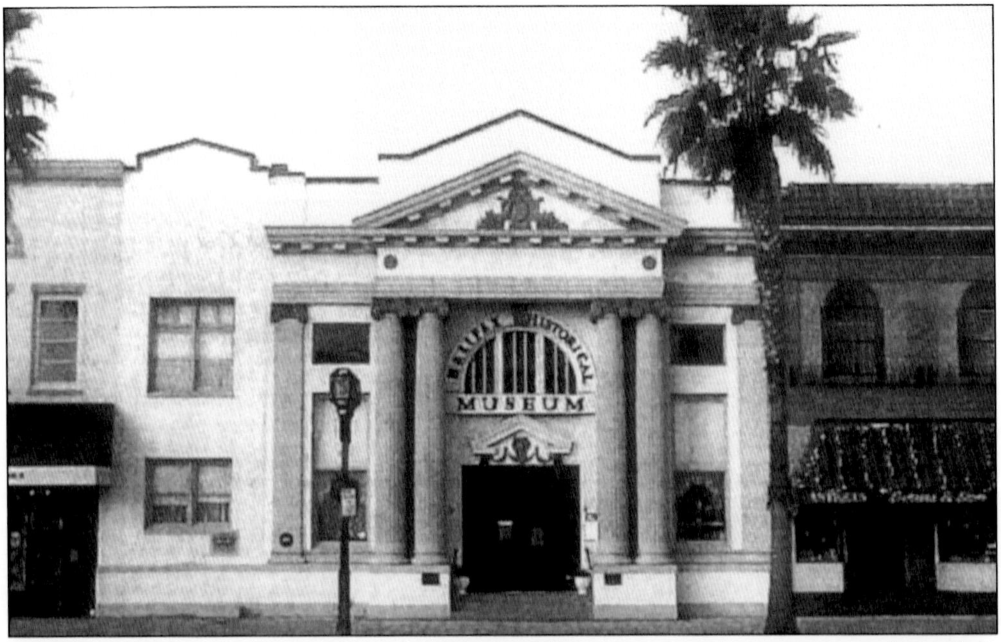

HALIFAX HISTORICAL SOCIETY AND MUSEUM. The society and museum are located at 252 South Beach Street in Daytona Beach and house the Lawson Diggett racing collection. Officers are as follows: Harold D. Cardwell Sr., president; Roy E. Midkiff, first vice president; Beth Mindlin, second vice president; Dr. Leonard Lempel, Ph.D., third vice president; John Mailhot, treasurer; Sonya Watkins, recording secretary; Virginia Buckner, corresponding secretary; Cheryl Atwell, museum director; and Joan Meyers, administrative assistant. (Courtesy of Paul Sexton.)

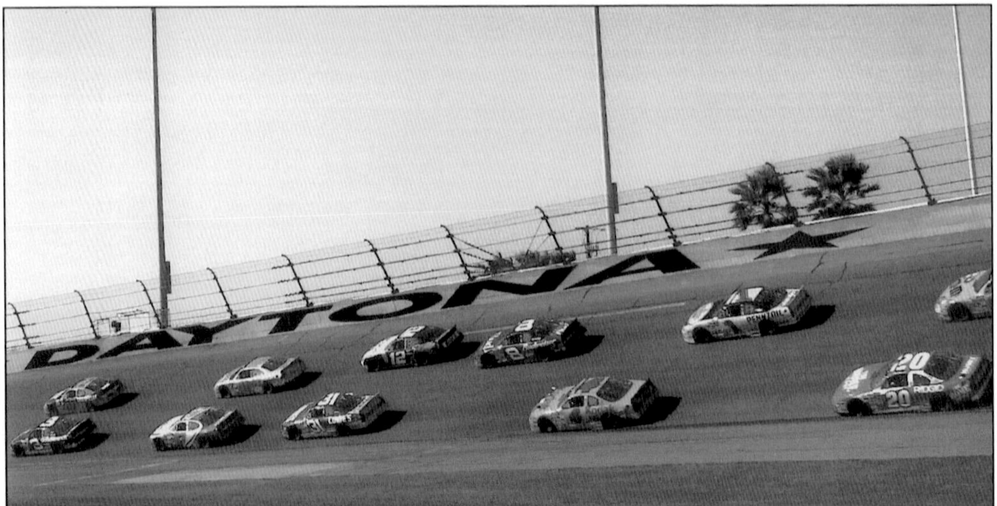

DAYTONA 500, FEBRUARY 18, 2001. Among the many drivers on the west bank are no. 3, the late Dale Earnhardt Sr.; no. 31, Mike Skinner; no. 12, Jeremy Mayfield; no. 8, Dale Earnhardt Jr.; no. 1, Steve Park; and no. 22, Ward Burton. The winners were as follows: first place, Michael Waltrip; second place, Dale Earnhardt Jr.; and third place, Rusty Wallace. (Courtesy of ISC Archives.)

IMAGES
of America

DAYTONA BEACH
100 YEARS OF RACING

Harold D. Cardwell Sr.

ARCADIA
PUBLISHING

ISBN 978-0-7385-1427-7

Published by Arcadia Publishing
Charleston, South Carolina

Printed in the United States of America

Library of Congress Catalog Card Number: 2002100886

For all general information contact Arcadia Publishing at:
Telephone 843-853-2070
Fax 843-853-0044
E-mail sales@arcadiapublishing.com
For customer service and orders:
Toll-Free 1-888-313-2665

Visit us on the Internet at www.arcadiapublishing.com

This book is dedicated to all the men and women who have attempted and broken speed records and won championships with automobiles or motorcycles at Daytona Beach, Florida—The World's Most Famous Beach.

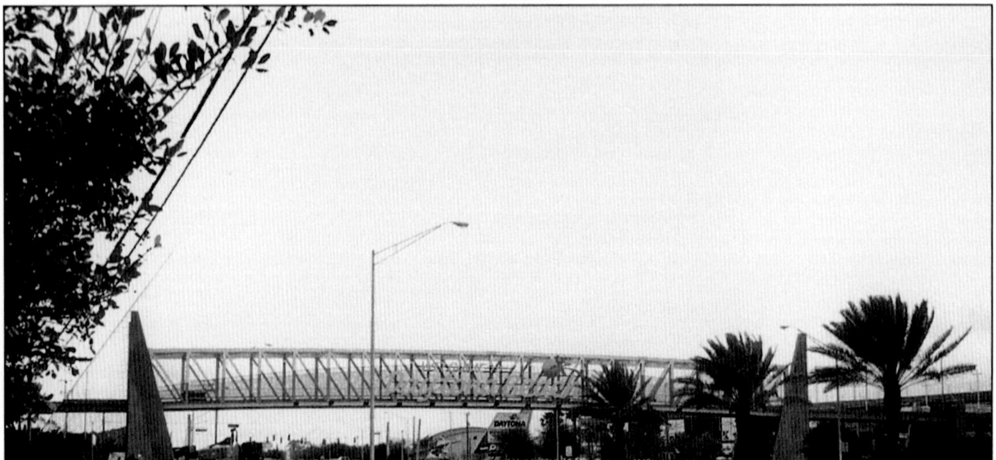

THE DALE EARNHARDT MEMORIAL BRIDGE. The bridge serves as a skywalk to the Speedway and is seen here in 2002. (Courtesy of Cardwell Family Collection.)

CONTENTS

About the Author

Harold D. Cardwell Sr. is a retired Senior Rehabilitation Specialist with the Florida Department of Labor and Employment Security, Division of Blind Services. He is a lifelong resident of Volusia County and a graduate of Florida Technological University. During World War II he was assigned to the Atomic Bomb Project at Oakridge, Tennessee and Los Alamos, New Mexico. Mr. Cardwell is currently chairman of the Daytona Beach Historic Preservation Board, president of the Halifax Historical Society, president of the Port Orange Historical Trust, and active in many other state historical and anthropological organizations.

Acknowledgments

The author wishes to recognize the following individuals for their contributions to this work: Buz McKim, Ron Edwards, John Gontner, Priscilla Cardwell, Diane M. Bara, Shirley Sheppard, Roy Midkiff, Tom Zane, Russ Atwell, Nancy Kendrick, Paul Sexton, Cheryl Atwell, and Glenn Landau.

INTRODUCTION

The 100th Anniversary of Speed, which will be held in 2003 at Daytona Beach, will celebrate a significant contribution to the automotive industry. Daytona Beach is made up of more than 20 miles of smooth, hard-packed sand from Ormond Beach to Ponce Inlet, and is appropriately known as The Origin of Speed.

The first speed records were set in Ormond Beach, at the foot of Granada Avenue, on the beach. This became known as the "flying mile," where speeds of earlier racers were calibrated. When cars became more advanced and could reach higher speeds, the full length of Daytona Beach was needed. Later, the Measured Mile was established south of the pier to allow cars to gain higher speeds. This timed section of the beach was located four miles south of the Main Street Pier. Such racers as Segrave and Campbell needed nine miles of the ocean beach—four miles north and four miles south including the measured mile. Campbell demanded a longer start and began his run at the Clarendon Hotel and proceeded south through the measured mile. These events were timed by the American Automobile Association (AAA).

A new 3.2-mile road/beach course was set up in 1936 at present-day Daytona Beach Shores. This was a point just north of City Hall running south to DeMotte Street, located below Dunlawton Avenue. This track operated from 1936 through 1947, with a hiatus from 1942 to 1946 due to World War II.

After the war, because of population growth and the development of new homes and businesses, the 3.2-mile road/beach course was no longer feasible. It was impossible to secure the track for paying fans and controlling safety measures required for larger racing events was difficult.

By 1948, the National Association of Stock Car Auto Racing (NASCAR) was organized. Through the efforts of Bill France Sr., NASCAR, the Volusia County Government, and the County Commissioners, a 4.1-mile road/beach course was developed at Ponce Inlet. This track was utilized from 1948 through 1958. However, due to the rapid growth of the south peninsula, this raceway was just as doomed as the Daytona Beach Shores track.

Bill France Sr. was farsighted enough by the 1950s to realize that with the growth of NASCAR and auto racing, a modern speedway had to be built.

This vision became a reality and on February 22, 1959, the Daytona Beach International Speedway opened. The first race had 47,000 fans in attendance and the Daytona 500 was born. This track was an engineering marvel and was completed at a cost of $3 million. It is located approximately four-and-a-half miles from the beach on the mainland. Today, these great events continue, with approximately 200,000 fans attending the Daytona 500 each year. The Pepsi 400 Sports Car events and motorcycle races attract thousands of fans to the area as well.

The following five chapters give a chronological study of the history of racing at Daytona Beach and the key figures in its development.

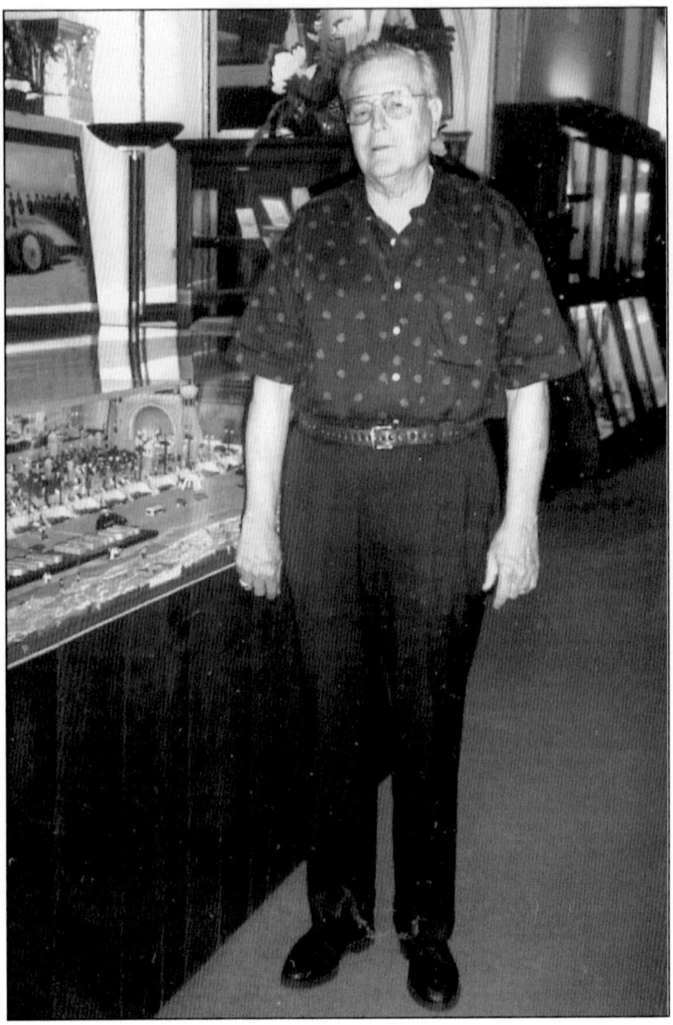

AUTHOR HAROLD D. CARDWELL SR. AT THE HALIFAX HISTORICAL SOCIETY'S BOARDWALK EXHIBIT, 2002. This award–winning model was constructed by Lawson Diggett, a local collector and model builder, of racing cars and landmarks. His entire collection was bequeathed to HHS and can be seen annually at the museum. Mr. Cardwell, president of the Society, stands proudly in front of this scale model of the Boardwalk area at the beach. (Courtesy of Halifax Historical Society.)

One

From Horseless Carriages to Streamline Race Cars 1903–1927

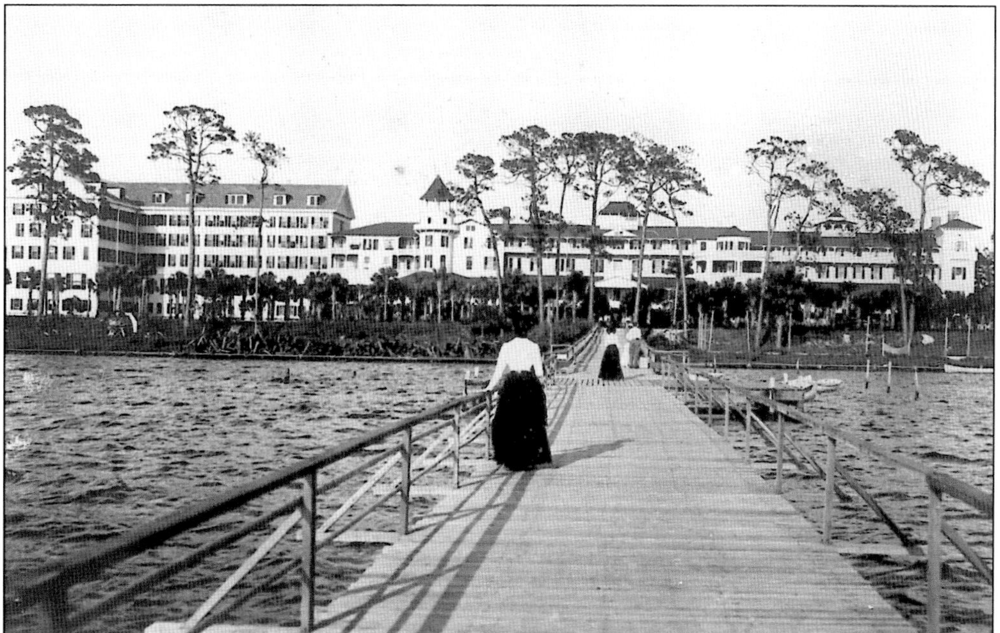

Ormond Hotel, 1903. This magnificent hotel was built by John Anderson and Joseph D. Price in 1887, and was sold to Henry Flagler in 1890. The hotel was a gathering place for gentleman automobile enthusiasts and wealthy winter guests. This created an atmosphere for trial speed runs on the nearby beach for the "horseless carriage." (Courtesy of John Gontner.)

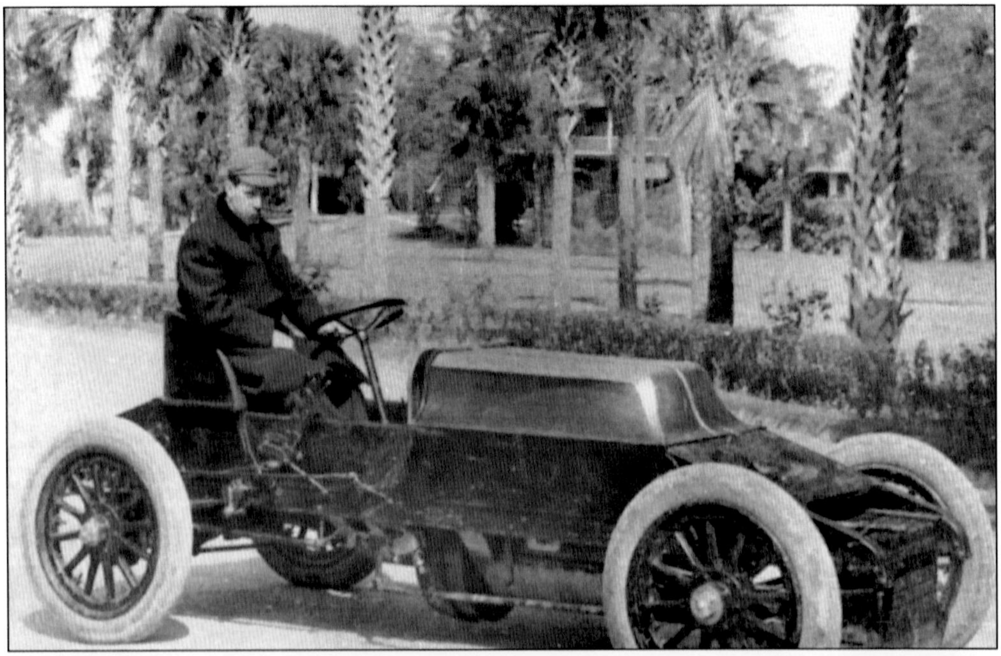

ORMOND BEACH, 1903. Alexander Winton breaks the speed record at 68.19 mph on Ormond Beach in *Bullet #2* on March 26, 1903. He attempted this feat in 1902 with *Bullet #1*, but failed due to carburetor trouble. Today both of Winton's cars are on display in the Smithsonian Museum. He was the first to challenge others to break new records. (Courtesy of John Gontner.)

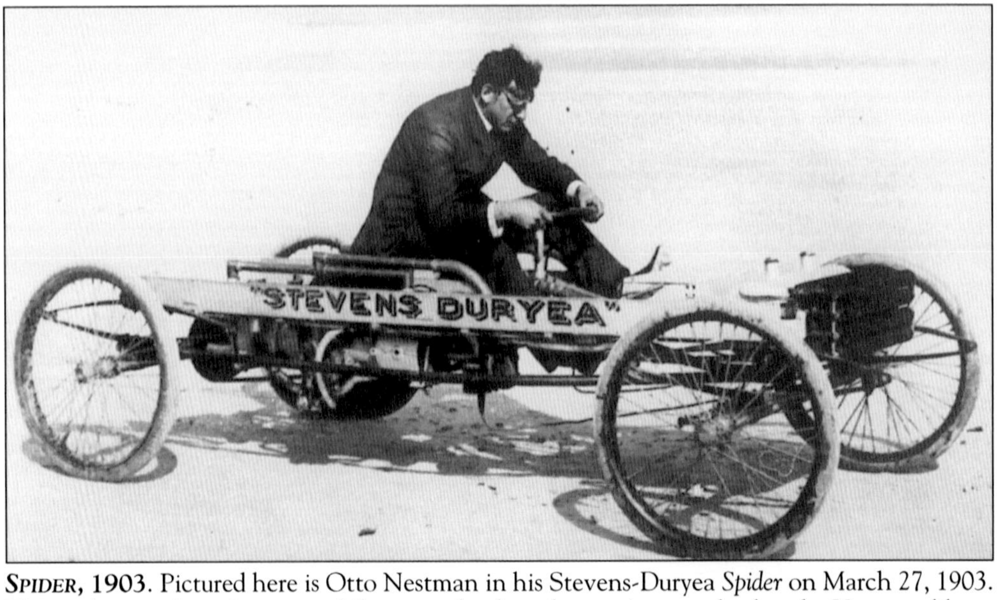

SPIDER, 1903. Pictured here is Otto Nestman in his Stevens-Duryea *Spider* on March 27, 1903. This rather crude early automobile created a lot of attention on the beach. He was able to reach a high speed, but because his solid tires separated from the rims, the officials declared his car unsafe. Nestman was unable to improve his wheel/tire construction and did not qualify for the event. However, in January of 1904, he set the record for a five-mile run at 60.443 mph. (Courtesy of John Gontner.)

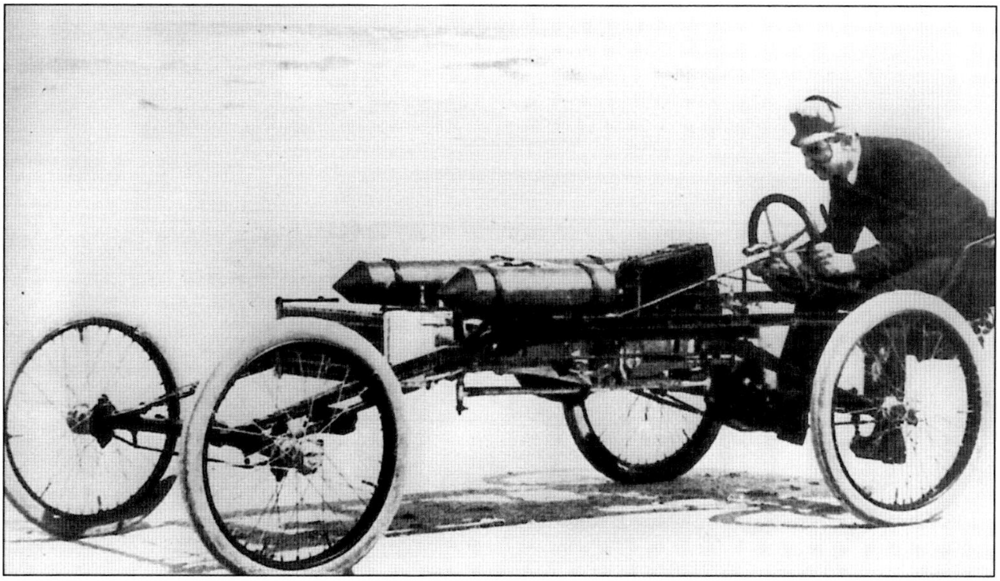

PIRATE, 1903. R.E. Olds was the owner and builder of this car and H.T. Thomas was the driver. Olds first brought his car to Ormond Beach for trial runs in 1902. When Olds started manufacturing the great Oldsmobile, Thomas was his supervising engineer. (Courtesy of John Gontner.)

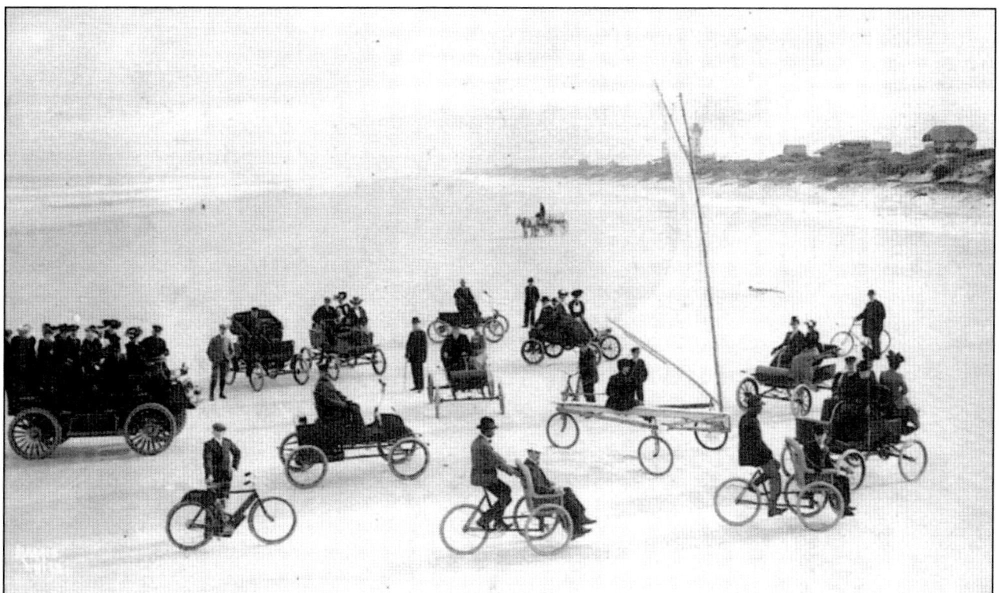

EARLY TRANSPORTATION, 1903. In this famous photograph by E.G. Harris, all forms of land transportation can be seen—horses, bicycles, and wind-sailing, along with steam-powered, electricity-powered, gas-powered, and man-powered vehicles. (Courtesy of Halifax Historical Society.)

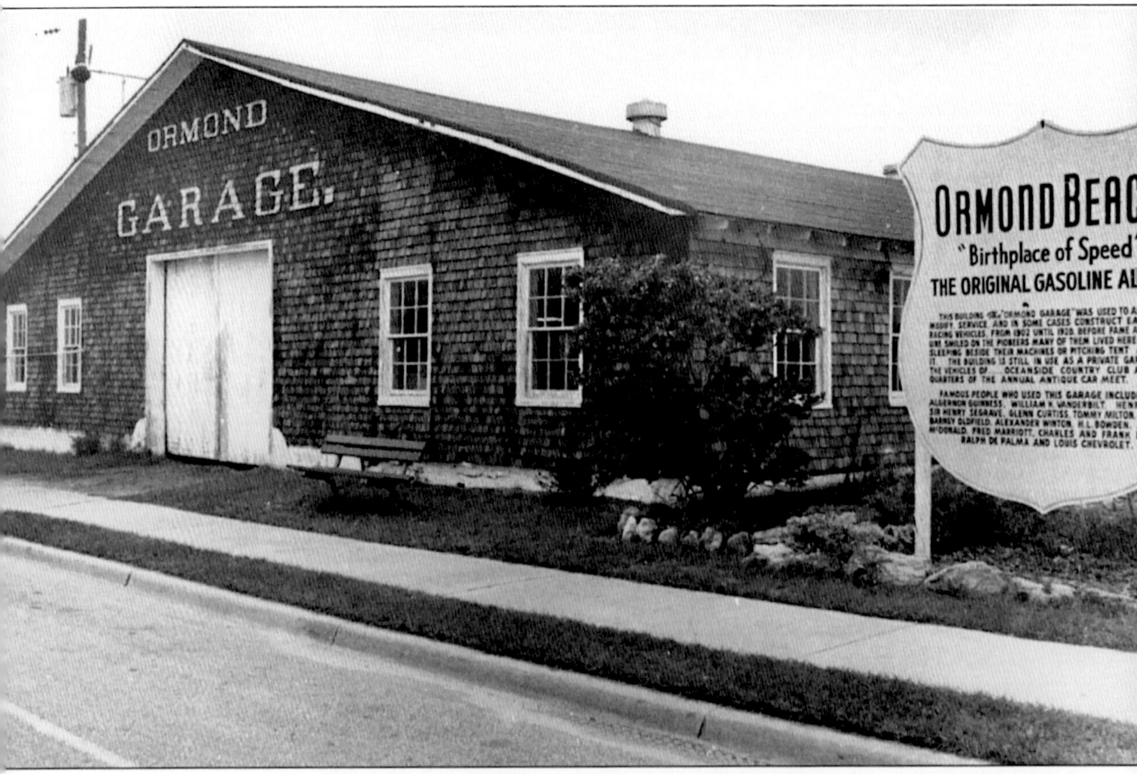

ORMOND GARAGE, 1904. Henry Flagler, owner of the Florida East Coast Railroad and the Ormond Hotel, built this garage, called "Gasoline Alley," to promote auto racing as a tourist attraction. In later years, three men whose names would be known the world over used this garage for their vehicles. The first was Henry Ford, who slept in the garage with his car. The second was Louis Chevrolet, the man who brought this famous name to the automotive industry. The third man to use this garage was Glenn H. Curtiss, who was the first to break the world's record on a V-8 powered, air-cooled motorcycle at 136.3 mph. Later, Curtiss was the first airplane pilot to get a license in the United States and gained notoriety throughout the aviation industry. (Courtesy of John Gontner.)

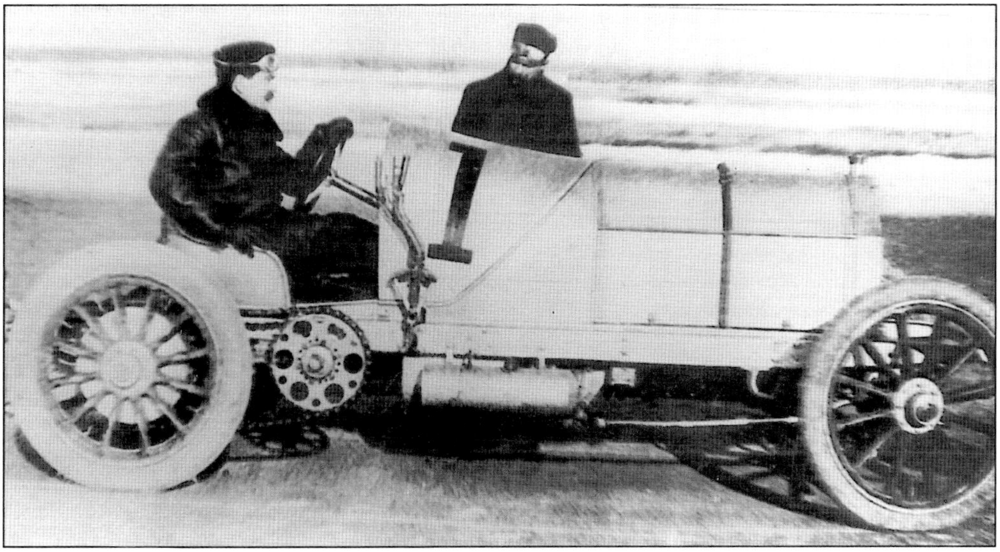

VANDERBILT, 1904. This photo is of William K. Vanderbilt in his *#1 Mercedes* on January 27, 1904. A gentleman race-driver and industrialist, he is seen here all decked out with goggles and gloves. He received a lot of attention at the fashionable Ormond Hotel, where all the drivers stayed during the winter season. Vanderbilt broke the record on the beach at 92.3 mph, setting the first world speed record. (Courtesy of Halifax Historical Society.)

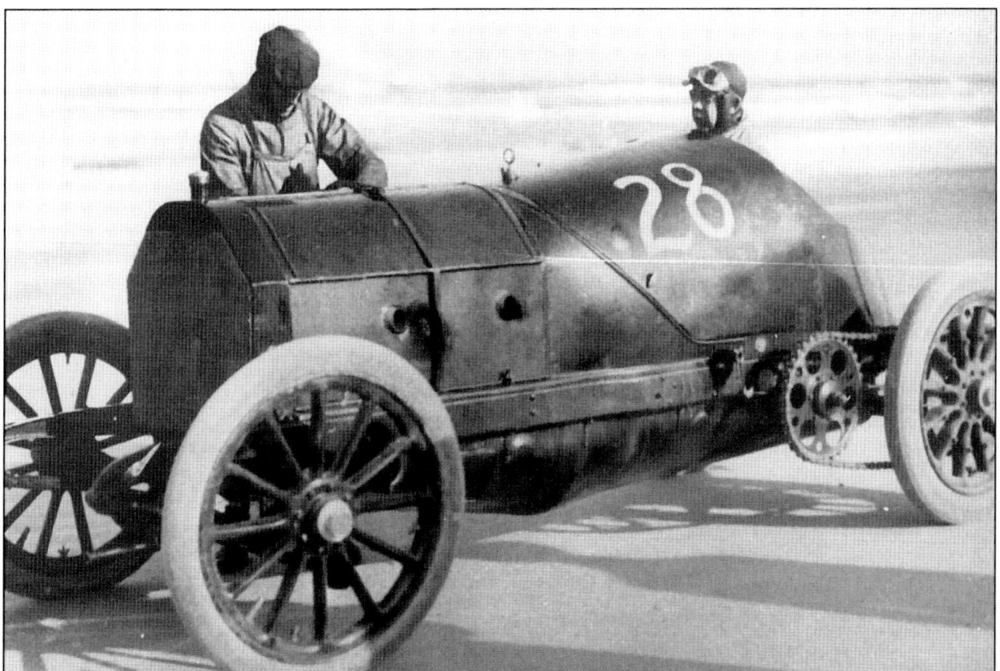

STEVENS, 1904. Pictured here is S.B. Stevens in his *Mercedes #28* on the beach in 1904. This popular automobile enthusiast created quite a stir with his leather headdress and goggles. Winter speed fans on the beach always commented on this car's unique new name. (Courtesy of John Gontner.)

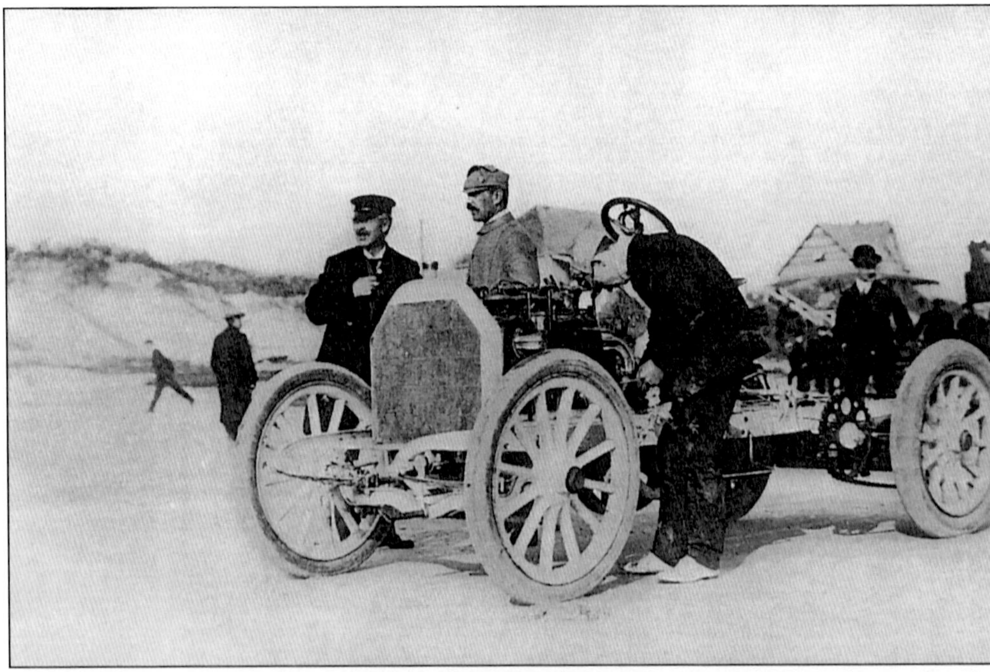

H.L. Bowden, 1904. Bowden is in the canvas jacket behind the car, and J.F. Hathaway is in the black cap. The mechanic is unidentified. Bowden is pictured with his 60 hp Mercedes, winner of the Hill-Climbing Contest at Boston, Massachusetts, in the spring of 1904. Bowden was also the winner of several events at Ormond in January 1904. (Courtesy of Halifax Historical Society.)

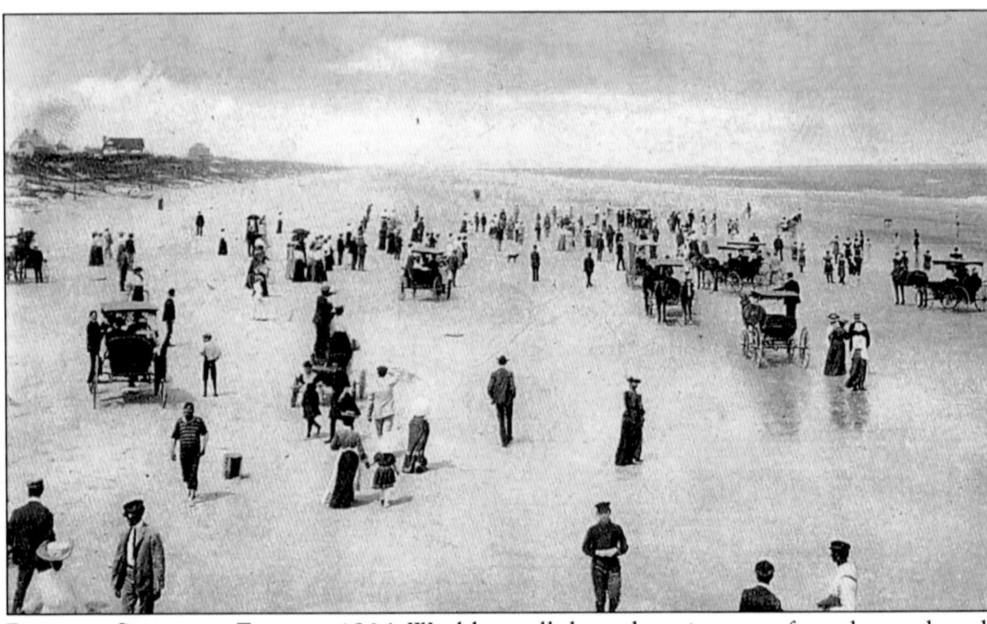

Beach at Seabreeze, Florida, 1904. Wealthy, well-dressed tourists came from the north each winter season to see and to be seen at the famous speed trials. They came to experience the subtropical environment, with its ocean breeze and orange and hibiscus blossoms, and to enjoy the abundant seafood. (Courtesy of Halifax Historical Society.)

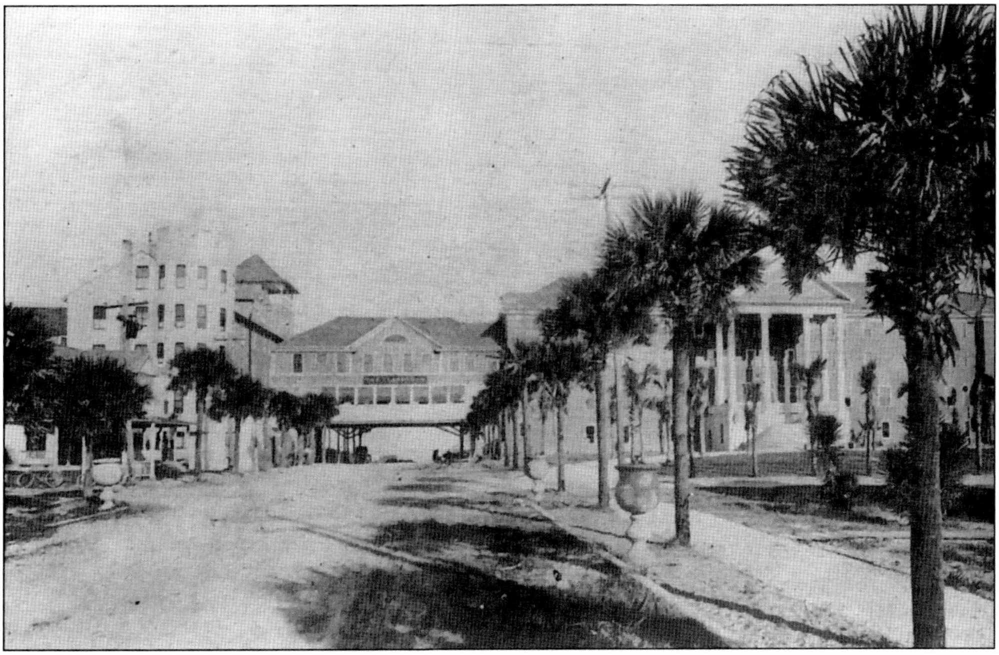

The Clarendon Inn, 1904. Northern tourists made this their destination in order to take part in the speed trials that were held on the beach. Other famous hotels were the Ormond Hotel and the Seaside Inn. Here, visitors could mingle with the sportsman drivers and learn about the "horseless carriage" that was flying at unbelievable speeds through a marked mile. (Courtesy of Halifax Historical Society.)

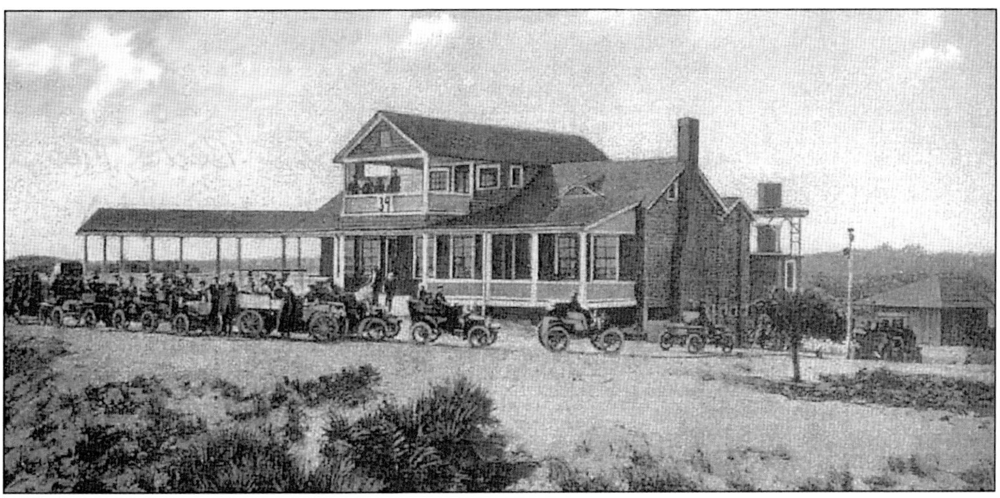

Florida East Coast Automobile Association Clubhouse, 1905. The "39" on the front of the building honors William K. Vanderbilt, who ran the Measured Mile (sometimes referred to as the Flying Mile) in 39 seconds. (Courtesy of Midkiff Family Collection.)

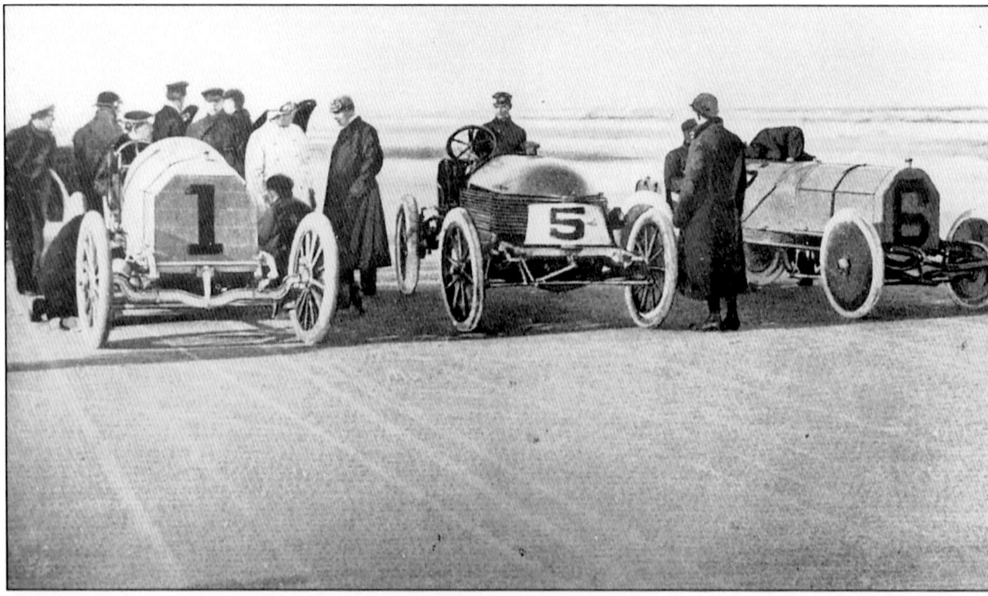

William K. Vanderbilt, Arthur MacDonald, and Horace T. Thomas (from left to right) on Ormond-Daytona Beach, February 17, 1905. These three well-known gentleman sports drivers were often seen in the Ormond Hotel lobby and at other places on the beach. Winter tourists were delighted to meet and socialize with these popular individuals. When the tourists returned north in early spring, they would show off autographs and photographs of these prestigious race drivers. (Courtesy of John Gontner.)

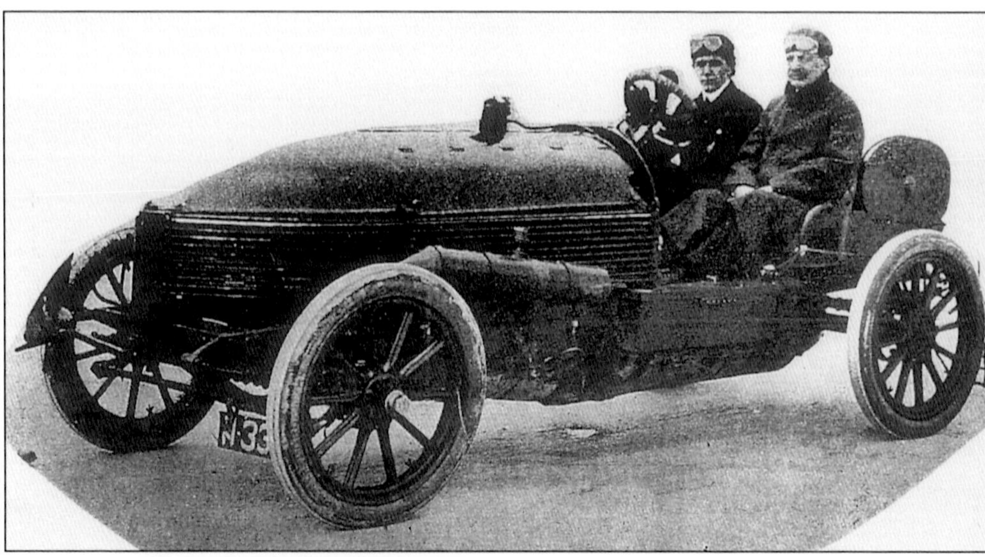

Arthur MacDonald in his English-built, Six-cylinder, Ninety-horsepower Napier. On January 31, 1905, he did the mile at a record speed of 104.651 mph. MacDonald, an Englishman, added a continental flair to the speed trials on the beach. The passenger is unidentified. (Courtesy of Halifax Historical Society.)

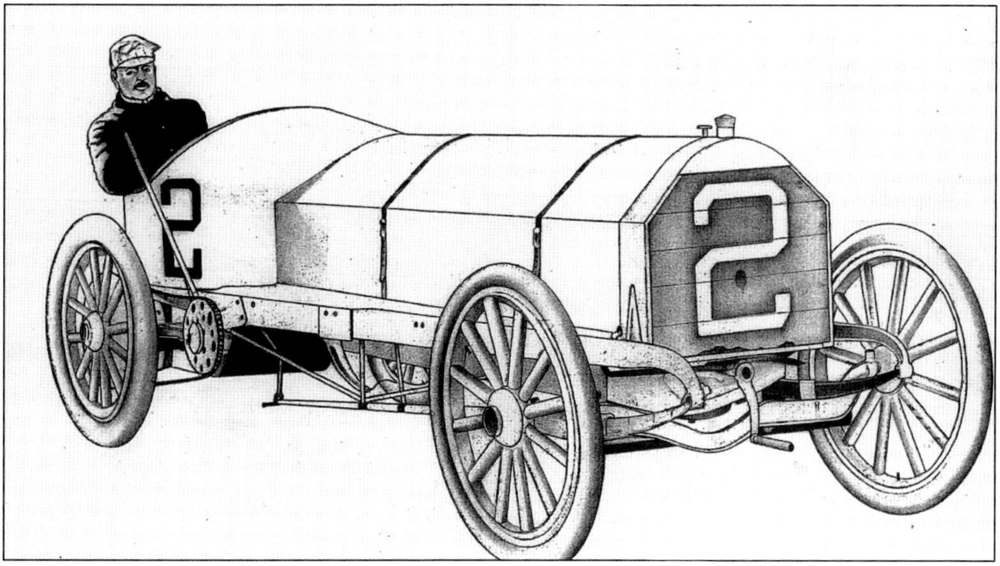

Flying Dutchman II, 1905. On the last day of the winter competition, H.L. Bowden set a new speed record of 109.76 mph. Bowden paid a considerable price to modify his Duesenberg by adding another engine to achieve an edge over other speedsters. There were several disputes over this addition between England's Arthur MacDonald and France's Paul Baras. The American Automobile Association (AAA) argued that Bowden's run was ineligible for an official record. However, the United States racing fans settled it in favor of Bowden's record run of 109.76 mph. (Courtesy of Halifax Historical Society.)

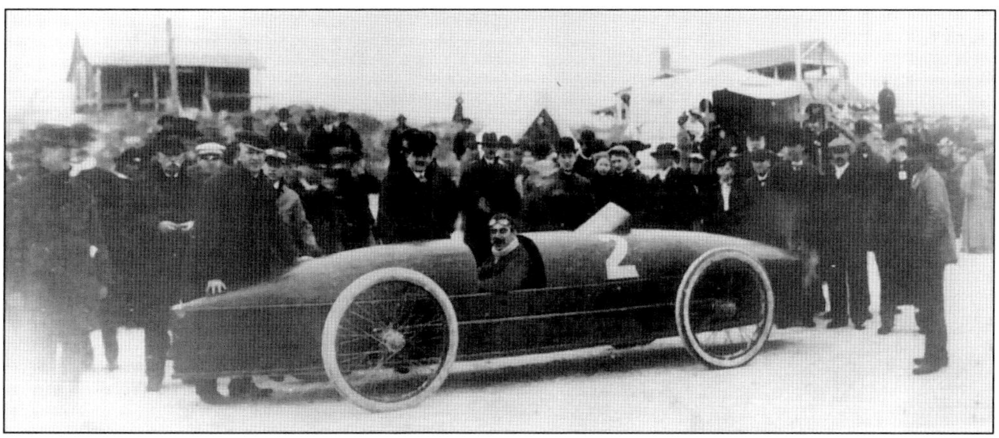

Fred Marriott in his #2 Stanley Steamer in 1906. The Stanley Brothers brought a new steam-powered car to the beach. Marriott stunned the racing world by achieving a new record of 127.66 mph. He was the first man to ever exceed a miraculous "two-miles-a-minute." (Courtesy of Halifax Historical Society.)

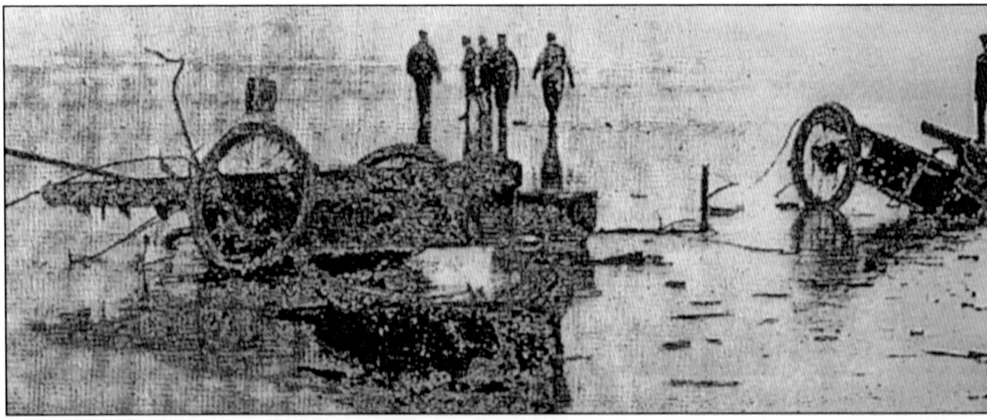

FRED MARRIOTT, JANUARY 31, 1907. Pictured here is Marriott in a wreck on the beach. He had waited several days for beach conditions to improve. However, the wind and high tide on the last day of the meet had left several uneven spots inside the Measured Mile course. Ultimately, Marriott made a last-minute decision to break the record with his *Stanley Steamer.* He entered the course at full speed, hit an uneven spot, and the steamer catapulted and careened in the air, landing near the surf. The machine broke into several pieces, slinging him and the boiler across the sand. He was injured and lost sight in one eye. The Stanley Brothers never returned to the beach with their steam-driven carriages. (Courtesy of Halifax Historical Society.)

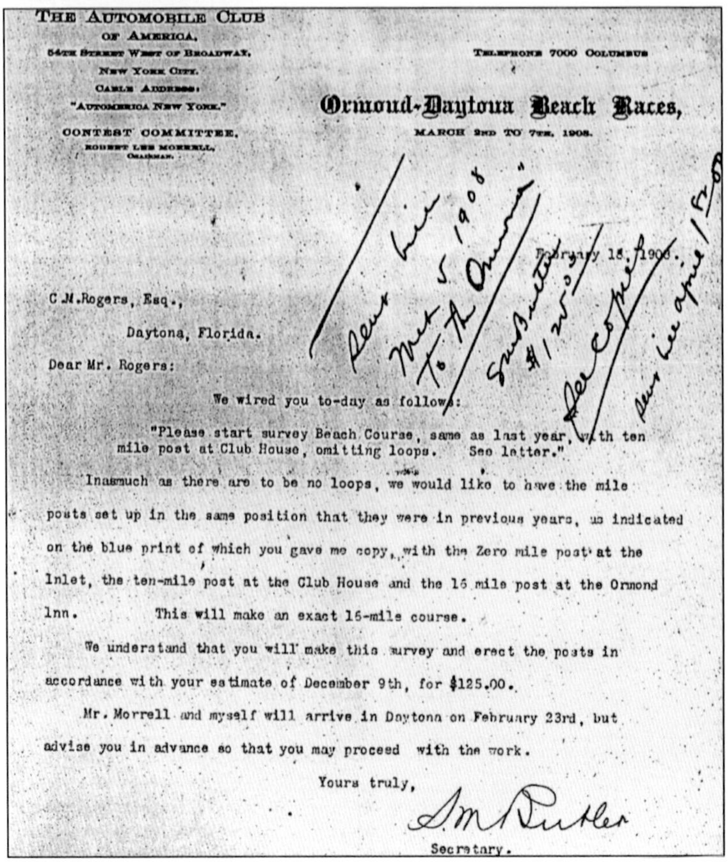

THE AUTOMOBILE CLUB
OF AMERICA.
54TH STREET WEST OF BROADWAY.
NEW YORK CITY.
CABLE ADDRESS:
"AUTOMERICA NEW YORK."
CONTEST COMMITTEE.
ROBERT LEE MORRELL,
CHAIRMAN.

TELEPHONE 7000 COLUMBUS

Ormond-Daytona Beach Races,
MARCH 2ND TO 7TH, 1908.

February 18, 1908.

C.M.Rogers, Esq.,

Daytona, Florida.

Dear Mr. Rogers:

We wired you to-day as follows:

"Please start survey Beach Course, same as last year, with ten mile post at Club House, omitting loops. See letter."

Inasmuch as there are to be no loops, we would like to have the mile posts set up in the same position that they were in previous years, as indicated on the blue print of which you gave me copy, with the Zero mile post at the Inlet, the ten-mile post at the Club House and the 15 mile post at the Ormond Inn. This will make an exact 15-mile course.

We understand that you will make this survey and erect the posts in accordance with your estimate of December 9th, for $125.00.

Mr. Morrell and myself will arrive in Daytona on February 23rd, but advise you in advance so that you may proceed with the work.

Yours truly,

S.M.Butler

Secretary.

CORRESPONDENCE BETWEEN S.M. BUTLER AND C.M. ROGERS REGARDING THE BEACH SURVEY FOR THE WINTER RACING SEASON, FEBRUARY 18, 1908. (Courtesy of Midkiff Family Collection.)

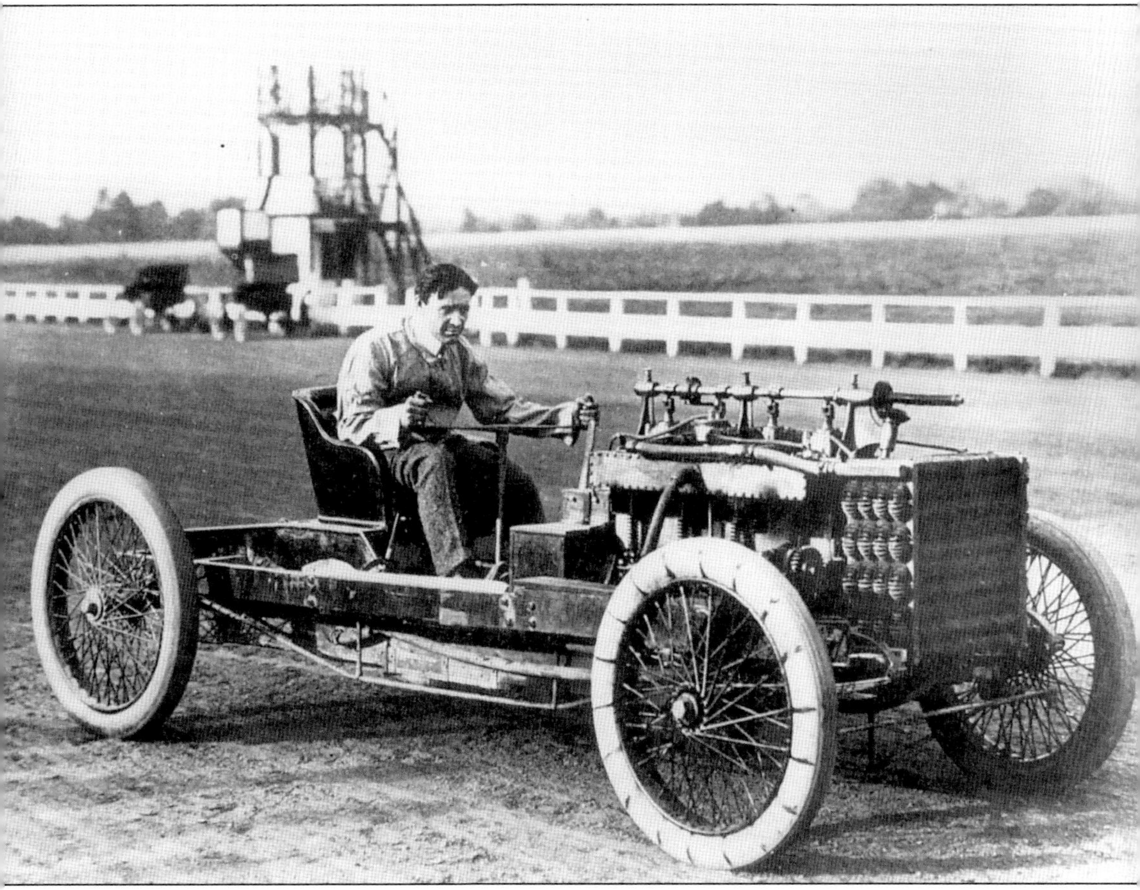

HENRY FORD'S 999, 1908. Barney Oldfield was a popular driver at the beach trials but was unable to break a record with Ford's car. It was reported that Ford was most interested in promoting his invention and making it highly visible to the public. When Ford brought his machine to the beach in previous years, he slept with his car at the Ormond Garage to avoid paying the high room rates at the Ormond Hotel. (Courtesy of John Gontner.)

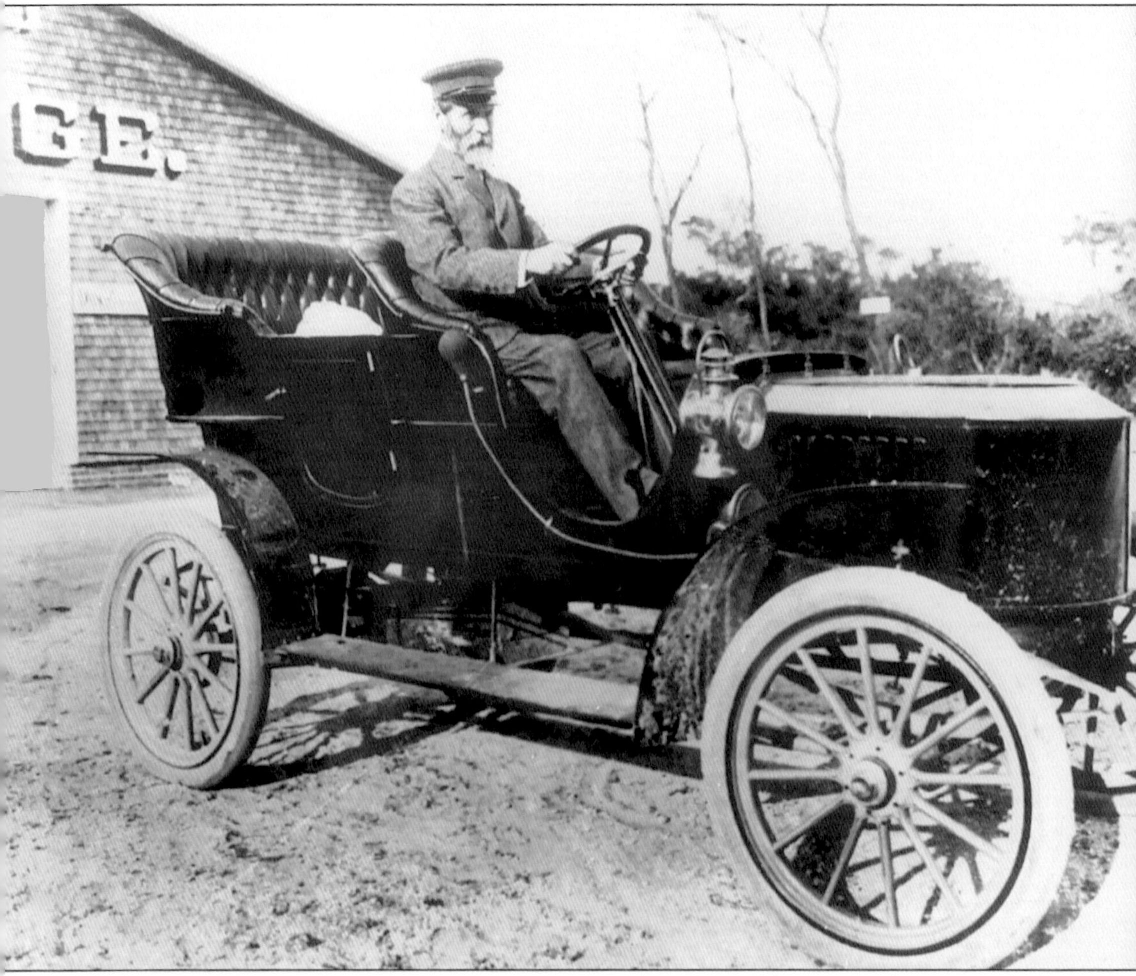

MODEL-M, STANLEY TOURING CAR, 1908. Pictured in front of the Ormond Garage, which was owned by Henry Flagler and the Florida East Coast Railroad (FEC), is Francis E. Stanley in his Model-M, Stanley Touring Car. Flagler owned the Ormond Hotel and the FEC Railroad from Jacksonville to Miami. Flagler was instrumental in accommodating the racing enthusiasts and special speed trials for the Flying Mile on the beach. (Courtesy of John Gontner.)

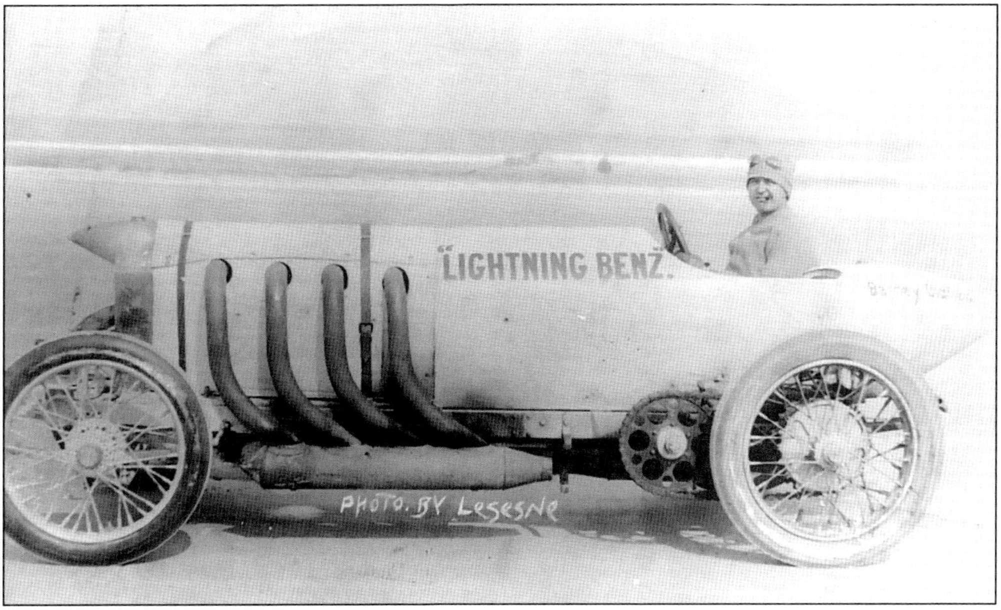

LIGHTNING BENZ, MARCH 16, 1910. Barney Oldfield broke the world record through the Measured Mile at 131.72 mph. Oldfield was one of the most popular and colorful drivers of all time. Following his record run, he stated that the acceleration gave him "the sensation of riding a rocket through space." (Courtesy of Halifax Historical Society.)

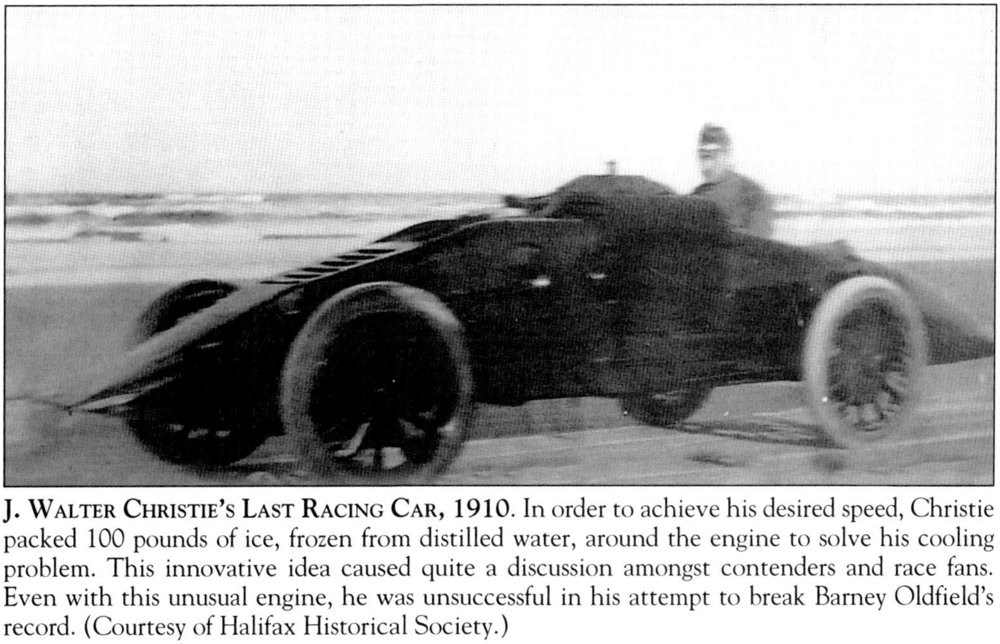

J. WALTER CHRISTIE'S LAST RACING CAR, 1910. In order to achieve his desired speed, Christie packed 100 pounds of ice, frozen from distilled water, around the engine to solve his cooling problem. This innovative idea caused quite a discussion amongst contenders and race fans. Even with this unusual engine, he was unsuccessful in his attempt to break Barney Oldfield's record. (Courtesy of Halifax Historical Society.)

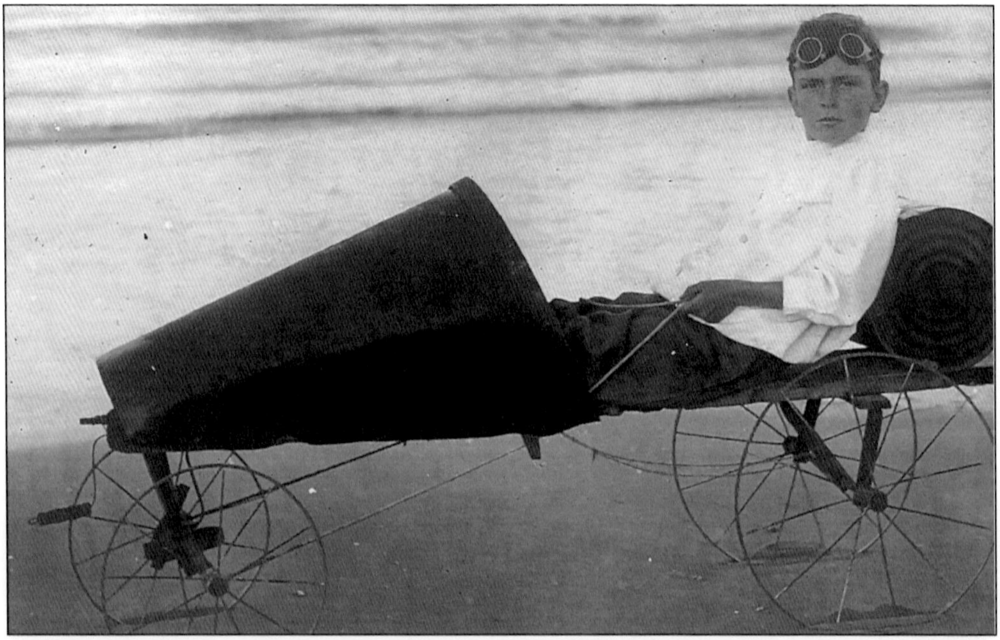

Lawson Diggett, c. 1912. Diggett, pictured here around eight years of age, devoted his whole life to racing and built models of cars and landmarks that were associated with racing. Diggett's entire estate was bequeathed to the Halifax Historical Society (HHS). Today his collections can be seen at the HHS Museum, 252 South Beach Street, Daytona Beach, Florida. (Courtesy of Halifax Historical Society.)

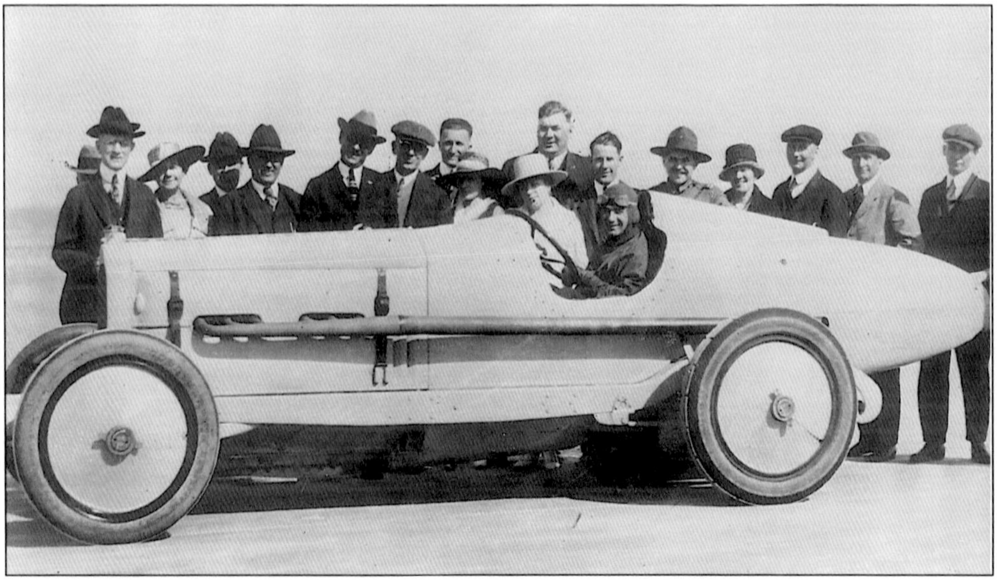

Ralph DePalma in a Packard with an Aviation Motor, 1919. On February 12, 1919, DePalma raced through the Measured Mile to set a new world record of 149.875 mph. DePalma had many achievements as a racer, including the Indianapolis 500, the Vanderbilt Cup, the National Driving Championship, and others. However, the Packard with a Liberty Aircraft V-12 engine he drove on the beach was his greatest accomplishment. (Courtesy of Halifax Historical Society.)

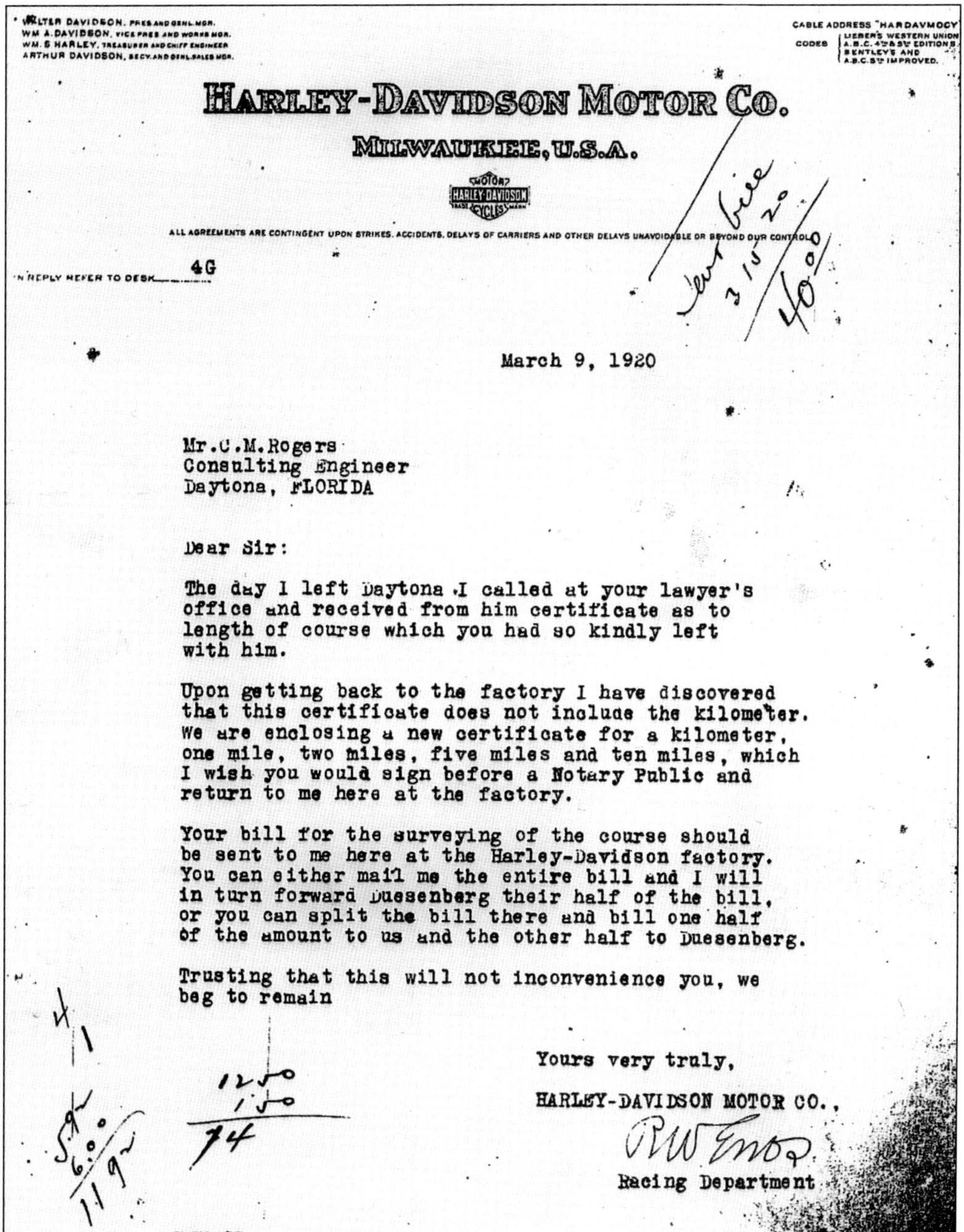
WALTER DAVIDSON, PRES. AND GENL. MGR.
WM. A. DAVIDSON, VICE PRES. AND WORKS MGR.
WM. S. HARLEY, TREASURER AND CHIEF ENGINEER
ARTHUR DAVIDSON, SECY. AND GENL. SALES MGR.

CABLE ADDRESS "HARDAVMOCY"
CODES: LIEBER'S WESTERN UNION; A.B.C. 4TH & 5TH EDITIONS; BENTLEY'S AND A.B.C. 5TH IMPROVED.

HARLEY-DAVIDSON MOTOR CO.
MILWAUKEE, U.S.A.

MOTOR HARLEY-DAVIDSON CYCLES

ALL AGREEMENTS ARE CONTINGENT UPON STRIKES, ACCIDENTS, DELAYS OF CARRIERS AND OTHER DELAYS UNAVOIDABLE OR BEYOND OUR CONTROL.

IN REPLY REFER TO DESK 4G

March 9, 1920

Mr. C. M. Rogers
Consulting Engineer
Daytona, FLORIDA

Dear Sir:

The day I left Daytona I called at your lawyer's office and received from him certificate as to length of course which you had so kindly left with him.

Upon getting back to the factory I have discovered that this certificate does not include the kilometer. We are enclosing a new certificate for a kilometer, one mile, two miles, five miles and ten miles, which I wish you would sign before a Notary Public and return to me here at the factory.

Your bill for the surveying of the course should be sent to me here at the Harley-Davidson factory. You can either mail me the entire bill and I will in turn forward Duesenberg their half of the bill, or you can split the bill there and bill one half of the amount to us and the other half to Duesenberg.

Trusting that this will not inconvenience you, we beg to remain

Yours very truly,
HARLEY-DAVIDSON MOTOR CO.,
R W Enos
Racing Department

RWE:GD

HARLEY-DAVIDSON MOTOR CO. CORRESPONDENCE, MARCH 9, 1920. This letter demonstrates how much engineering was involved in the preparation of racing events, motorcycle and automobile alike. (Courtesy of Midkiff Family Collection.)

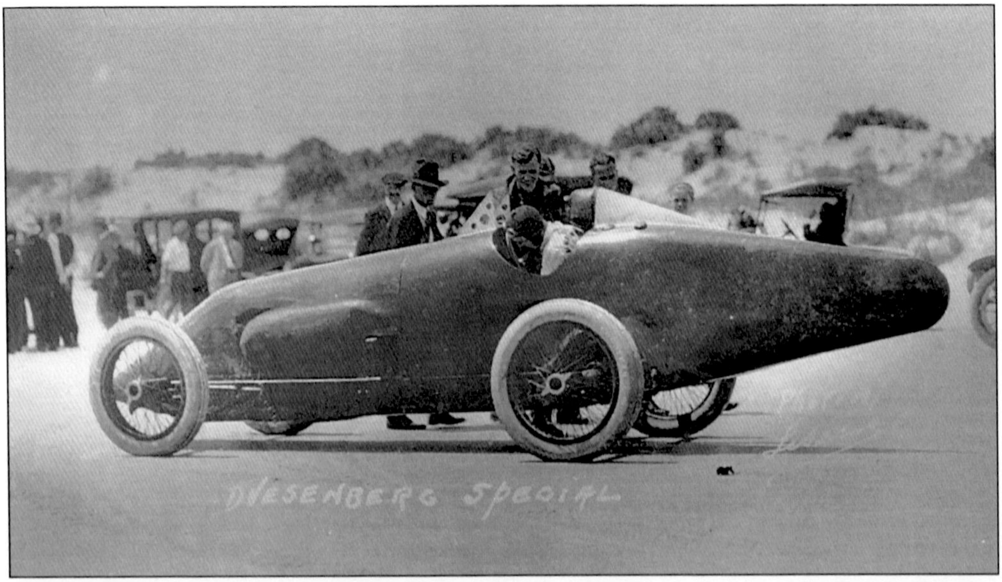

Jimmy Murphy in Milton's Deusenberg Special, 1920. As head mechanic for Tommy Milton, Murphy was so thrilled at the performance of this car that he took it upon himself to drive through the Measured Mile. To his surprise, he broke the world's speed record at 152 mph. When Milton returned to Daytona from his trip to Cuba, he learned of this unauthorized event and dismissed Murphy as head mechanic. Milton took the car and broke another world's speed record with an amazing 156.046 mph. Murphy went on to achieve further racing acclaim in his own right, and in 1922, he won the Indianapolis 500. (Courtesy of ISC Archives.)

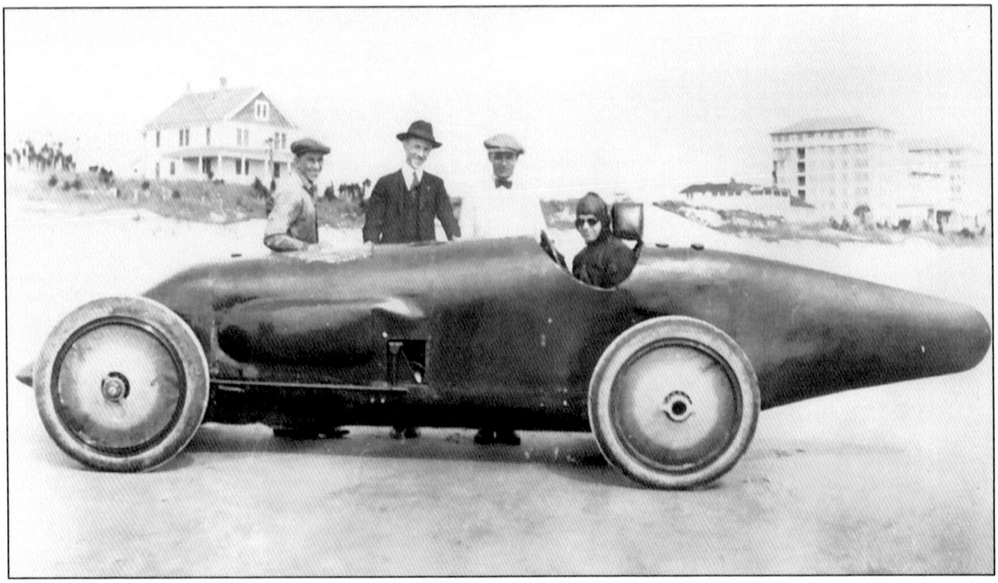

Tommy Milton in his Deusenberg, 1920. Notice the wheel hub changes which gave the car an extra high-speed advantage over the old spoke wheels. This enabled Milton to break the world's ground speed record. Milton was very popular with the spectators that came to the beach to witness speed events. (Courtesy of John Gontner.)

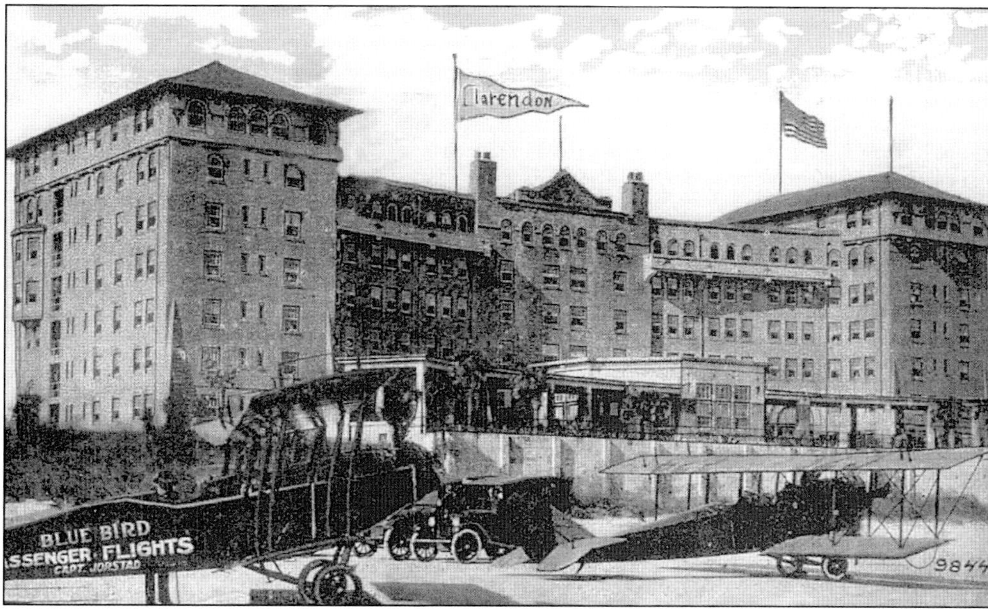

Capt. J.O. Jorstad's The Bluebird, c. 1920. This plane, parked in front of the Clarendon Hotel, was available for passenger flights. Captain Jorstad was a veteran of World War I and was regarded as a safe pilot to fly an airplane. He took off and landed on the beach on many chartered flights. (Courtesy of Halifax Historical Society.)

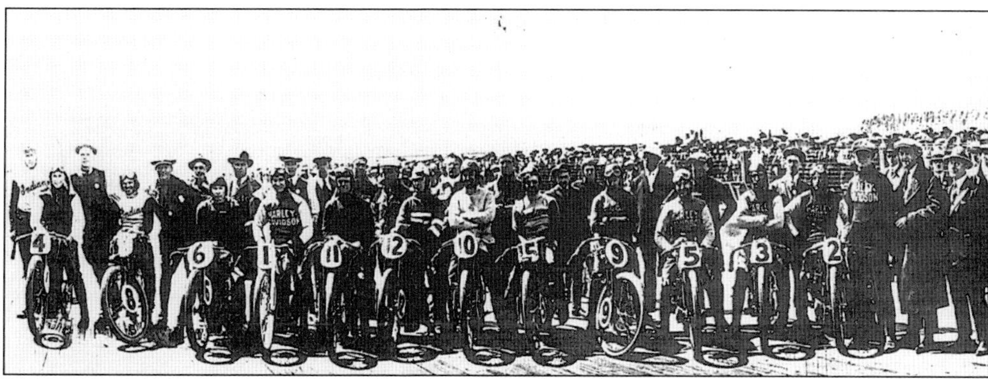

Jim Davis, April 24, 1921. Davis (fifth from the left) was an internationally renowned motorcycle racer who raced on Indian Motorcycles. He broke many records and retired in 1939. Davis was a flagman for the American Motorcycle Association racing events at Daytona Beach for many years. His knowledge of racing made him an excellent flagman. He was honored in 1996 at a motorcycle breakfast for the "Over The Hill Gang." (Courtesy of Midkiff Family Collection.)

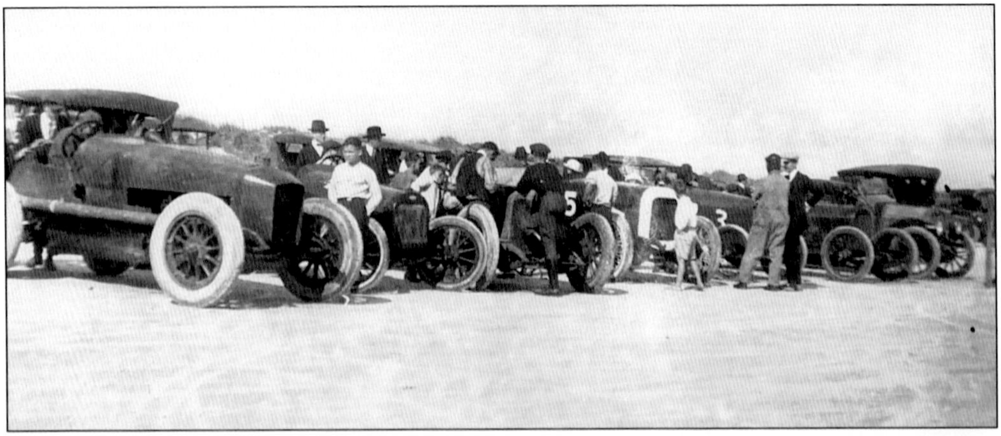

OFFICIALS READYING THE ENTRIES IN A SPECIAL BEACH BARREL RACE IN THE EARLY 1920S. During the winter season, many small events were held. Racing enthusiasts called them "barrel" or "pillar" races. These objects marked the boundaries of the race course on the beach. (Courtesy of John Gontner.)

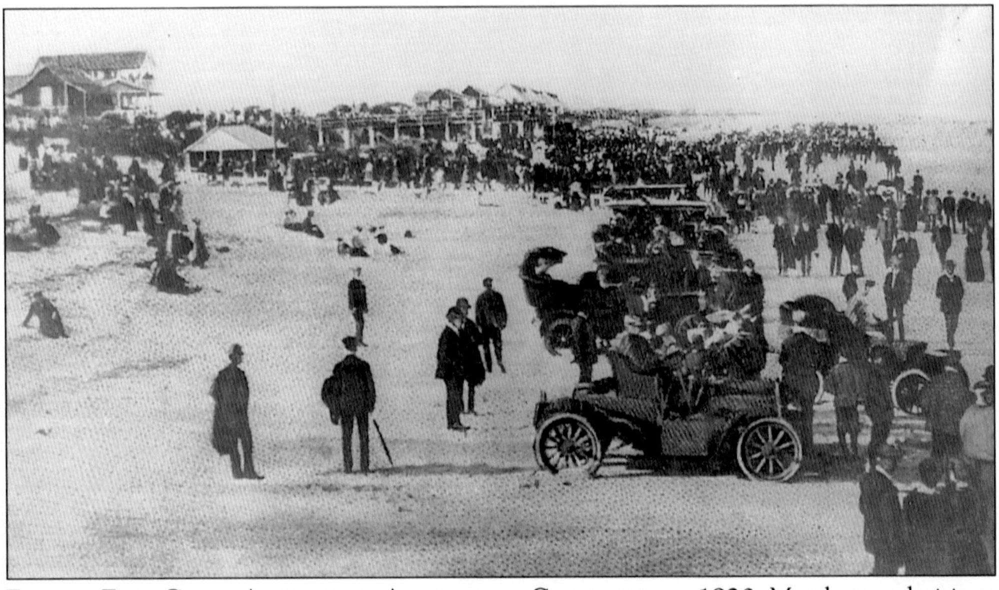

FLORIDA EAST COAST AUTOMOBILE ASSOCIATION CLUBHOUSE, C. 1920. Members and visitors gather for the barrel racing competition on the beach at Daytona. The club was organized with over 200 members in 1903. A few of the more prominent, wealthy members were W.K. Vanderbilt, Henry M. Flagler, Howard Gould, and John Jacob Astor. The clubhouse was originally located near the Silver Beach approach. (Courtesy of Halifax Historical Society.)

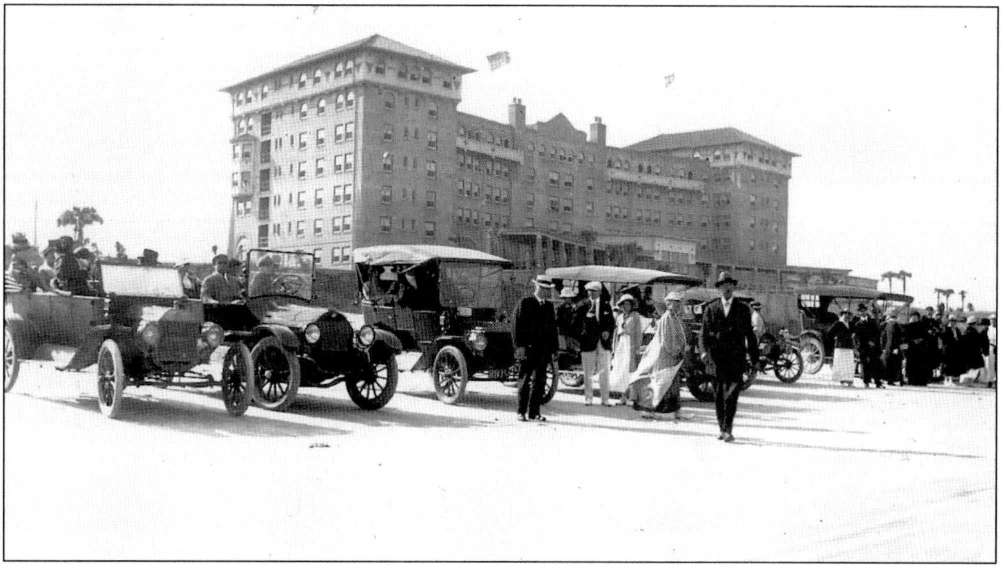

CLARENDON HOTEL, C. 1922. Winter visitors and race fans gather in front of the old Clarendon Hotel to "show off" their horseless carriages. The marvel of the barrel races and the speed trials thrilled these guests, along with the glamour of socializing with the sportsman race drivers from the north and abroad. These gatherings made Daytona the racing capital of the world. (Courtesy of John Gontner.)

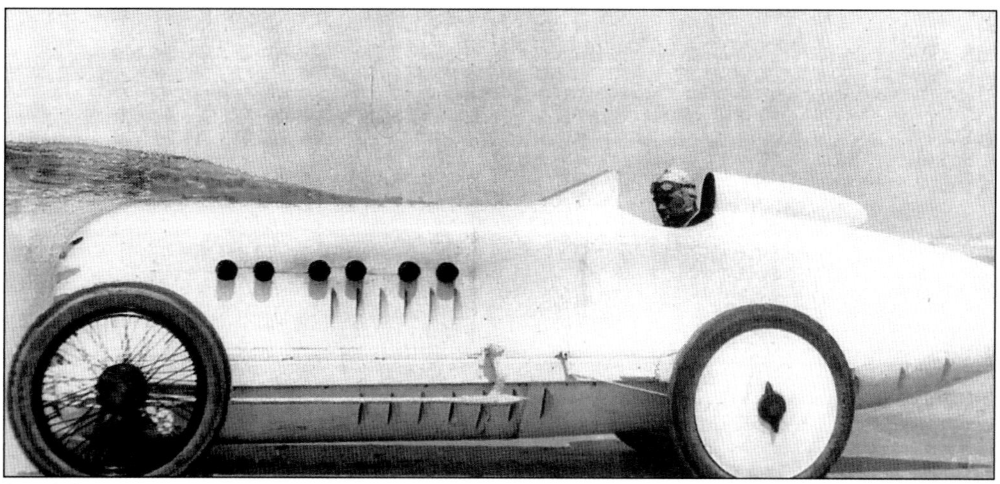

SIG HAUGDAHL, FAMED MOTORCYCLE AND AUTOMOBILE RACER, 1922. Haugdahl broke the unofficial world's speed record at 180.27 mph with his *Wisconsin Special.* The American Automobile Association (AAA) deemed the event invalid due to unsanctioned sponsorship. Haugdahl had a racing shop in Daytona where he set up his special race car. He installed a 652-cubic-inch modified aircraft engine. In 1936, he helped organize stock car racing and planned the first road/beach race course, a 3.2-mile track. (Courtesy of Halifax Historical Society.)

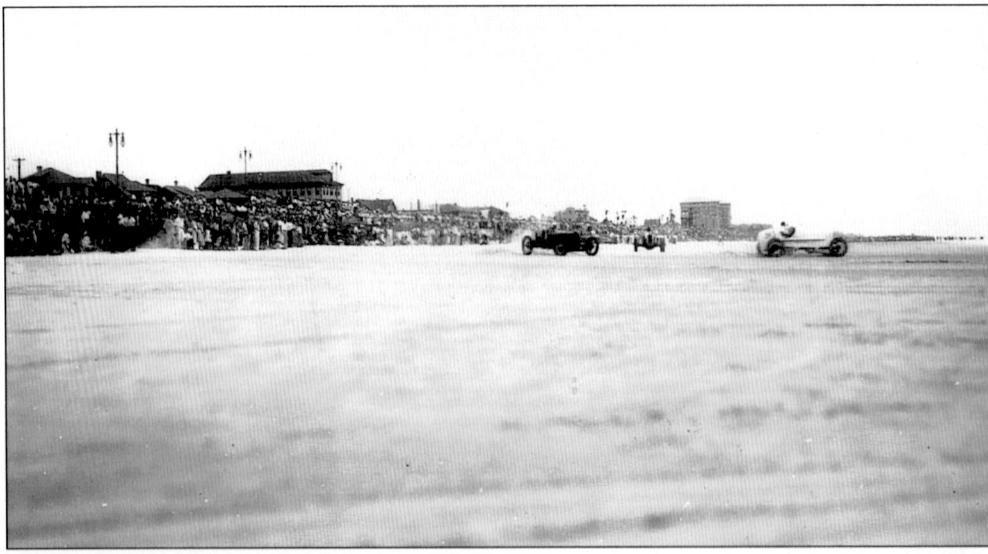

Barrel Racing, Early 1920s. Races were held just south of the Clarendon Hotel, near where the Band Shell and boardwalk stand today. These events were popular with race enthusiasts and it is alleged that a wager was often placed on these race cars. (Courtesy of Halifax Historical Society.)

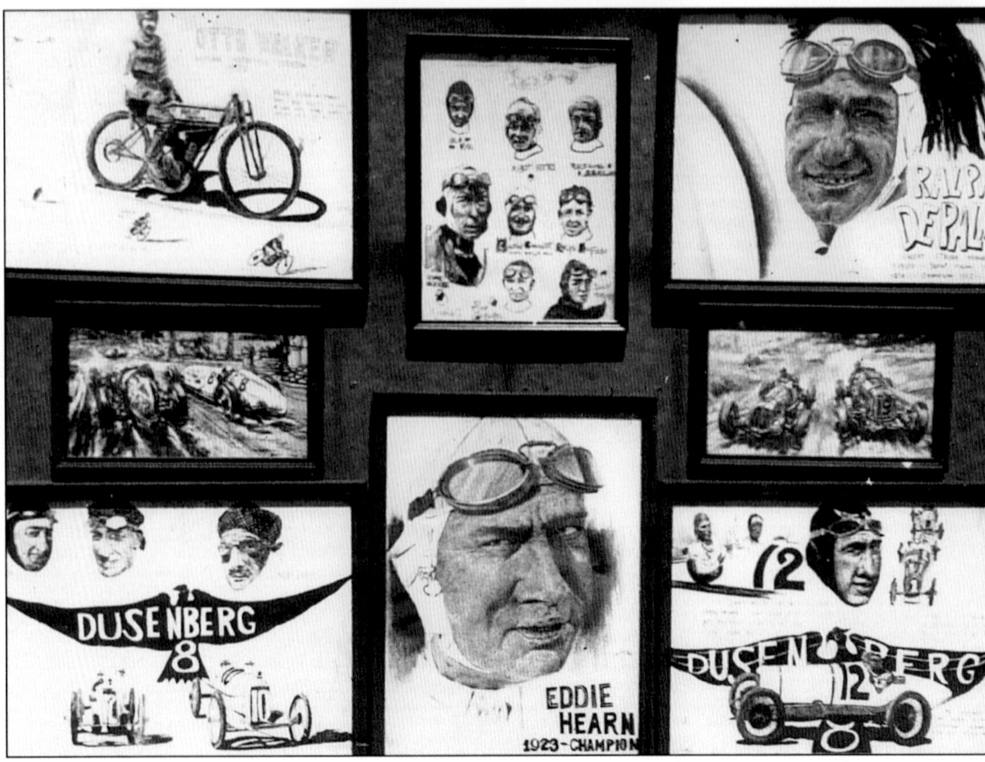

Champion Display Honoring Ralph DePalma and Eddie Hearn, 1923. This was a year in Daytona when barrel racing was very popular with the racing enthusiasts who came here to enjoy the special events, the sun, and the surf. (Courtesy of John Gontner.)

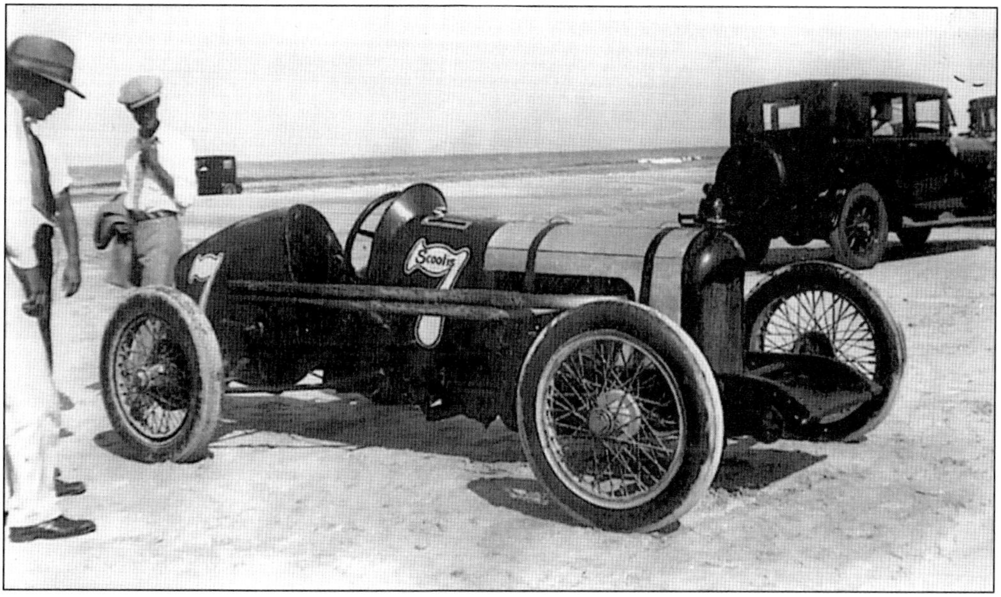

SCOOTIS 7, 1924–1925. This car was one of the more popular race cars used in the barrel, or pillar, events. These cars took a beating from the beach sand and salt air and required a rigid maintenance program to keep them tuned for high performance. (Courtesy of Halifax Historical Society.)

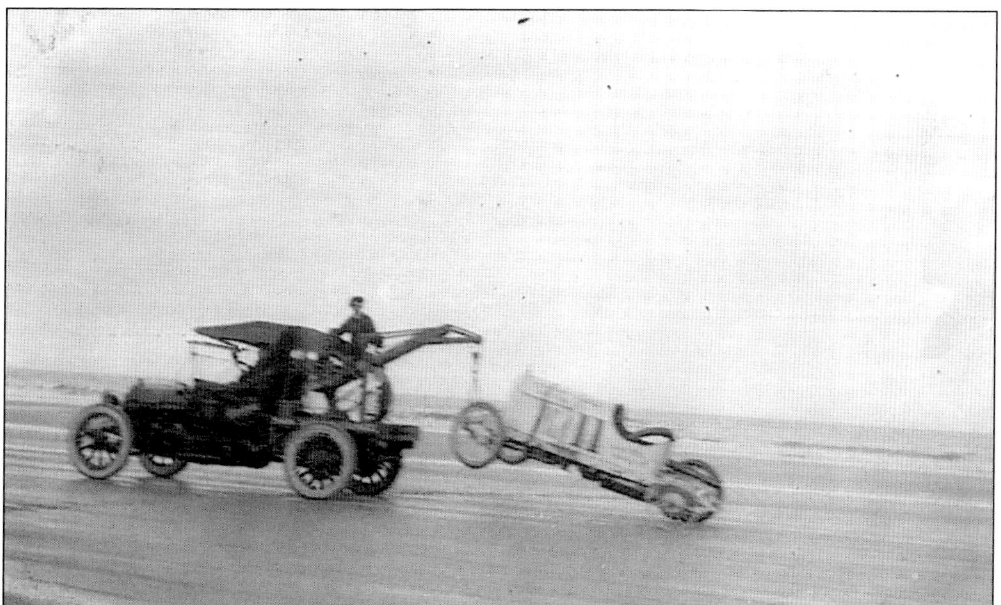

SPROCKET DRIVE TOW TRUCK, C. 1920S. All of the special racing events had their breakdowns and misfortunes and racers had to be towed through the soft sand to their garages off the beach. (Courtesy of Halifax Historical Society.)

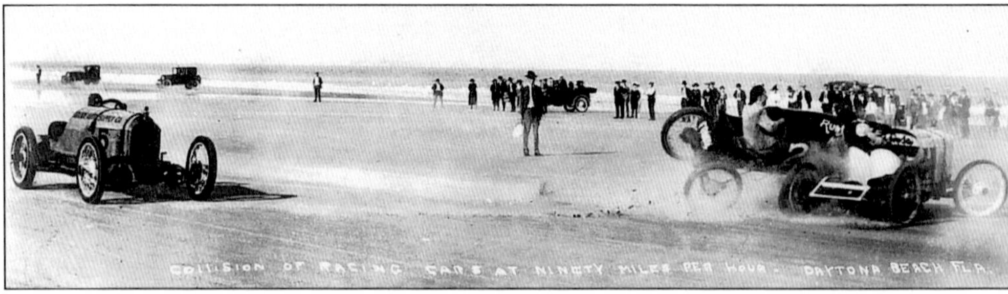

RACING COLLISION, C. 1926. Every now and then, an accident would occur at a racing event. When this took place, a driver ran the risk of losing everything unless he could find a sponsor. The drivers and onlookers are unidentified. (Courtesy of Halifax Historical Society.)

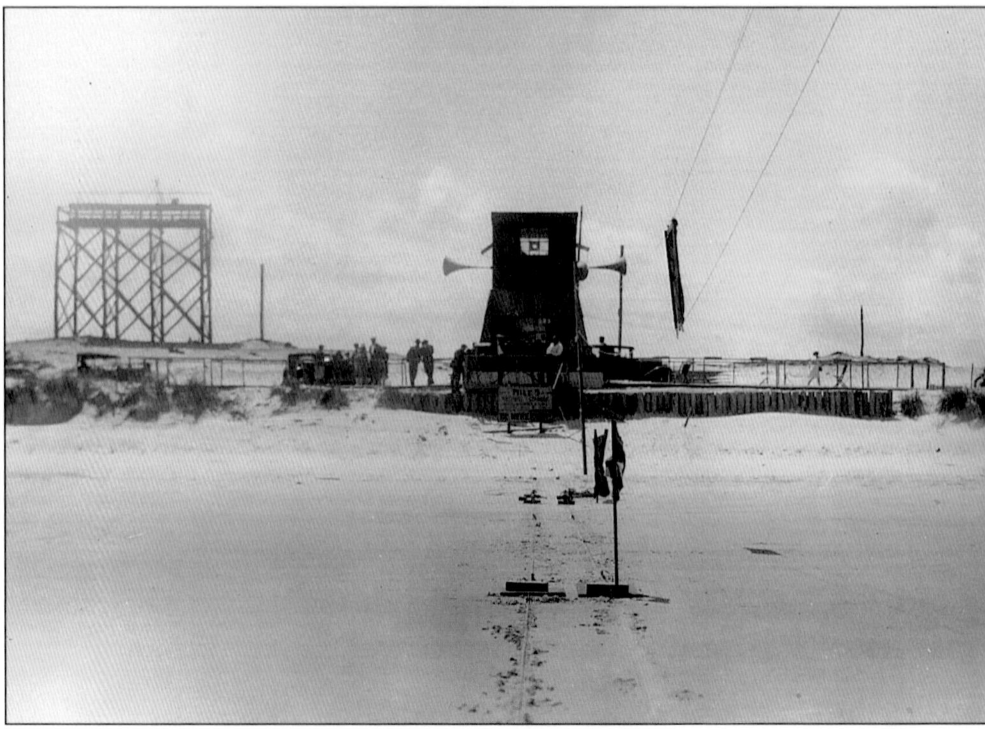

FIRST MEASURED MILE TIMING TOWER, C. 1927. This tower was constructed of pine and cypress wood. Odis Porter was given credit for the first timing devices. He invented an electric timing mechanism, which consisted of trip-wires stretched across each end of the measured mile. The elapsed time was recorded by utilizing an electric clock, running tape, and a printing device which was accurate to one one-hundredth of a second. (Courtesy of Halifax Historical Society.)

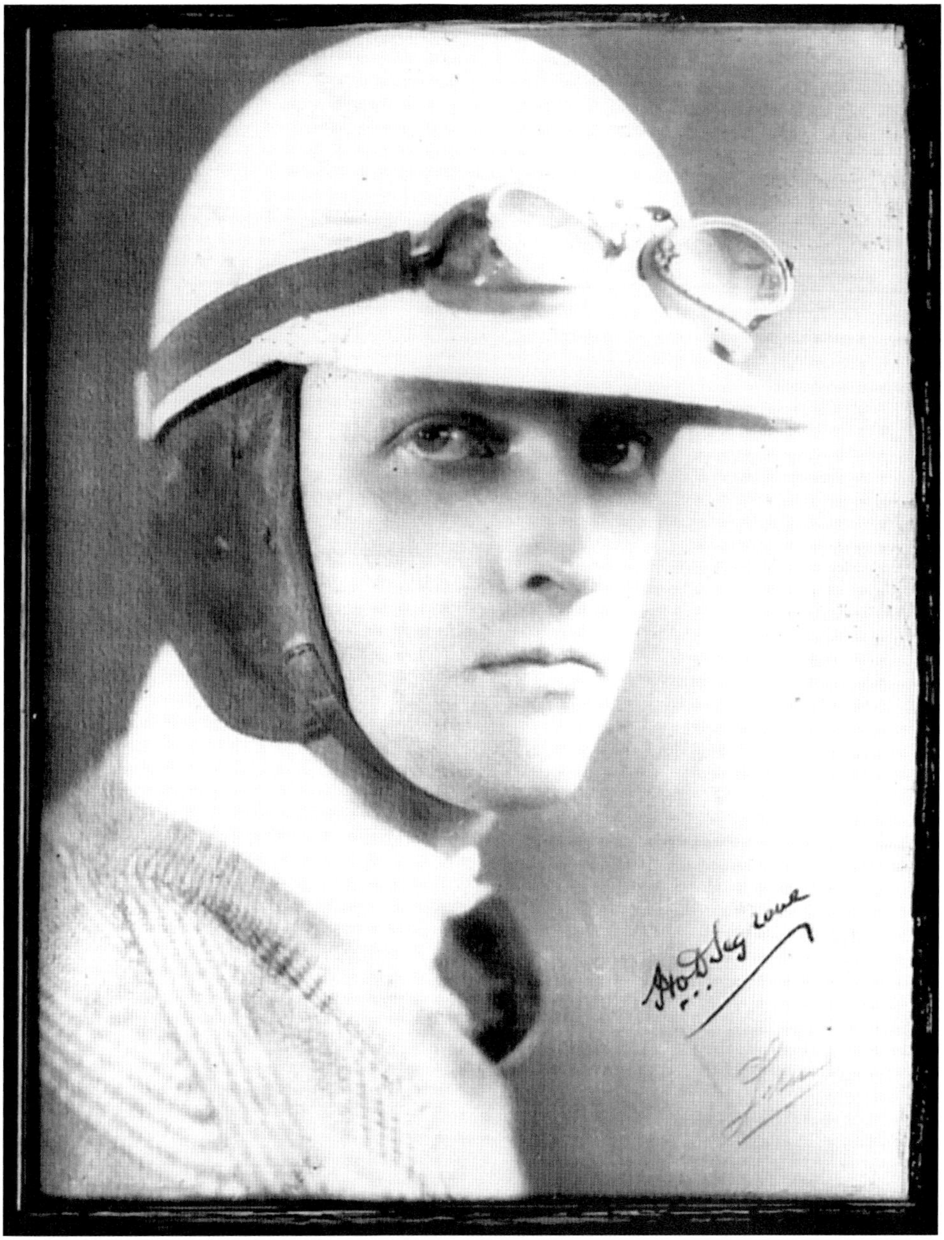

MAJ. HENRY O'NEILL DEHANE SEGRAVE, C. 1927. Segrave received the title of knighthood when he returned to England after breaking the World's Ground Speed Record at Daytona Beach. One of Daytona's prominent streets bears the name of Segrave, and many other honors were given to him. He is credited with wearing the first safety helmet. (Courtesy of Halifax Historical Society.)

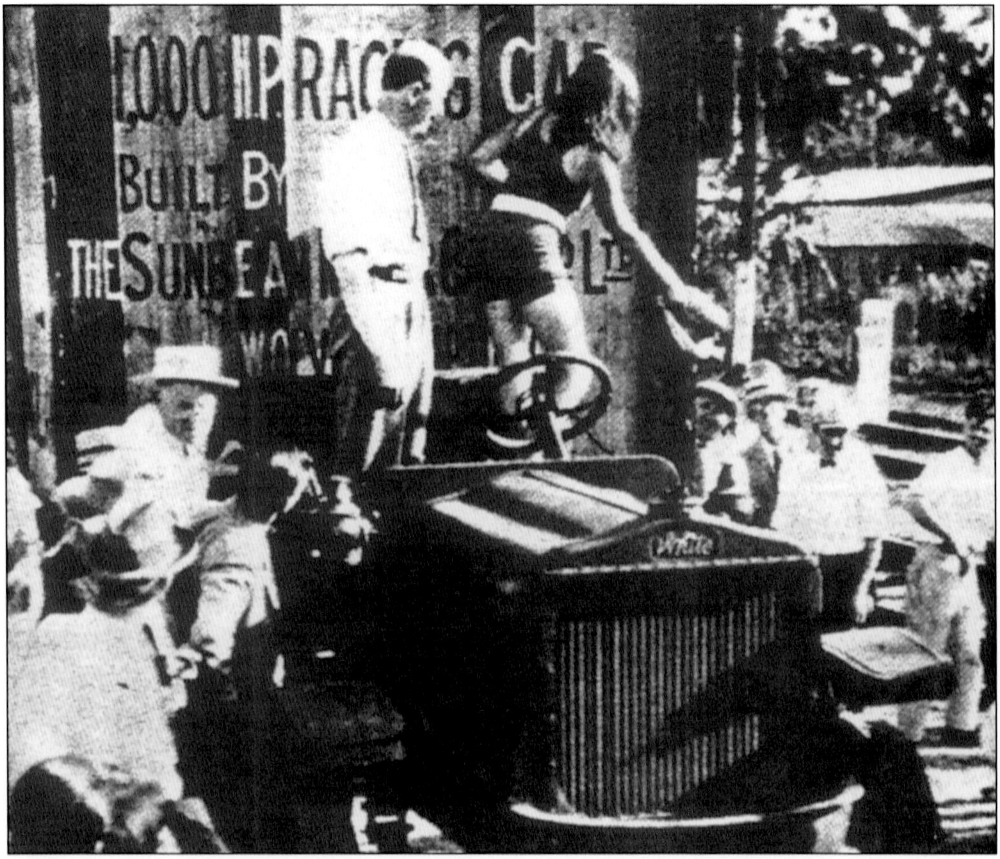

Segrave's *Mystery-S*, 1927. The *Mystery-S* arrived in New York from England by steamship. It was transferred to a freight car, and arrived by rail at Daytona on March 15. This was a great event for the town's inaugural run by Segrave. Fire sirens heralded in the speed trials. Officials and journalists gathered in town to be a part of this spectacular occasion on March 29, 1927. (Courtesy of Halifax Historical Society.)

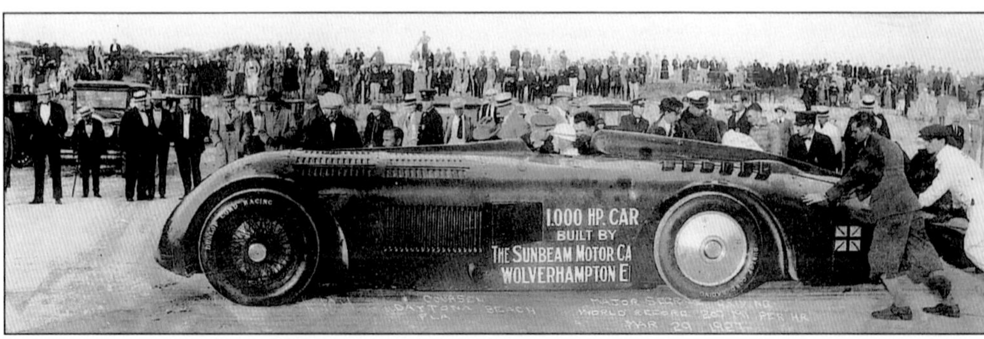

Maj. Henry O'Neill DeHane Segrave in His Sunbeam *Mystery-S*, March 29, 1927. Segrave returned to Daytona Beach in 1929 and broke the world record through the Measured Mile at 231.36 mph in his *Golden Arrow*. Segrave was killed in a speedboat accident in England in the summer of 1930. (Courtesy of Halifax Historical Society.)

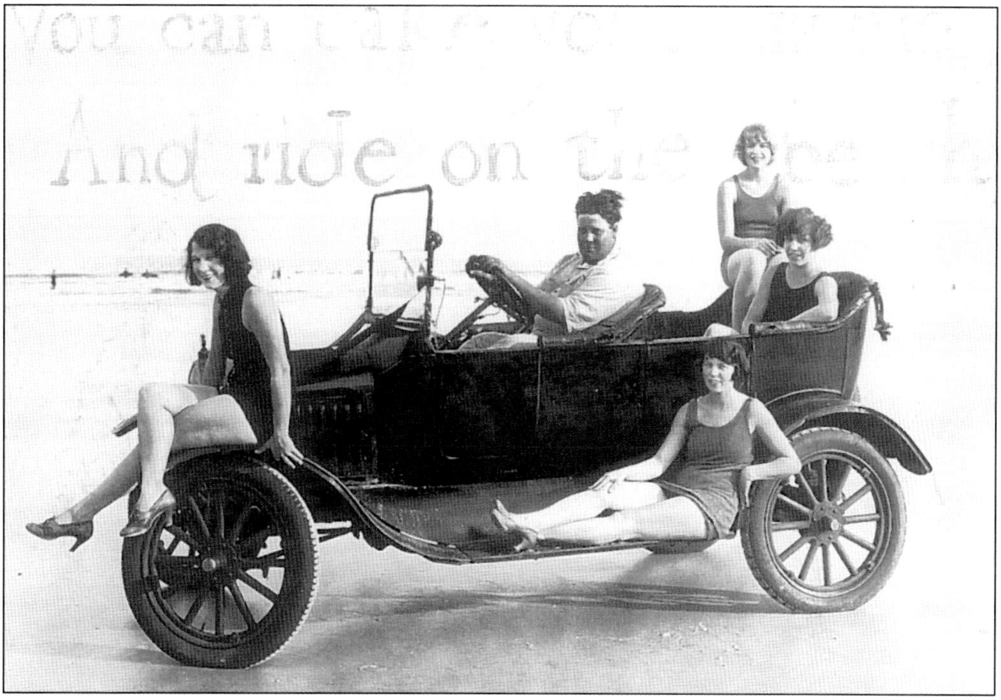

A Day at the Beach, c. 1927. This was a common sight along the beach—young people enjoying the surf and the sand. This Tin-Lizzie was a popular car for the young and old. In the back seat are Mary Nunn and Mildred ?. Jewel Cox is seated on the running board. The driver and the young lady on the front wheel are unidentified. (Courtesy of Cardwell Family Collection.)

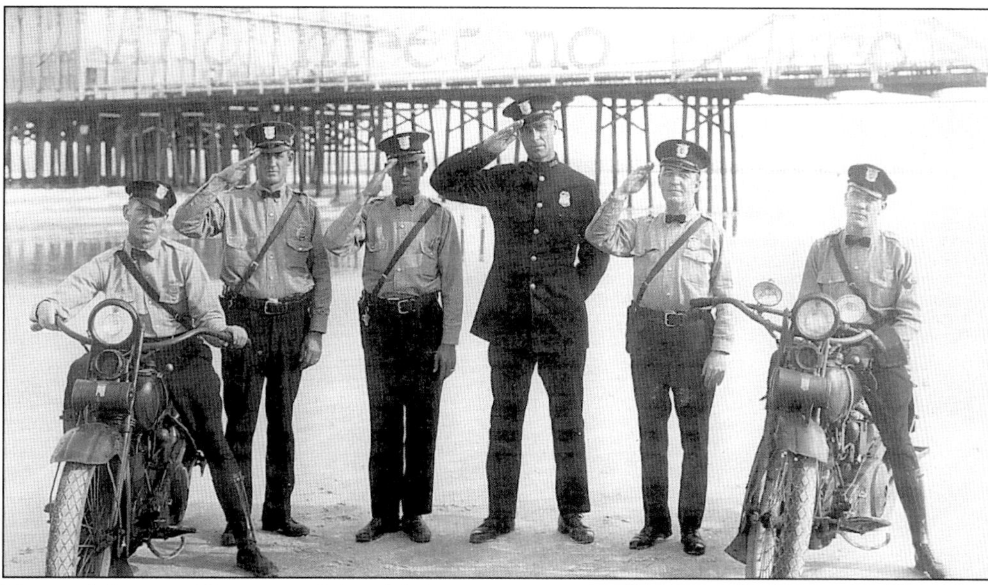

Ninety Miles an Hour and Meet No Police, c. 1927. The City of Daytona Beach bragged about their police department and their officers who helped with the racing festivities on the beach each winter. The Ocean Pier and Casino can be seen in the background. (Courtesy of Cardwell Family Collection.)

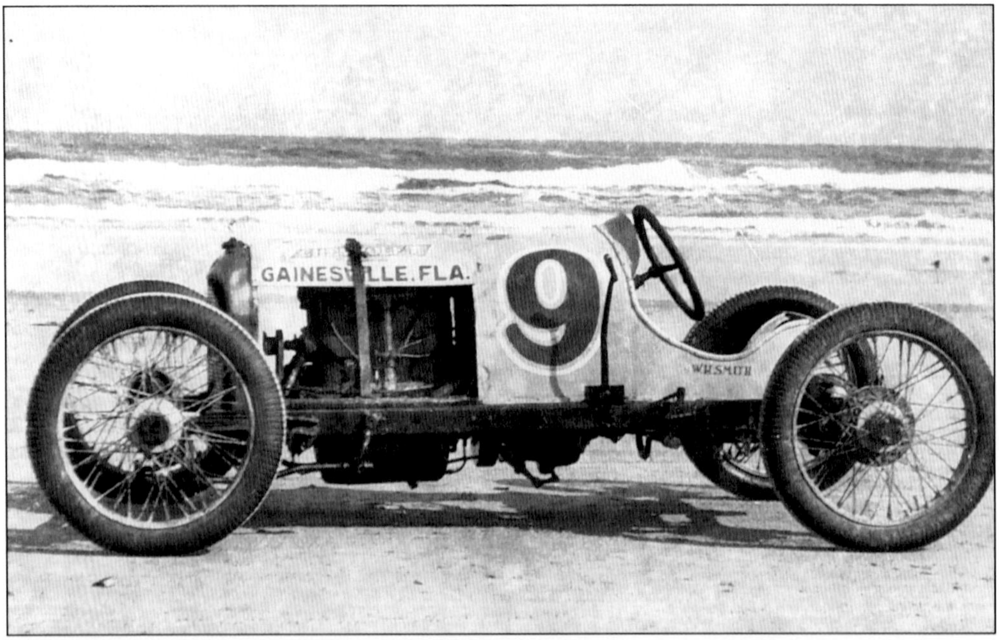

W.H. Smith's Chevrolet Race Car, 1927. Many car owners came from places all over the United States, as well as Florida, to compete in the Barrel Races on the beach. The competition was varied and there were many awards for their achievements. Little did they know they were helping the evolution of speed by participating each year. (Courtesy of John Gontner.)

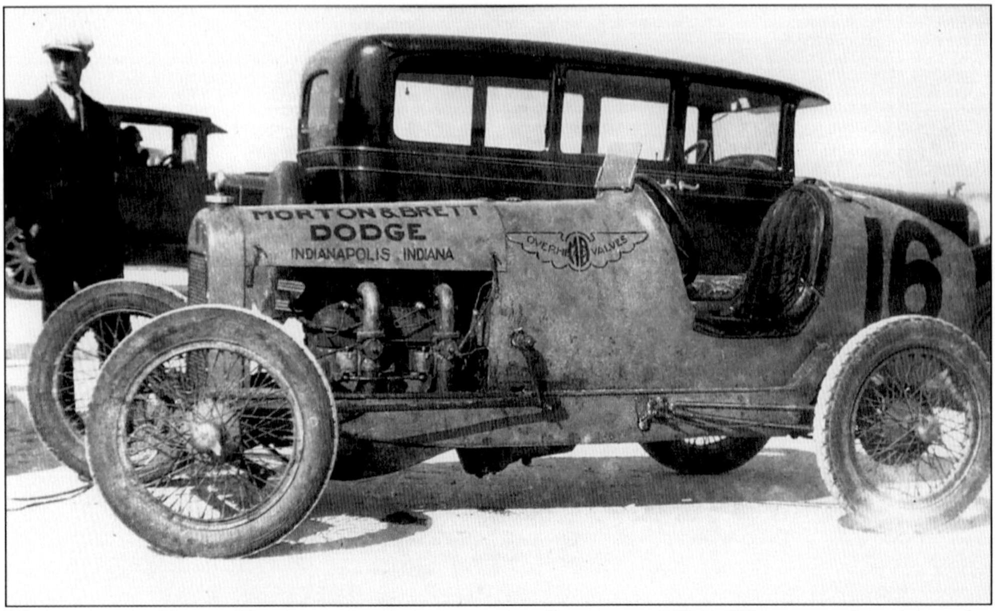

Morton and Brett Dodge from Indianapolis, Indiana, 1927. This car, advertising the Dodge engine, was in competition with other famous names in the automobile industry. The races and speed trials on the beach helped the industry develop better vehicle safety features and speed performance. The barrel or pillar races were favorites throughout the years. (Courtesy of John Gontner.)

Two

Racers Break New World's Ground Speed Records 1928–1935

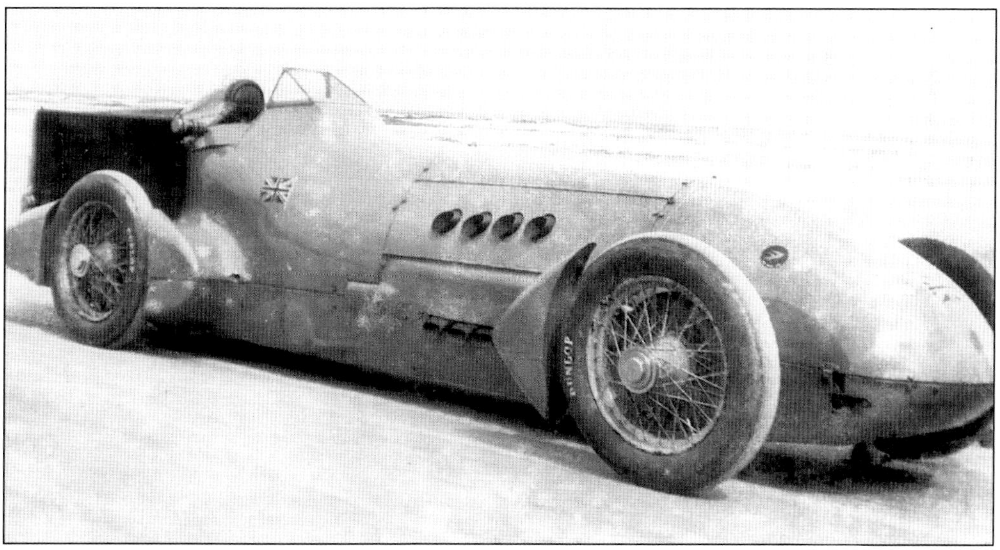

Capt. Malcolm Campbell's Napier *Bluebird I*, 1928. On February 19, Campbell broke the world record at 206.96 mph at Daytona Beach. He was an Englishman who owned an estate in England. Although his wealth came from real estate, insurance, and the diamond industry, he devoted his time to designing, building, and driving the world's fastest cars. His five famous racecars were the record-breaking *Bluebirds* from 1928 to 1935. (Courtesy of John Gontner.)

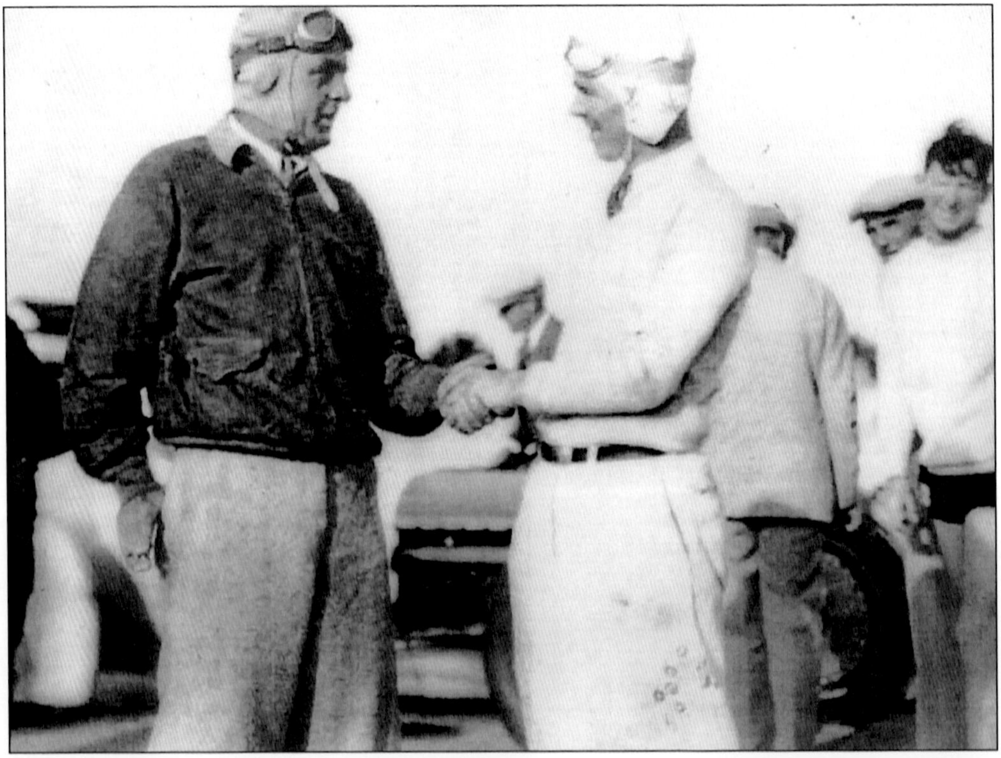

Sir Malcolm Campbell and Frank Lockhart, 1928. Campbell congratulated Lockhart before running the Measured Mile. He described beach conditions and advised him to check his tires before entering and leaving the Measured Mile. Campbell established a record of 206.96 mph. Lockhart survived his first crash on February 19, 1928. Unfortunately, he was killed in a second crash, on April 22, 1928, attempting to break the world record. (Courtesy Halifax Historical Society.)

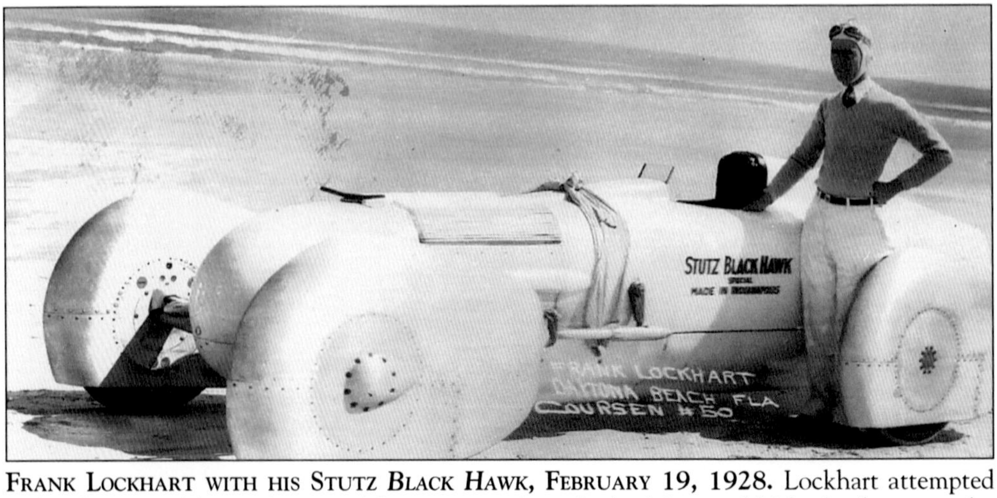

Frank Lockhart with his Stutz *Black Hawk*, February 19, 1928. Lockhart attempted to break the world record twice. After running through the Measured Mile the first time, he survived a crash on the beach. On his second run six weeks later, he crashed and was killed instantly. (Courtesy of Halifax Historical Society.)

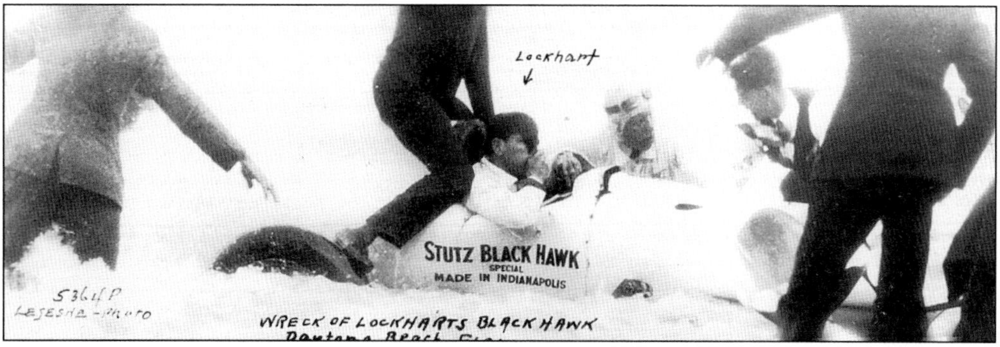

FRANK LOCKHART AND HIS STUTZ *BLACK HAWK*, FEBRUARY 19, 1928. Lockhart won the Indianapolis 500 before coming to Daytona Beach to try for the world record. The V-16, 182-cubic-inch engine, aided by two superchargers, was wrecked on his first attempt through the Measured Mile. He was rescued from the surf and the car was towed to safety. He rebuilt the car in just four weeks and was ready to seek the world record again. (Courtesy of Halifax Historical Society.)

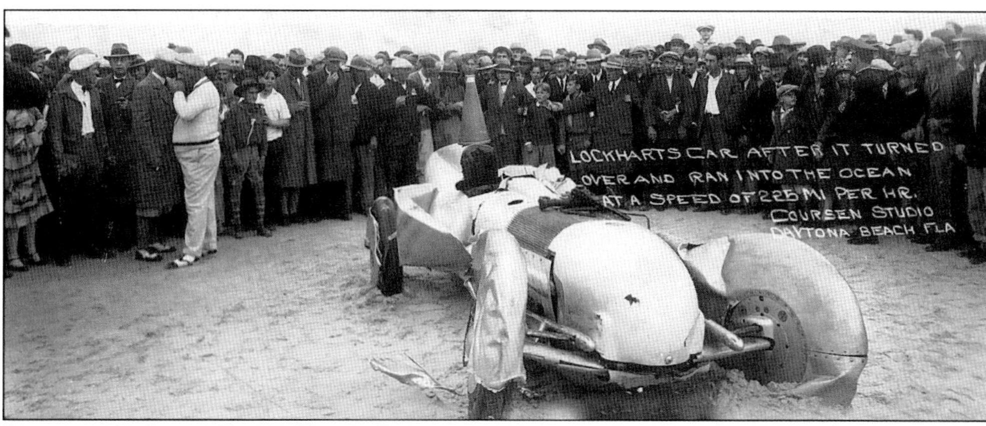

LOCKHART'S STUTZ *BLACK HAWK*, FEBRUARY 19, 1928. Bearing the name *Black Hawk*, this 2,800-pound vehicle was bright white, low, sleek, narrow, and capable of record-breaking speed. Onlookers thought it could never run again. However, after a short convalescence, Lockhart quickly rebuilt the car and was ready to try again for the world record. (Courtesy of Halifax Historical Society.)

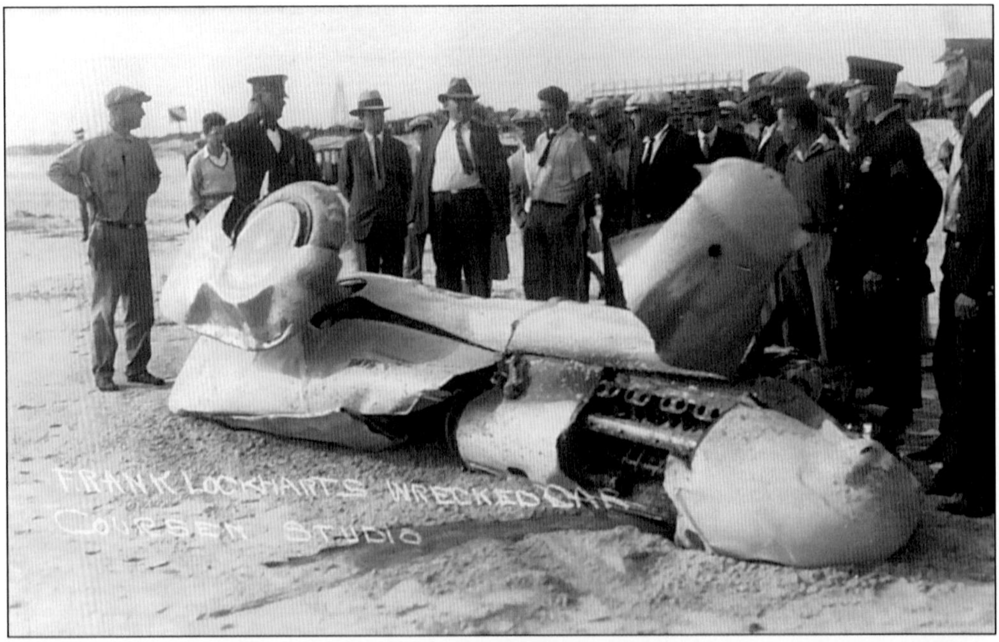

FRANK LOCKHART'S FATAL CRASH, APRIL 22, 1928. Officials gather to inspect the wreckage after Lockhart's car catapulted and rolled in a 1,000-foot skid. Lockhart was killed instantly as his wife and onlookers watched in horror. The promising life of the 26-year-old racer ended early in the morning, at the famed Measured Mile on Daytona Beach. (Courtesy of Halifax Historical Society.)

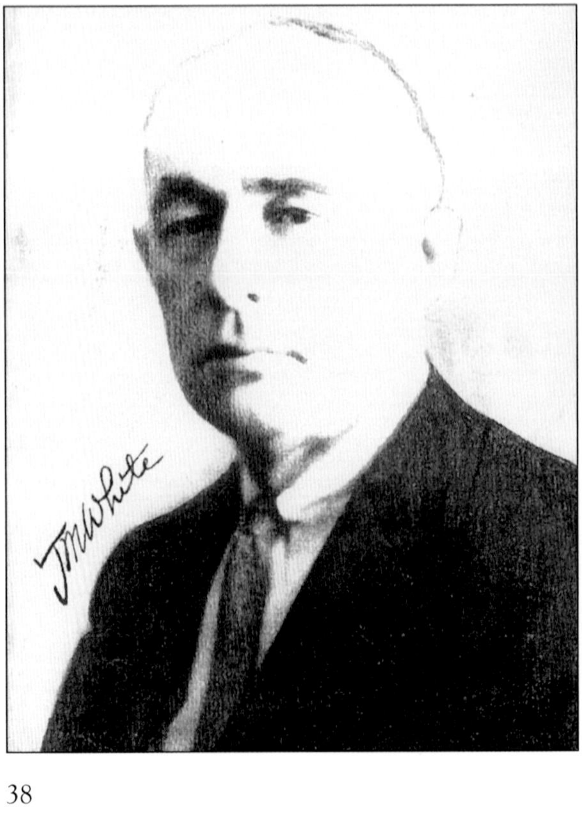

J.M. WHITE, 1928. White was an inventor from Philadelphia, Pennsylvania, and the owner and builder of the *Triplex* race car. White utilized three 500-horsepower Liberty motors. He hired Ray Keech, who broke the World's Speed Record on April 22, 1928, doing the mile in 17.34 seconds at a speed of 207.55 mph. In 1929, Lee Bible was killed in a crash in the *Triplex* that also took the life of photographer Charles Traub. (Courtesy of Halifax Historical Society.)

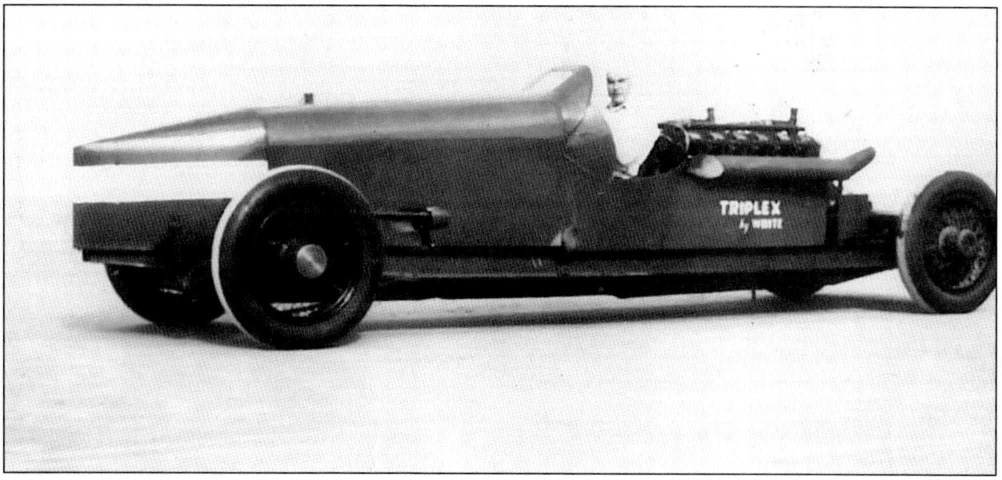

Ray Keech in the *Triplex*, April 22, 1928. On this memorable day, the *Triplex* race car, owned by J.M. White, made a record run of 207.552 mph. This famed Indianapolis race driver was signed to make the run in the *Triplex* with its three V-12, 5,000-cubic-inch engines, which ran in unison, to break the World's Ground Speed Record and the title was once again claimed by America. (Courtesy of Halifax Historical Society.)

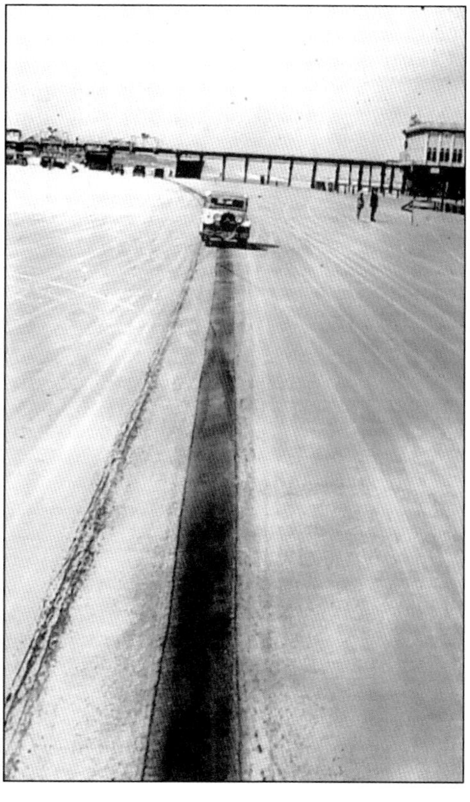

Famous Black Line, c. 1929. There were many innovative ways to help the race driver keep on track during his high-speed run through the Measured Mile. This black line was put down on the sand using blackened oil from an oil-tank truck with a spout at the rear. Today, this method would be considered an environmentally unsafe practice. Eventually, the drivers preferred flags, which were used throughout the years on the beach. (Courtesy of Halifax Historical Society.)

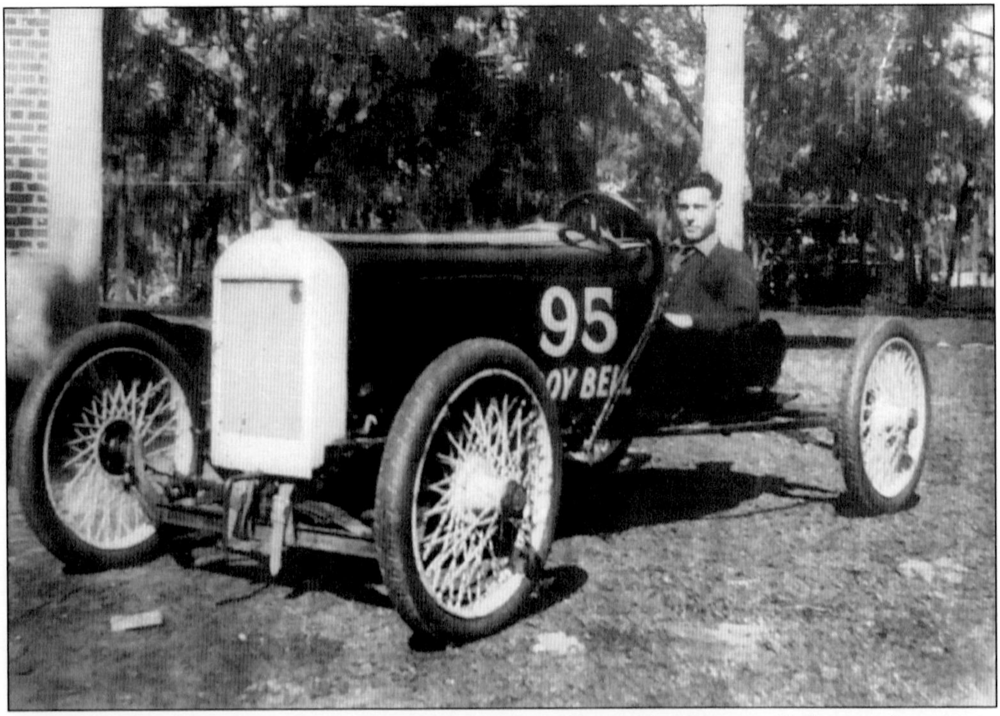

LeRoy R. Bell, Daytona Beach Businessman and Race Car Driver. Bell was a favorite in many of the barrel and pillar races, events held on July 4 and Labor Day each year. Bell won the Volusia County Frolics race in 1928. He died in 1950. (Courtesy of Gloria Bell-Tow.)

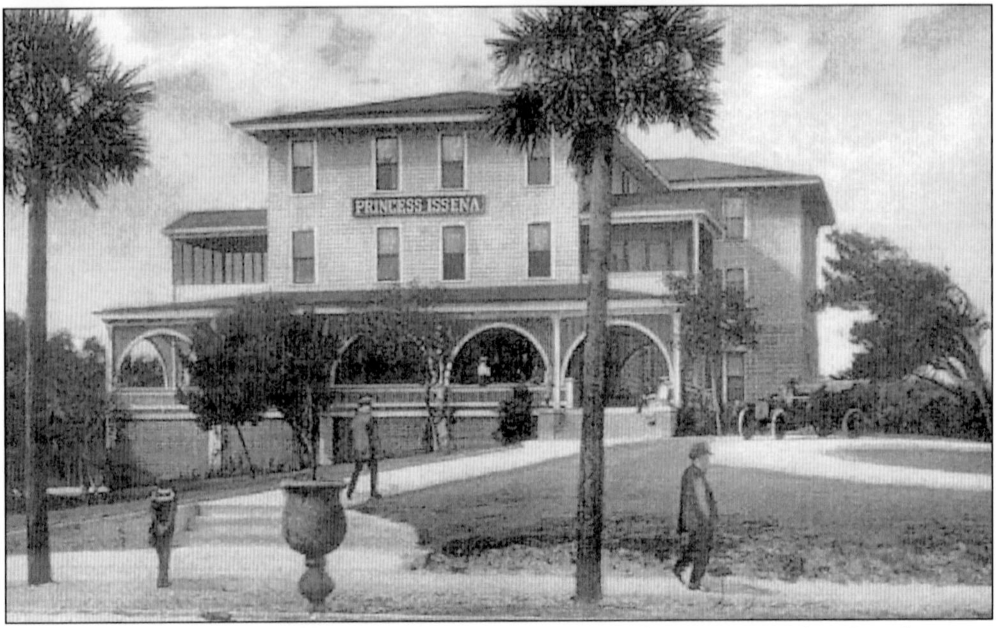

Princess Issena Hotel, 1928. Wealthy tourists came to this prestigious hotel each winter to escape the cold weather and view the barrel races, speed trials, and other events that were held on the beach. Many of the notable guests that signed the hotel register were from the automotive and racing industry. (Courtesy of Midkiff Family Collection.)

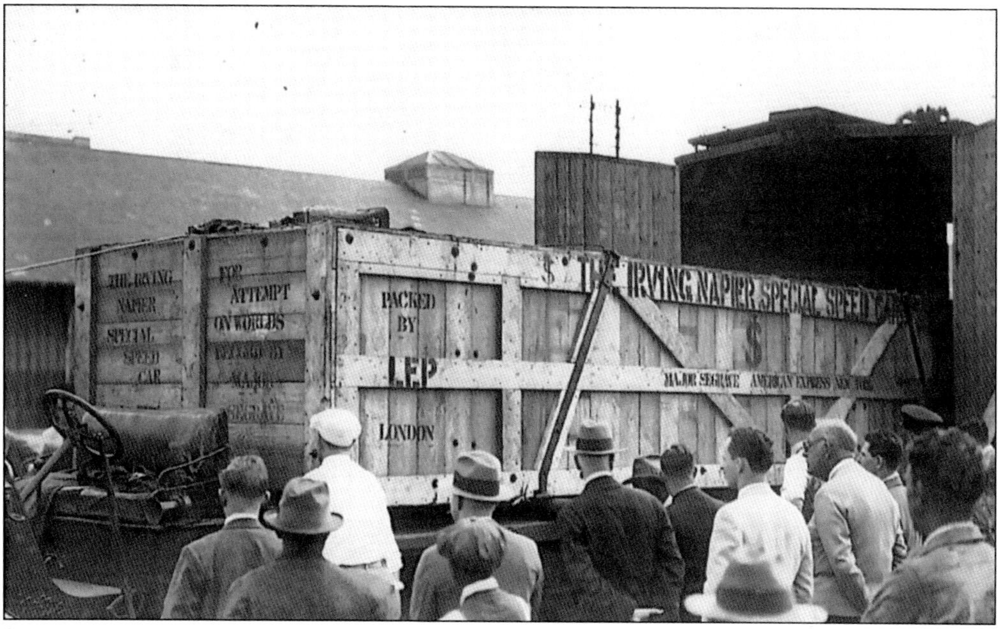

SEGRAVE'S *GOLDEN ARROW* ARRIVAL, 1929. This race car was shipped from England via steamship and rail. Segrave arrived later in Daytona Beach to the Clarendon Hotel. To avoid a stir of notoriety he avoided public places, but citizens and officials were too alert to let him escape recognition. He broke the ground speed record on March 6, 1929, at a speed of 231.36 mph. At this same time, Segrave brought his famous speedboat to Daytona for a trial run on the Halifax River. (Courtesy of Halifax Historical Society.)

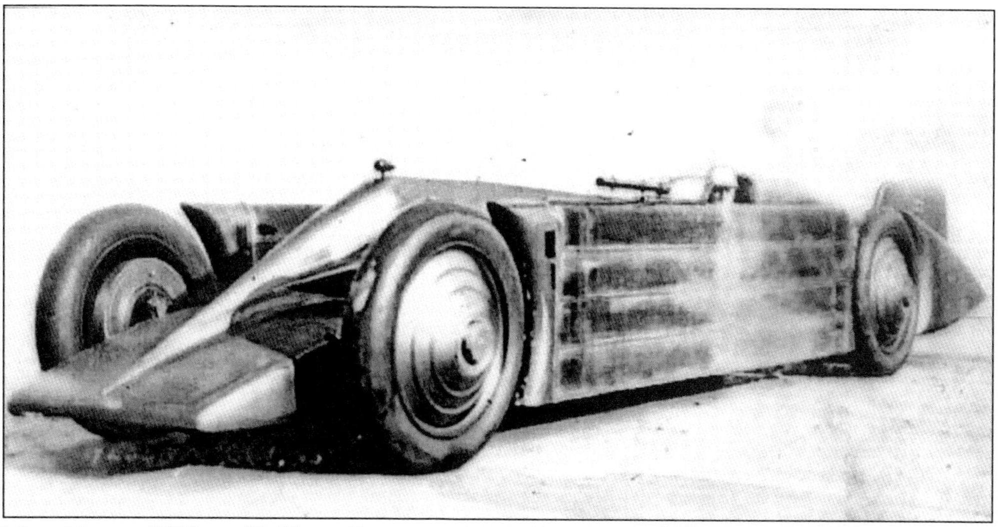

MAJ. HENRY O'NEILL DEHANE SEGRAVE, 1929. Segrave made his trial run on the beach in his *Golden Arrow*. The Measured Mile was calculated by the speed of the racer through marked mileposts, which were read from instruments atop a timing tower. The racer had to build up speed several miles before entering the measured mile area. This was done by making the run going north, and then south, to obtain the average calculated speed. Segrave broke the World's Ground Speed Record at 231.36 mph—his last attempt at Daytona. (Courtesy of Halifax Historical Society.)

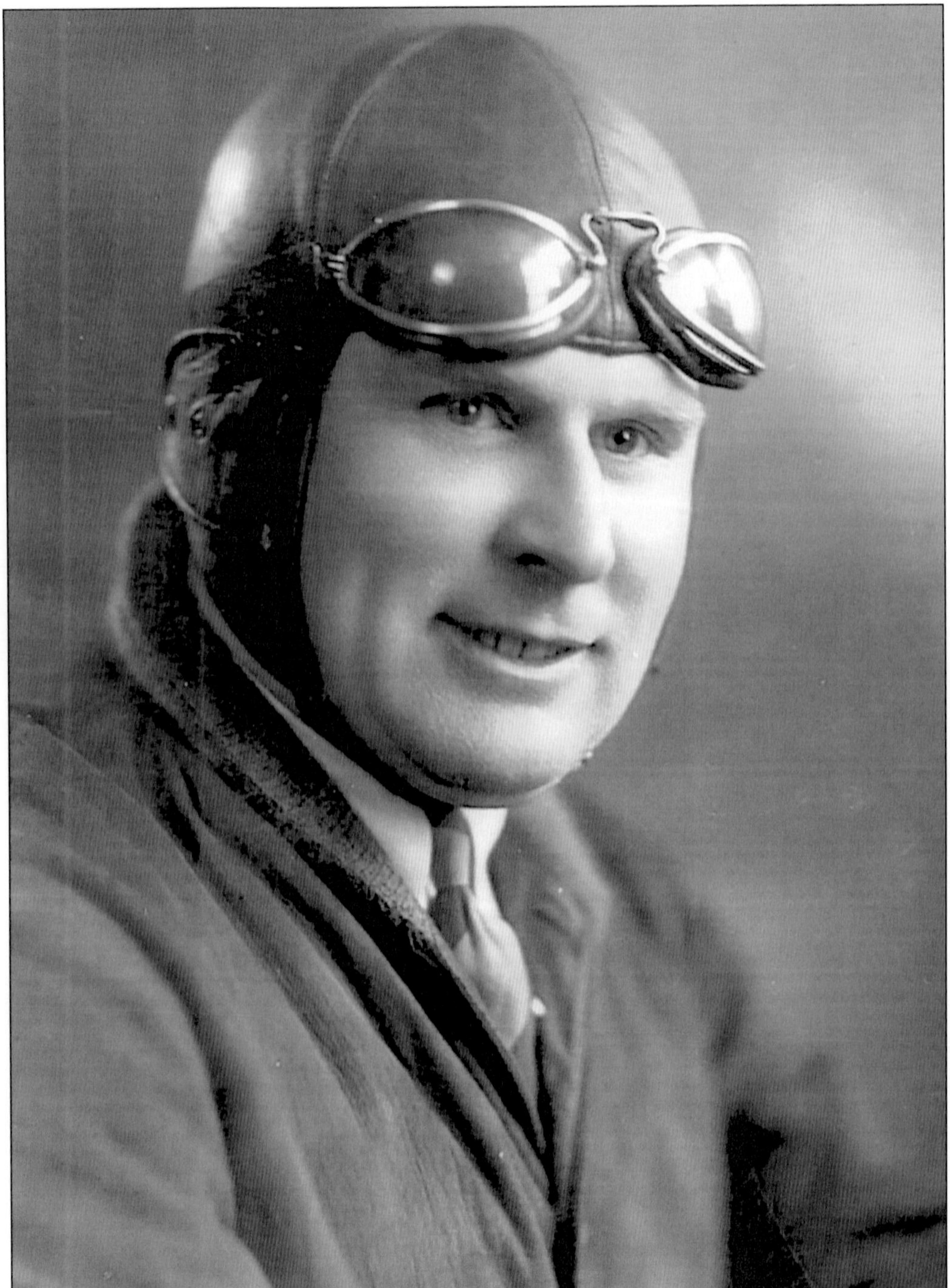

RAY KEECH, 1929. Keech was a famed Indianapolis race car driver. He was hired by J.M. White to drive the massive *Triplex* at Daytona Beach in 1928. He suffered serious burns while behind the wheel, but did push the car through the measured mile at a speed of 207.552 mph, breaking the record for America. Keech refused to drive the *Triplex* in 1929 and White was forced to find a new driver. Daytona Beach honored him by naming a street after him. (Courtesy of Halifax Historical Society.)

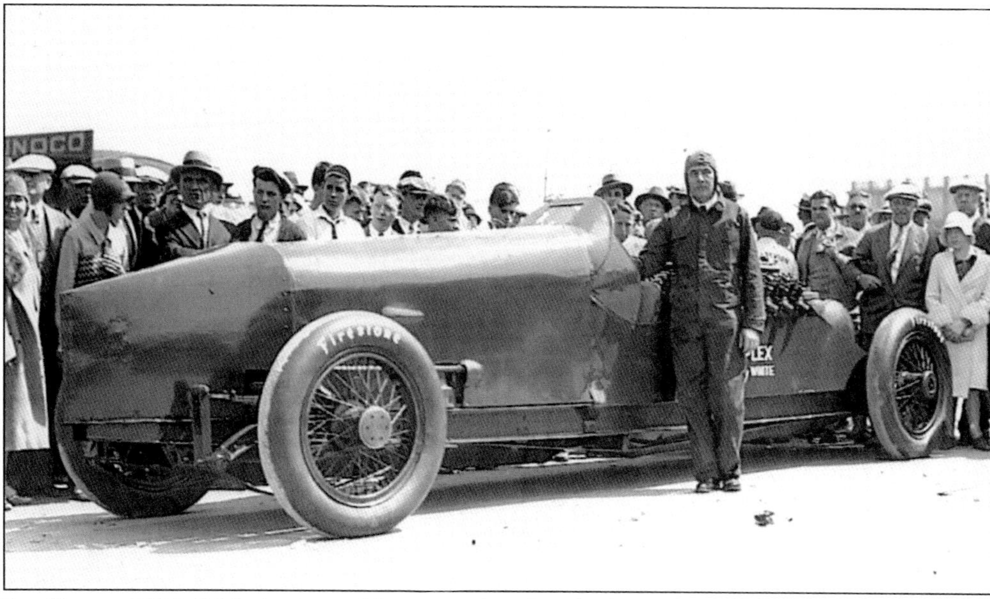

Lee Bible, 1929. Bible is pictured here standing beside the massive *Triplex* 20 minutes before his fatal crash. Many of the officials and onlookers gave him their best wishes for a successful run. J.M. White was pleased with his choice of driver and was hoping for a record run. It was a chance for Bible to achieve notoriety but fate took away his chance for an opportunity of a lifetime. (Courtesy of Halifax Historical Society.)

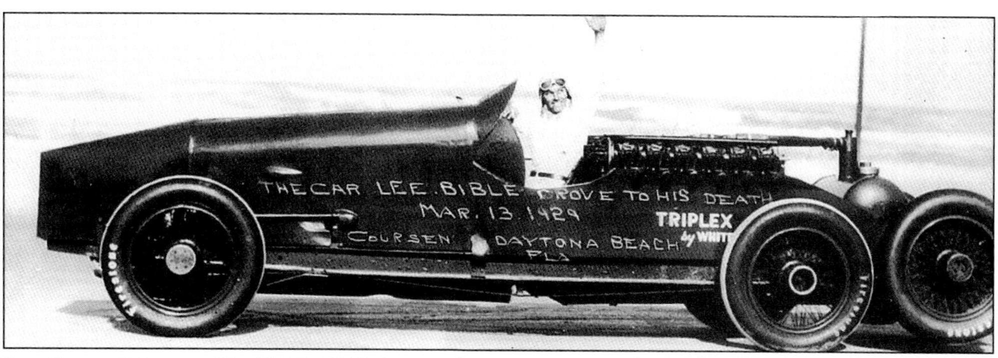

Lee Bible, March 13, 1929. Bible is seen here waving to the enthusiastic crowd of onlookers just before firing up the engines. He was hoping to break the World's Ground Speed Record for J.M. White. (Courtesy of Halifax Historical Society.)

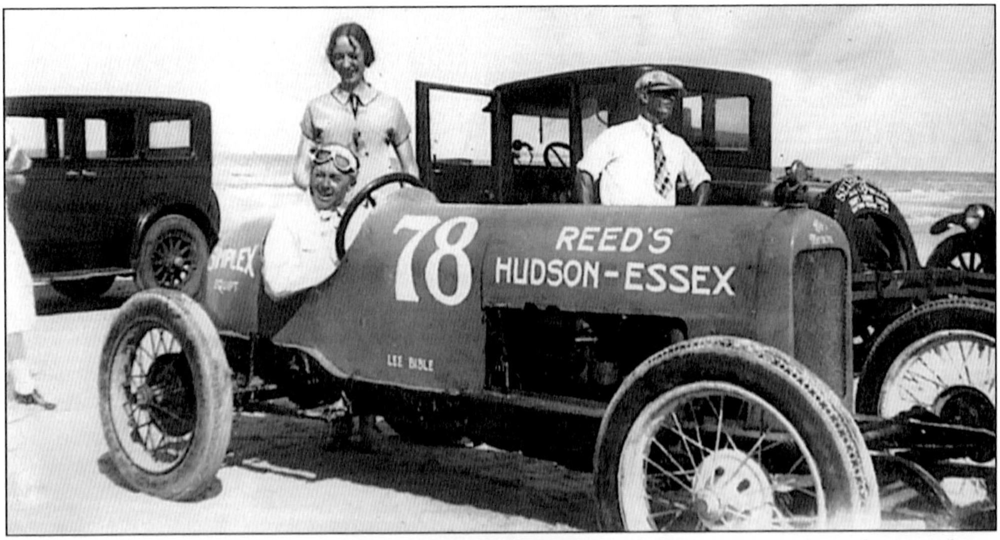

LEE BIBLE IN *REED'S HUDSON-ESSEX*, 1929. Bible was a garage owner and mechanic whose racing experience had been limited to half-mile dirt tracks. Bible proved himself to be an outstanding race driver in small competitions. J.M. White needed a driver for the 1929 season and Lee Bible happened to be chosen for the *Triplex*. Little did he know that he would meet his fate in the Measured Mile on March 13, 1929. (Courtesy of Halifax Historical Society.)

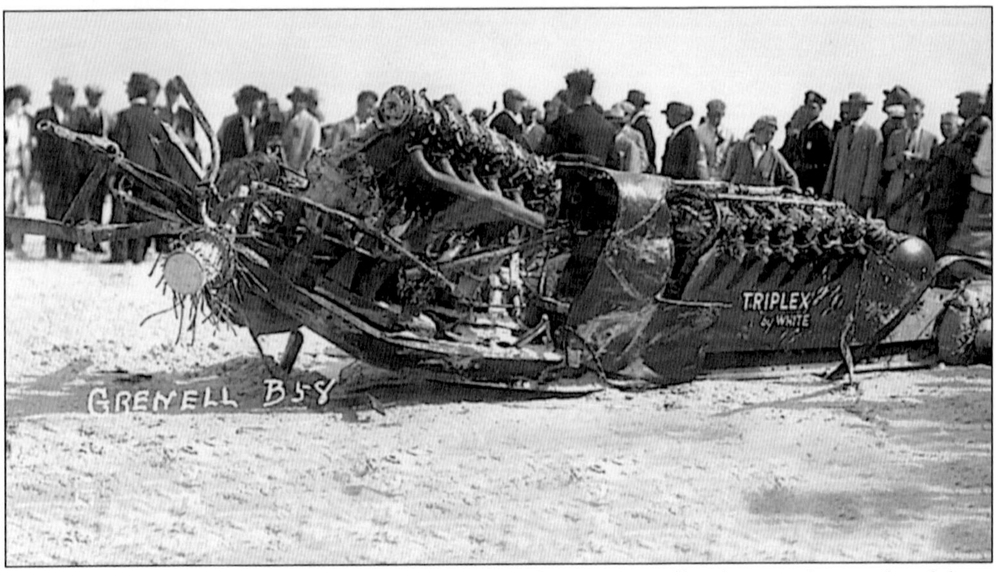

FATAL CRASH OF LEE BIBLE, MARCH 13, 1929. When racing officials gave the go-ahead from the timing tower, the signal was flagged to Lee Bible and he started his preliminary run. He headed north, through the measured mile at a speed of more than 200 mph and seemed to lose control just past the timing tower. The car swerved into heavy sand near the dunes, where it careened off course and struck a news photographer. The car rolled over several times and pieces of the *Triplex* were scattered along the beach. When it was over, the photographer had been killed instantly and Lee Bible lay dying near the wreckage. Among the many onlookers were Bible's wife and daughter. The legend of Lee Bible has never died. A ballad was written in his memory and can be heard to this day at the Halifax Historical Museum. (Courtesy of Halifax Historical Society.)

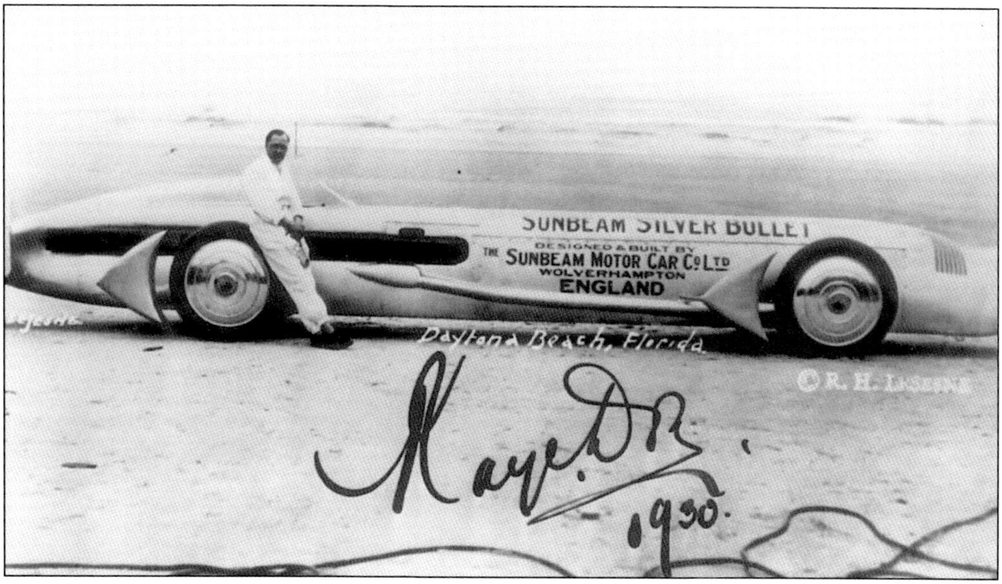

KAYE DON AND HIS SUNBEAM *SILVER BULLET*, MARCH 14, 1930. This race car was 31 feet long with adjustable tail fins and a pair of Sunbeam V-12 engines mounted in tandem. Don drove this through the measured mile at over 190 mph but was unable to make a successful timed run. This project completely failed at the beginning of the Depression Era in the United States. However, it did help to motivate future timed trial runs. (Courtesy of John Gontner.)

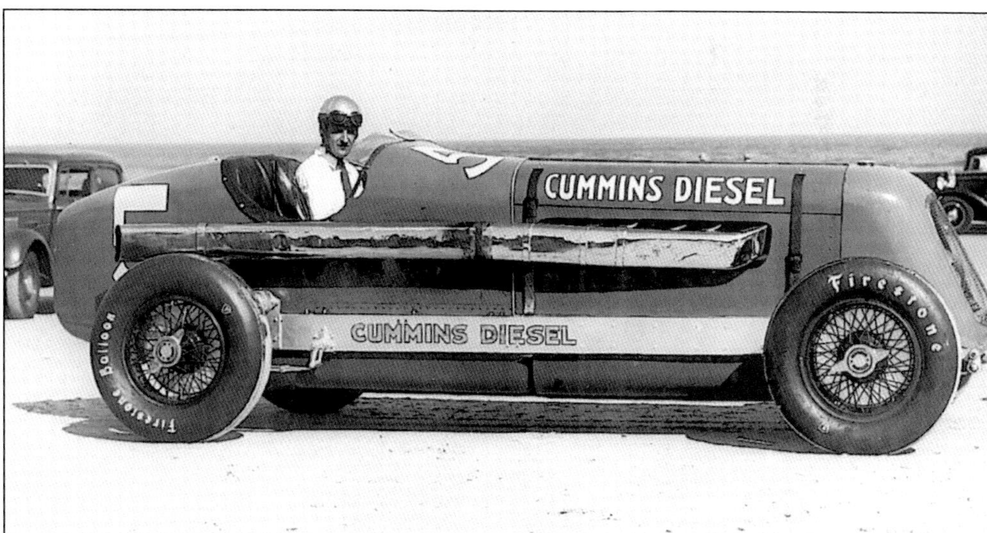

CLESSIE L. CUMMINS, 1930. Cummins set a record of 80 mph through the measured mile with a diesel-powered truck engine on a Packard frame. The American Automobile Association awarded him a certificate for the first record ever set by a diesel-powered automobile. He was also commended as the designer and builder of this special car. (Courtesy of Halifax Historical Society.)

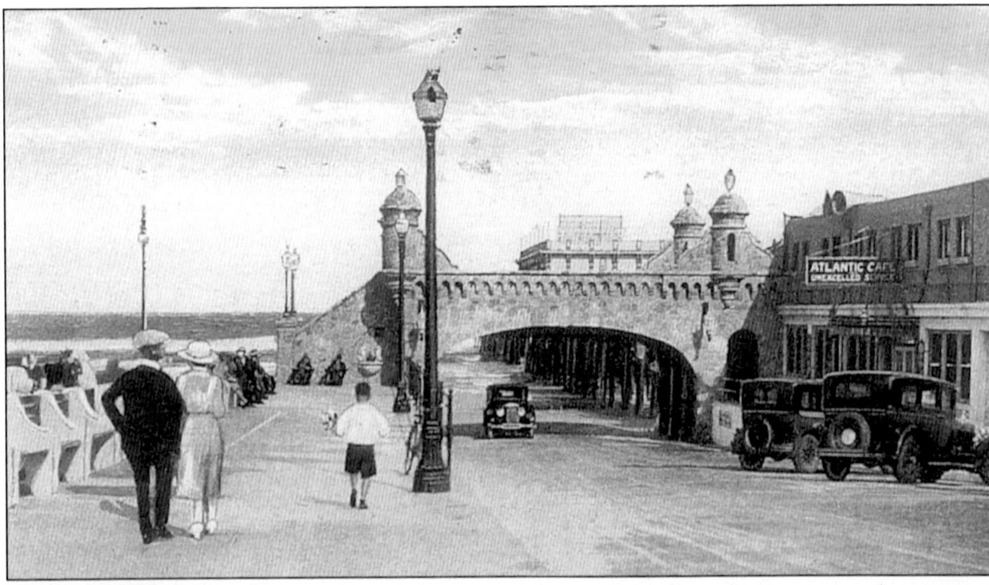

HISTORIC LANDMARK, 1931. This is a view of the first boardwalk and entrance to the pier and beach. Notice the sign for the Atlantic Cafe stating that they provide "unexcelled service." (Courtesy of Halifax Historical Society.)

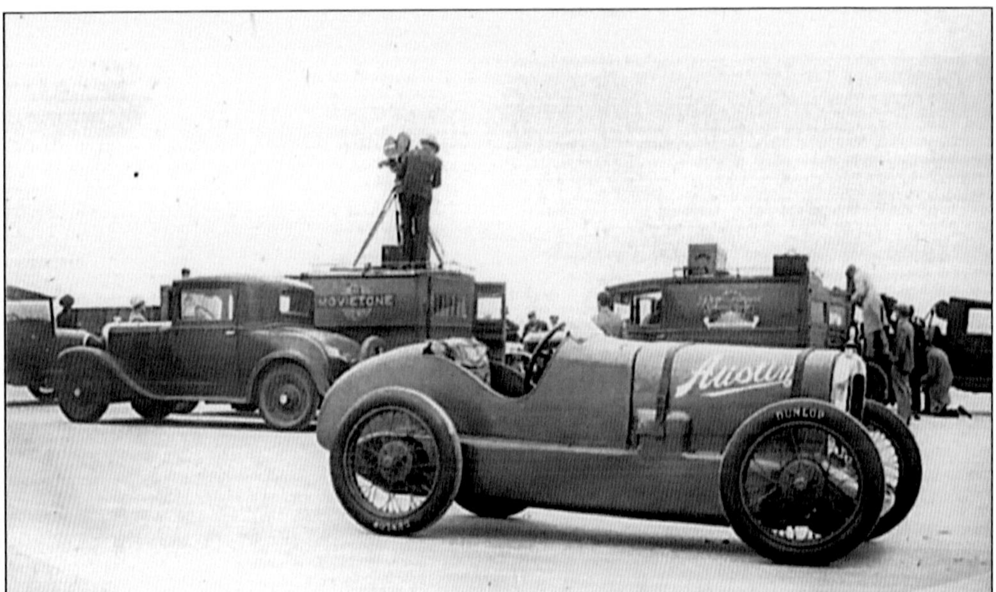

FILMING THE RACES, 1931. This "Movietone" news photographer is adjusting the camera to be ready for Sir Malcolm Campbell's record run. Notice the Austin in the foreground with the spoke wheels. (Courtesy of Halifax Historical Society.)

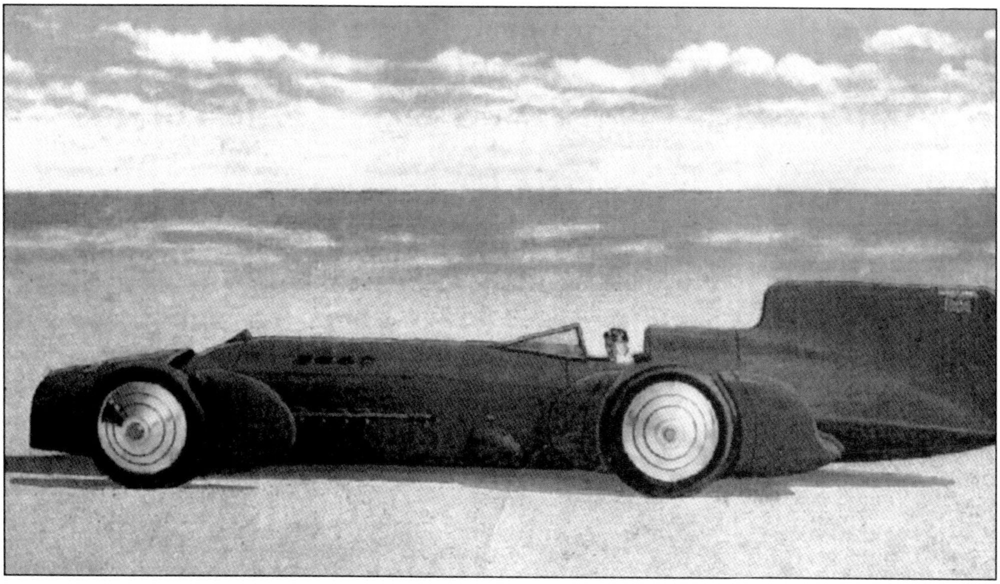

Sir Malcolm Campbell's *Bluebird II*, 1931. The *Bluebird* was completely rebuilt with a new streamlined profile. The driver's seat was relocated to an offset position, alongside the drive shaft. The horsepower was raised to 1,350, and the tires were improved to provide better traction in the sand. Campbell beat Segrave's record of 240 mph and raised the World's Ground Speed Record to 245.73 mph. (Courtesy of Halifax Historical Society.)

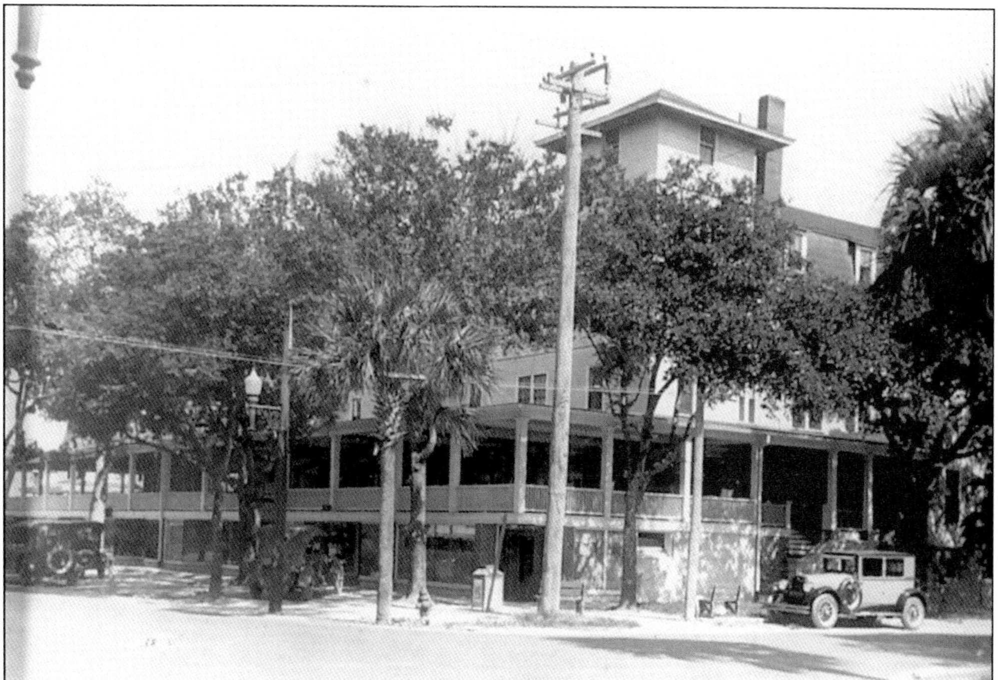

Williams Hotel, c. 1931. Winter visitors stayed in this mainland hotel where they could shop and attend the speed events beachside. The hotel was in walking distance of the Florida East Coast Railroad Depot. It was located on the southeast corner of Magnolia and Palmetto Avenues. (Courtesy of Halifax Historical Society.)

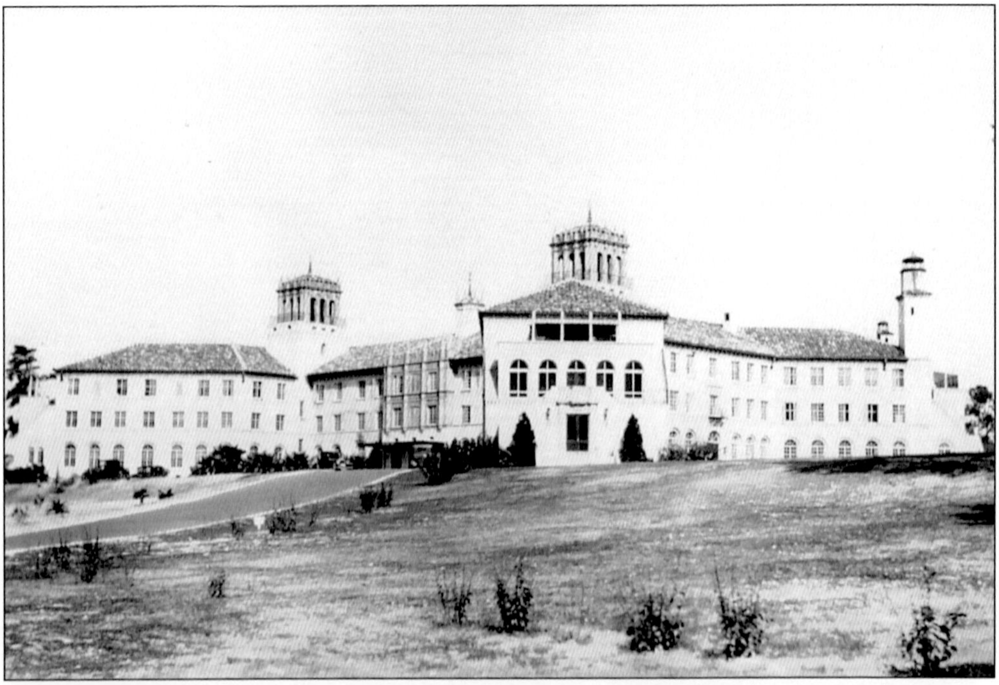

HALIFAX HOSPITAL, 1931. The architectural style of this beautiful landmark is Mediterranean Revival. This hospital has served the needs of the community for many years. All race-related injuries were brought to this medical facility. (Courtesy of Cardwell Family Collection.)

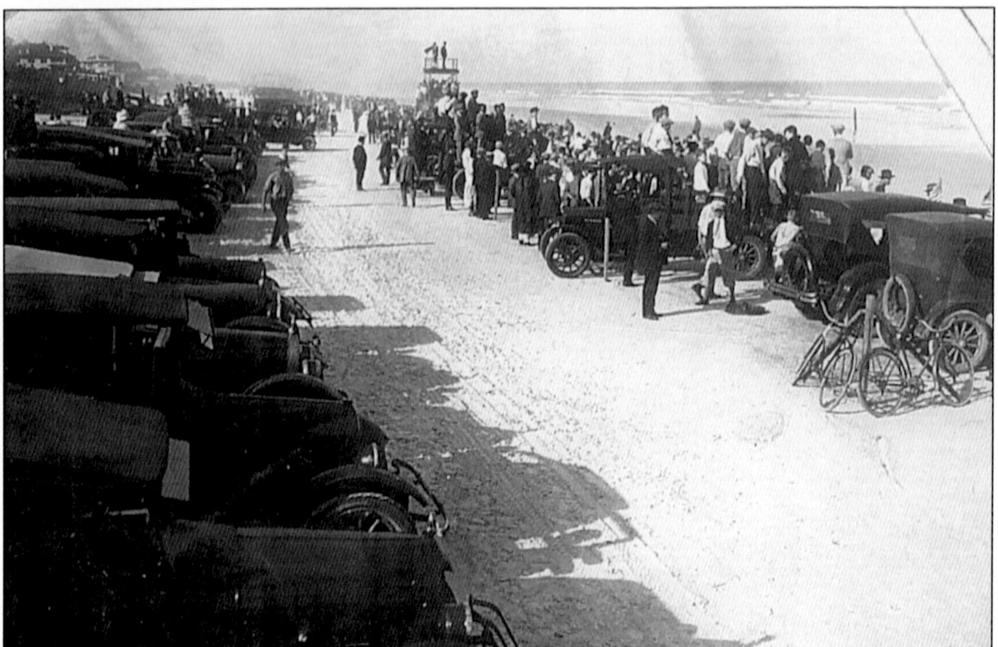

TIMING TOWER AT THE MEASURED MILE, C. 1931. Notice the man with the megaphone, which was necessary among the race officials to control the crowds and to announce the approaching driver making his speed run. (Courtesy of Halifax Historical Society.)

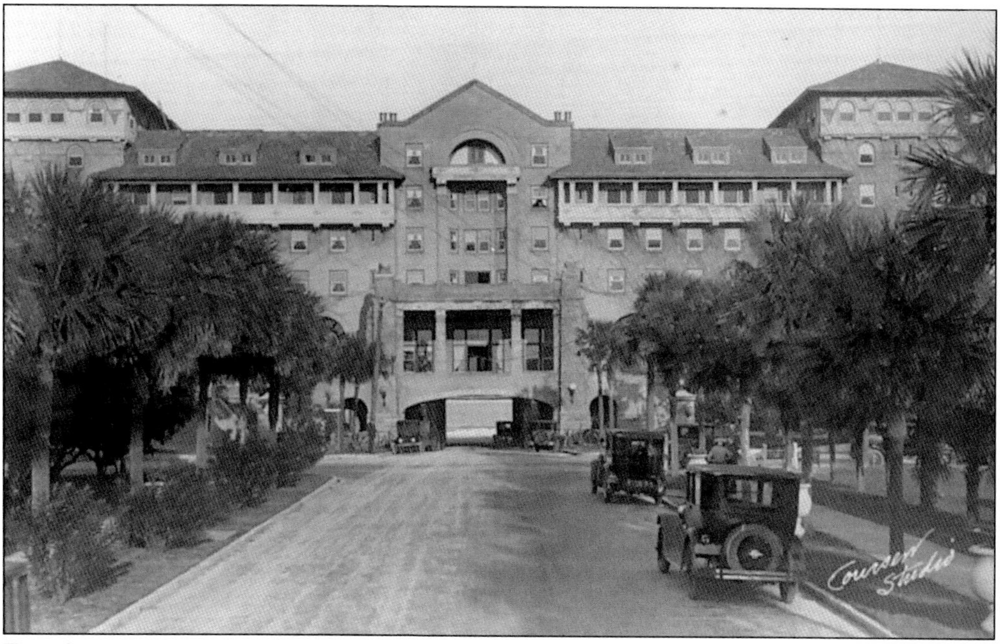

THE CLARENDON HOTEL, C. 1931. This was the favorite hotel of many of the race drivers during the speed events. The Princess Issena and the Seaside Inn were also popular gathering places for all of the winter visitors. Among the well-known speedsters were Segrave, Keech, and Campbell. Many tourists only wanted to get a glimpse of these famous drivers. They would stand in the lobby of the hotel for hours for a chance to witness the pandemonium. (Courtesy of Halifax Historical Society.)

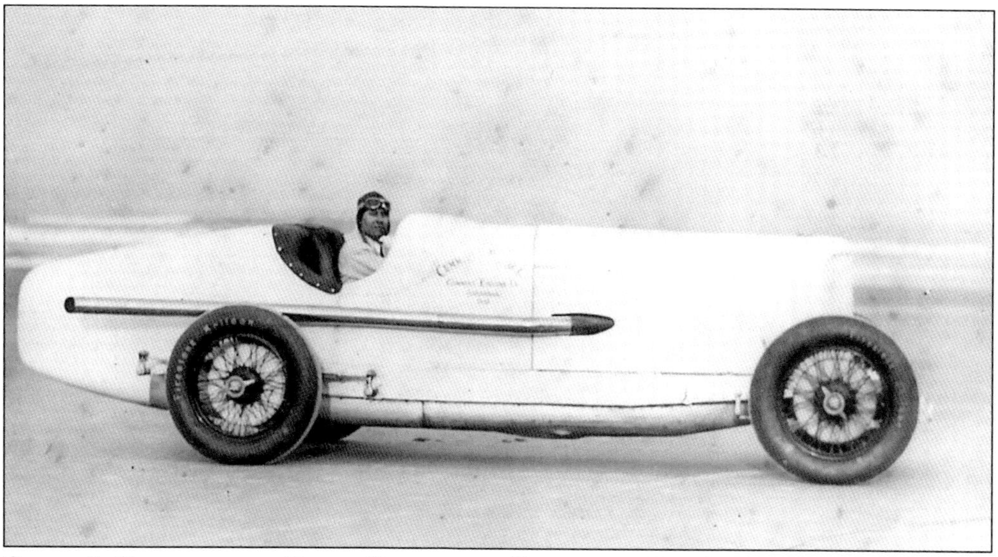

CLESSIE L. CUMMINS IN HIS DIESEL-DUESENBERG, FEBRUARY, 1931. Cummins opened the racing season by breaking the diesel engine record with a speed of 100.755 mph. This was the first record for a diesel engine running over 100 mph on Daytona's beach. Later, this car would run nonstop at the 1931 Indianapolis 500 in May. The evolution of the diesel engine was advanced at these winter speed trials through the measured mile. Cummins was the designer and builder, and beat his own 1930 record of 80 mph. (Courtesy of Halifax Historical Society.)

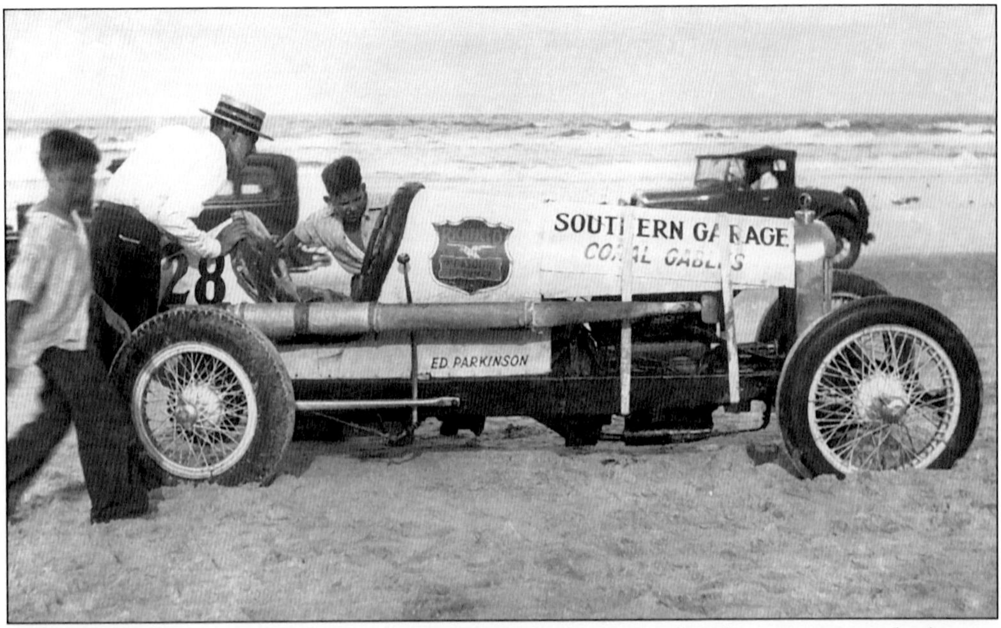

RACE CAR FOR THE 100-MILE BEACH RACE, 1932. The winter beach racing events had many entries. This car, owned by Ed Parkinson, was a real challenger for the 100-mile race. (Courtesy of Halifax Historical Society.)

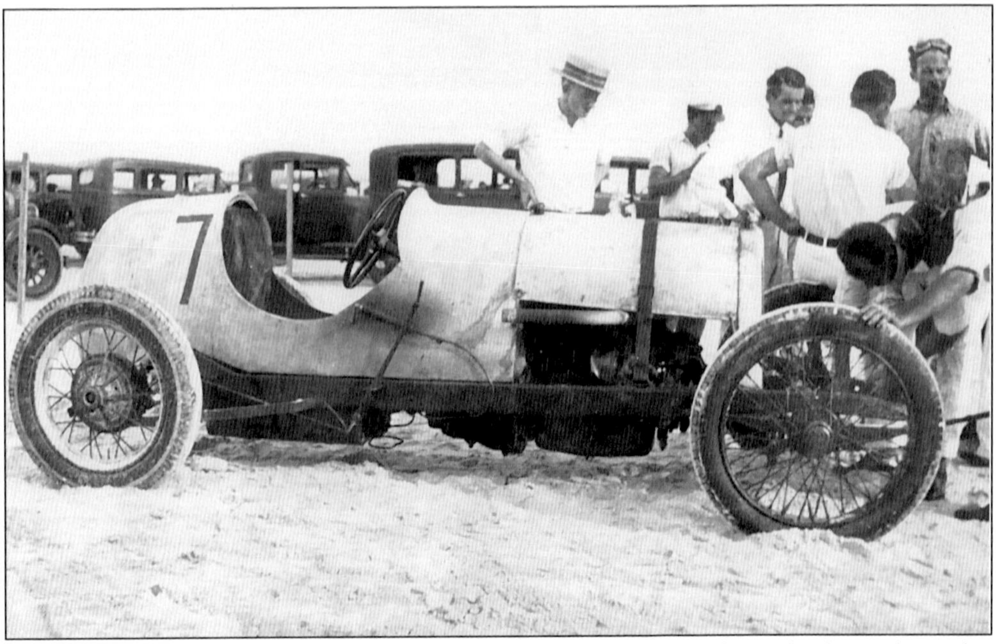

BARREL AND PILLAR RACING, SEPTEMBER 1932. Race enthusiasts, a driver (with goggles on his head), and mechanics inspect the well-maintained car before entering a special event on the beach. Notice the spoke wheels. (Courtesy of Halifax Historical Society.)

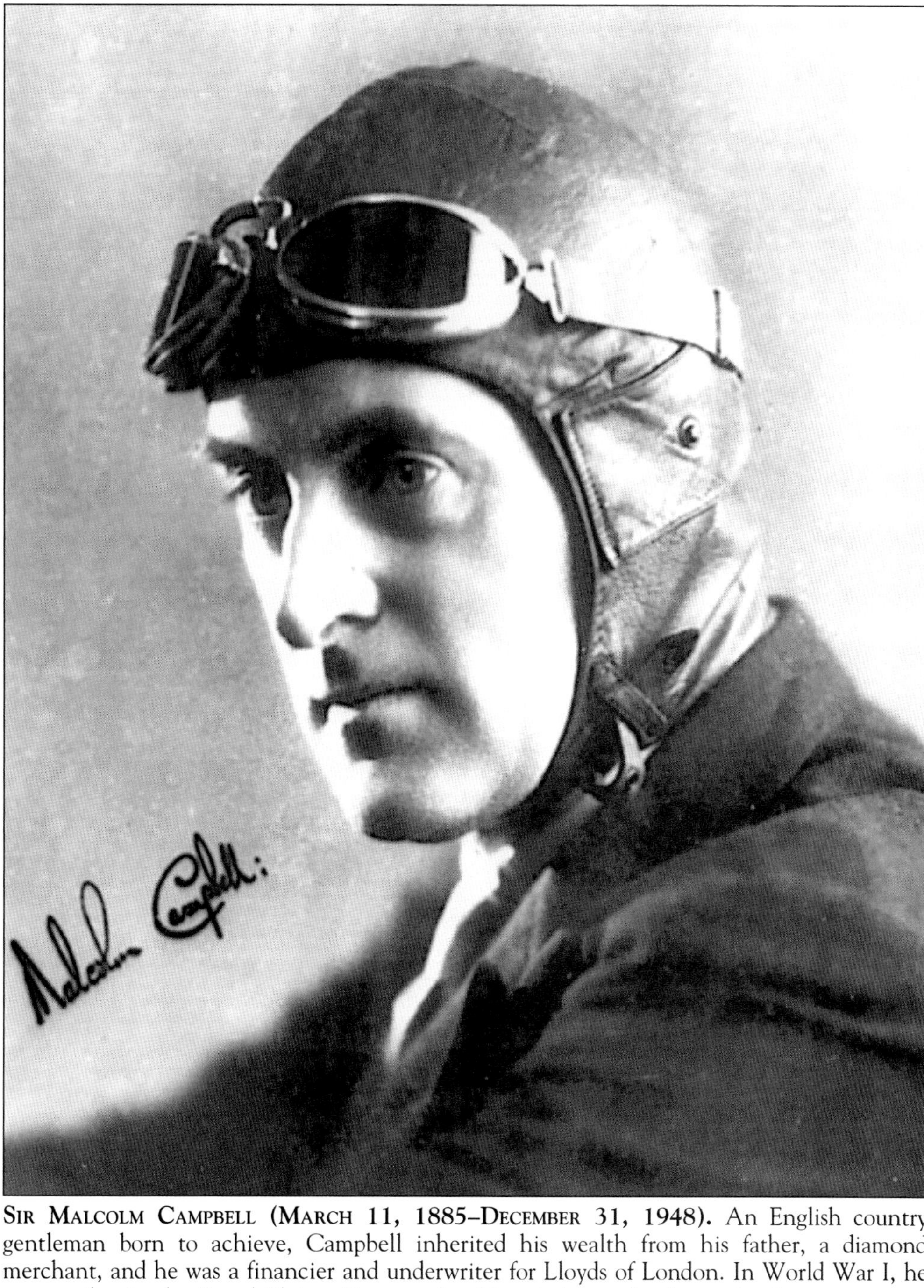

Sir Malcolm Campbell (March 11, 1885–December 31, 1948). An English country gentleman born to achieve, Campbell inherited his wealth from his father, a diamond merchant, and he was a financier and underwriter for Lloyds of London. In World War I, he was a pilot in the Royal Flying Corps and achieved the rank of captain. In a seven-year period, Campbell set five world records in his famed *Bluebirds* on Daytona Beach from 1928 to 1935. He was unable to break the 300 mph barrier on Daytona Beach, but his lifetime goal was reached on the Salt Lake Flats in Utah. In 1931, Campbell was knighted by King George VI for his 245.73 mph world record on Daytona Beach in his *Bluebird II*. (Courtesy of Halifax Historical Society.)

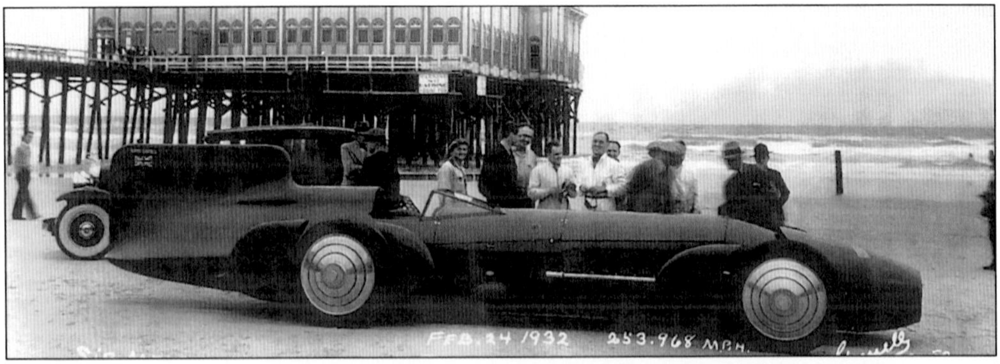

SIR MALCOLM CAMPBELL'S *BLUEBIRD III*, FEBRUARY 24, 1932. The *Bluebird*, with its improved design and Rolls-Royce engine, was readied, crated, and shipped to the United States aboard the S.S. *Aquitania*, and was then transported by rail to Daytona Beach. Included in the shipment was the petrol, the distilled water for the cooling system, the specially made tires, and the tools. Leo Villa, crew chief, headed up the team that was to prepare the *Bluebird* for the world record. Campbell was unsatisfied with his World's Ground Speed Record for 1932 and immediately had the car shipped back to England for refitting and design to ready the car for the 1933 season. (Courtesy of Halifax Historical Society.)

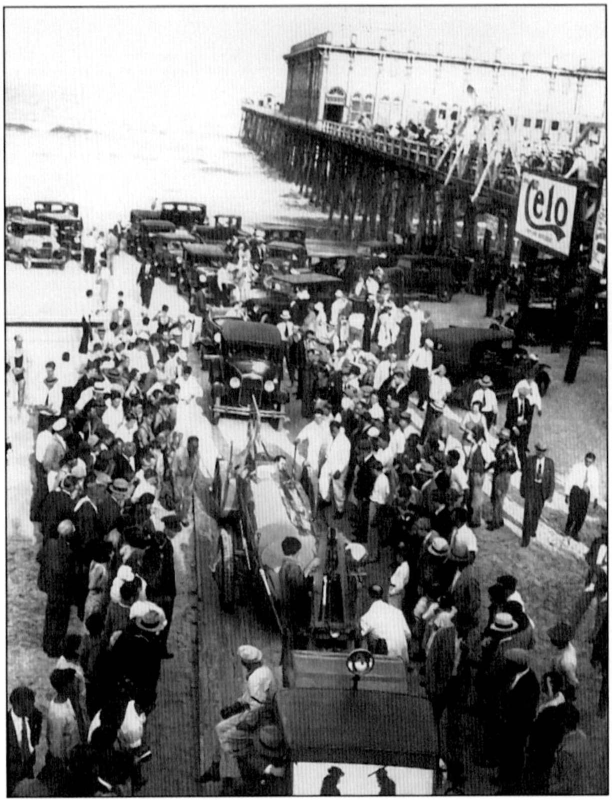

SIR MALCOLM CAMPBELL'S *BLUEBIRD III*, 1932. It was a monumental task to place or remove the *Bluebird* on the beach. First, the Bluebird had to be removed from the freight car at the Florida East Coast Railroad (FEC). Then it had to be towed through the streets of Daytona to the maintenance garage on the Peninsula, and from there to the beach where its engine was started and it was finally able to operate under its own power. Crowds gathered at every opportunity to view the Bluebird each year at speed trial time. (Courtesy of Halifax Historical Society.)

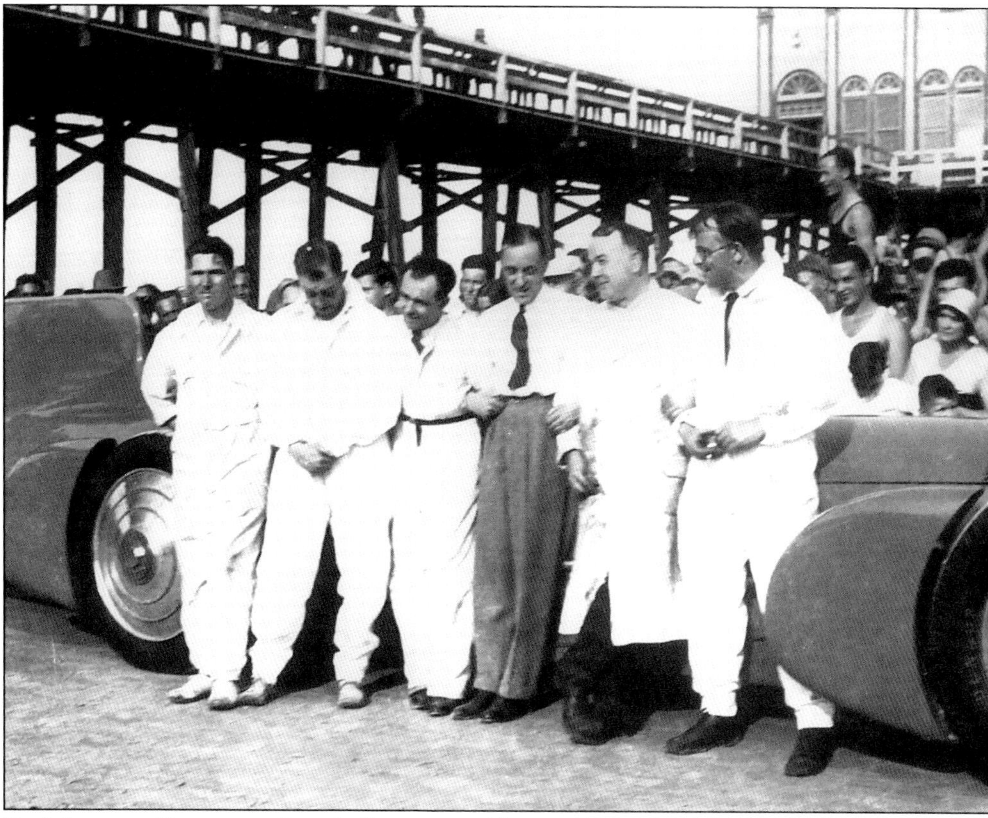

SIR MALCOLM CAMPBELL. Campbell is pictured here with his crew chief and team near the Pier Casino on February 24, 1932. Crew chief Leo Villa began his employment with Campbell in 1921 and stayed with him until he reached his 300 mph goal on the Bonneville Salt Flats in Utah. The crew always accompanied the *Bluebird* from South Hampton, England, to New York. (Courtesy of John Gontner.)

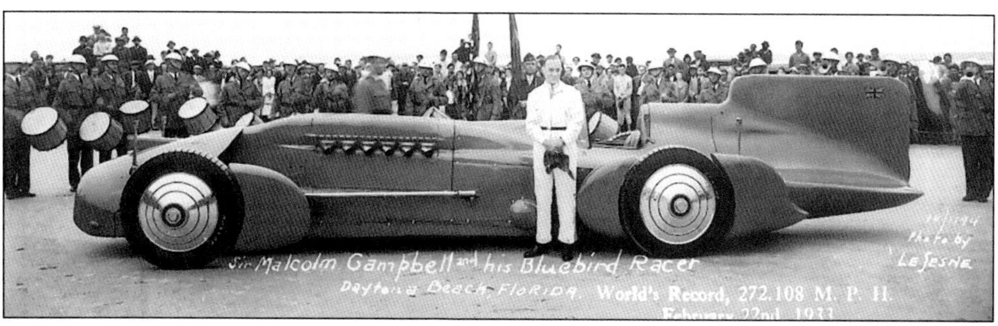

SIR MALCOLM CAMPBELL'S *BLUEBIRD IV*, FEBRUARY 22, 1933, WORLD'S GROUND SPEED RECORD OF 272.108 MPH. After several attempts through the measured mile, Campbell realized that the *Bluebird IV* could not achieve 300 mph. The slippage of the tires on the sand and the incorrect design to withstand the power of the Rolls-Royce engine would not allow the amount of RPMs needed to reach the desired goal. Again, Campbell shipped the *Bluebird* back to England for redesigning and engineering. (Courtesy of Halifax Historical Society.)

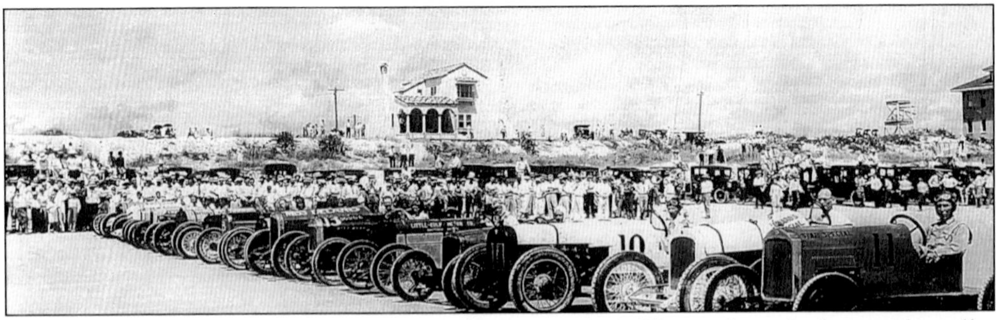

POST AND PILLAR RACING NEAR THE OCEAN DUNES, C. 1933. The track was laid out with a pillar on the north and south turn. A post was placed to warn racers that they were approaching their turn at the pillar. These pillars were placed at various intervals in order to calculate multiple racing records. These racing events were very popular during the late 1920s and early 1930s. (Courtesy of Halifax Historical Society.)

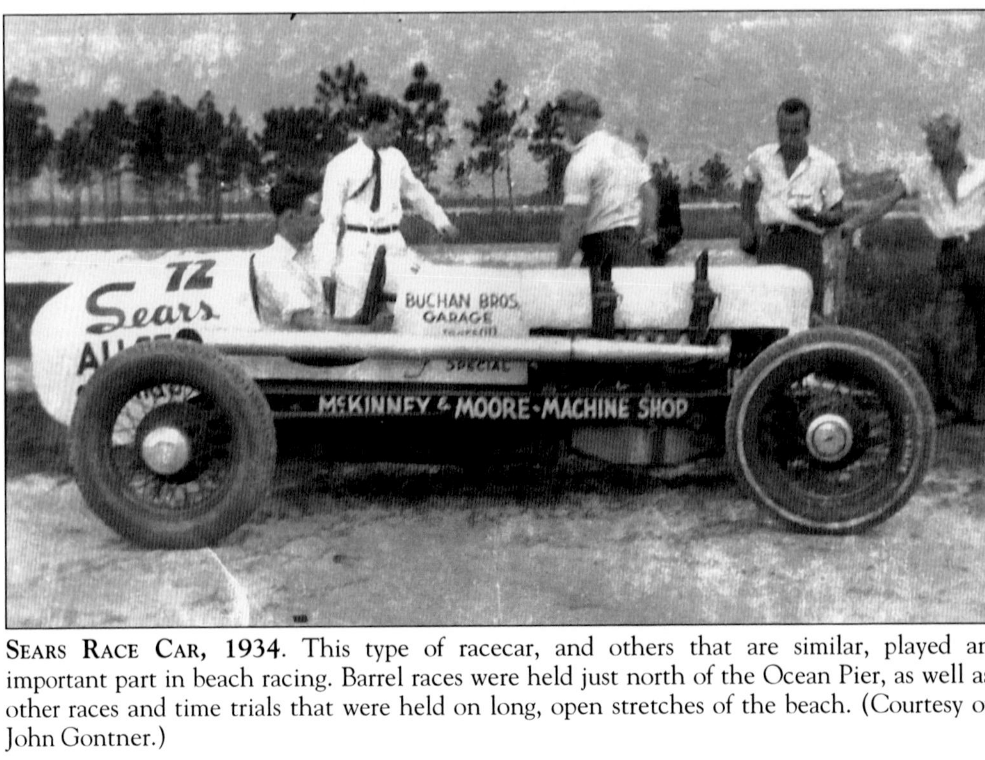

SEARS RACE CAR, 1934. This type of racecar, and others that are similar, played an important part in beach racing. Barrel races were held just north of the Ocean Pier, as well as other races and time trials that were held on long, open stretches of the beach. (Courtesy of John Gontner.)

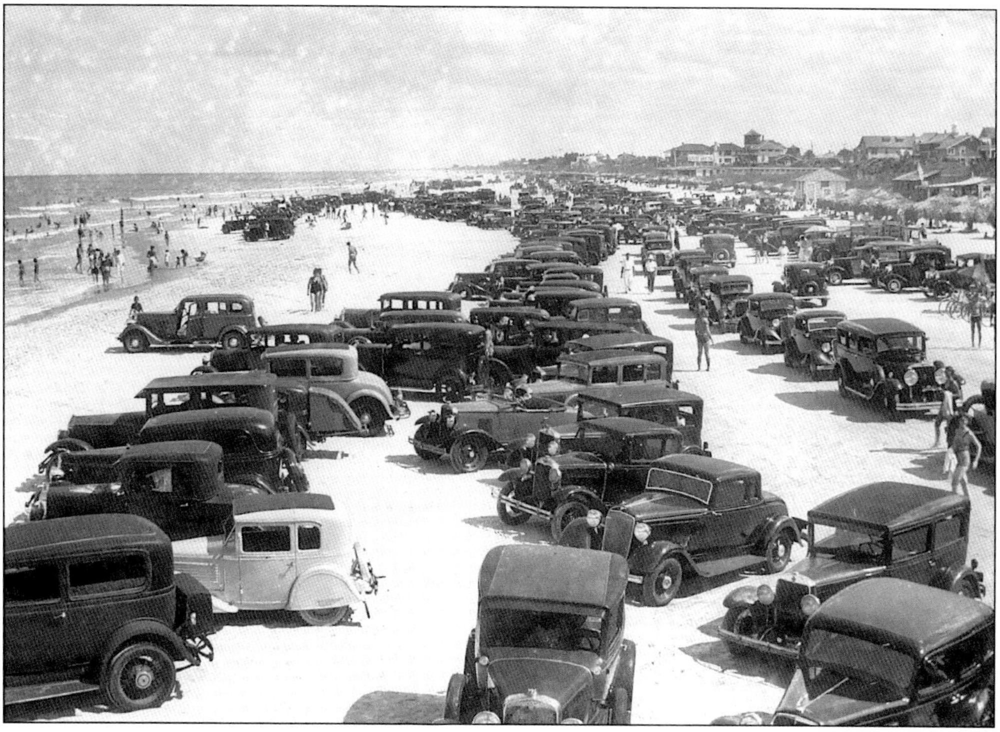

TYPICAL BEACH SCENE, 1934. Among the many automobiles on the beach, the light-colored vehicle in the left foreground belonged to Lawson Diggett. He recorded much of the history of auto racing and built many models of racing which can be seen today at the Halifax Historical Museum, located at 252 South Beach Street, Daytona Beach, Florida. (Courtesy of Halifax Historical Society.)

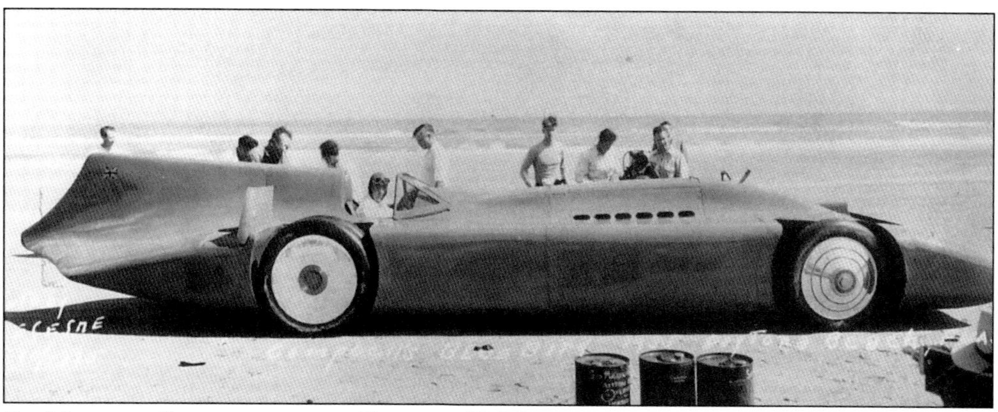

SIR MALCOLM CAMPBELL AND HIS *BLUEBIRD* V, MARCH 7, 1935. Campbell's record still stands at 276.82 mph. This car had dual rear wheels to help eliminate the wheel-spin that plagued the 1933 car. The Rolls-Royce engine, with special spark plugs and supercharger, was engineered to break the 300 mph barrier. It was reported that the Rolls-Royce engine performance was monitored by the British Defense Ministry's special team responsible for research for improved airplane development. Today this car remains on display at the Daytona USA Museum. (Courtesy of Halifax Historical Society.)

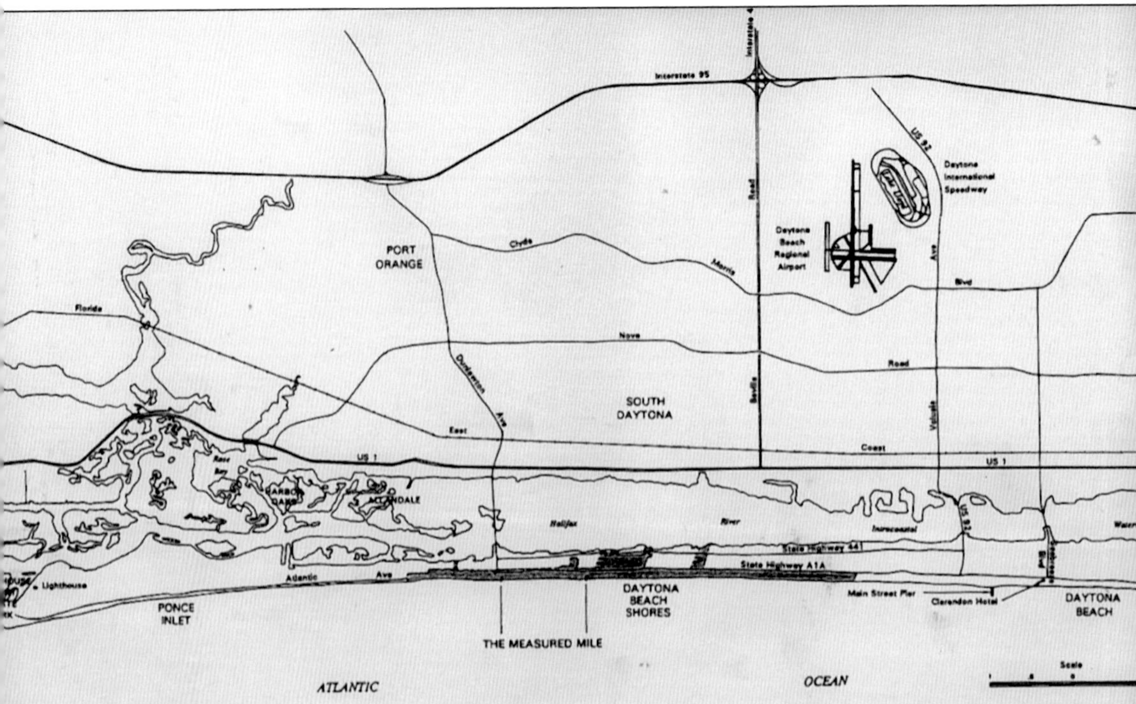

The Measured Mile, 1935. This famous mile was used by Campbell for his time trials through his last speed record—276.816 mph. This stretch of beach was traversed earlier by Segrave in 1927, and again in 1929. Other drivers, including Lockhart, Keech, Bible, and Don also utilized this beach area for their famous speed records. The Measured Mile is located within the southern boundary at Dunlawton Avenue and running one mile north. (Courtesy of Port Orange Historical Trust.)

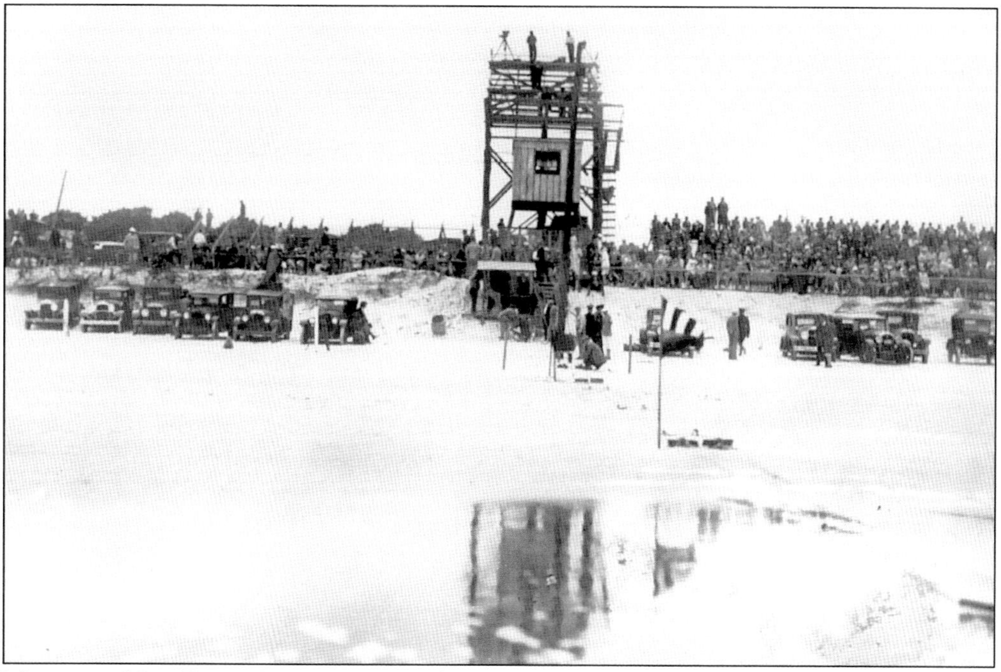

MEASURED MILE BEACH TOWER, 1935. This structure served many of the ground speed record trials through the measured mile. The more famous drivers who set records were Segrave, Keech, and Campbell. This tower was an improvement over the earlier structure, which was made entirely of wood. (Courtesy of Port Orange Historical Trust.)

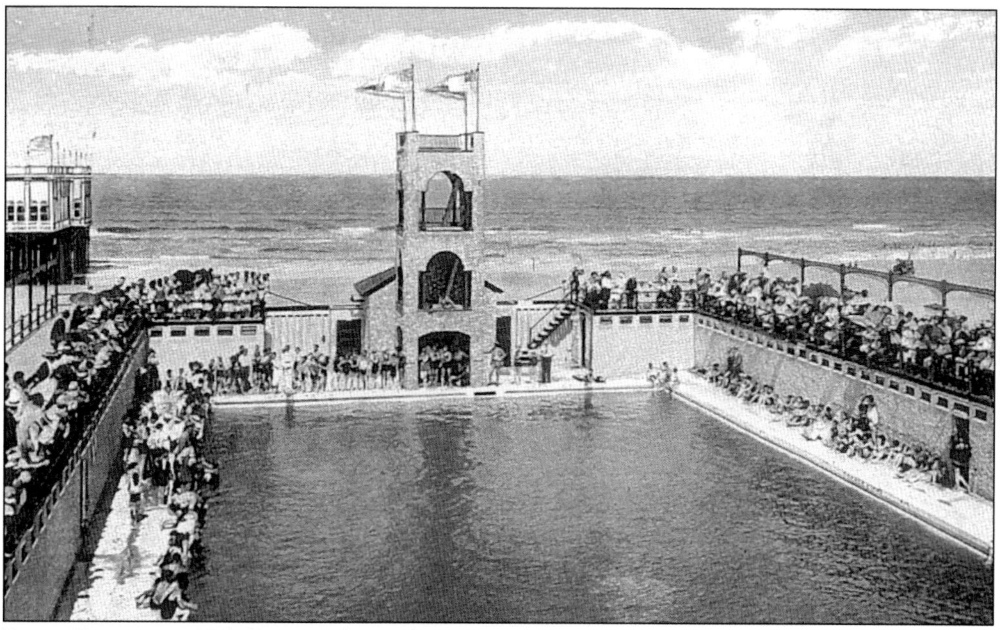

PEPPS POOL, C. 1935. During the early 1930s, this was a popular gathering place for young people wearing their wool bathing suits and trunks. This pool was saltwater fed by a pump that drew the water from the ocean. It was located near the Ocean Pier and Main Street. (Courtesy of Halifax Historical Society.)

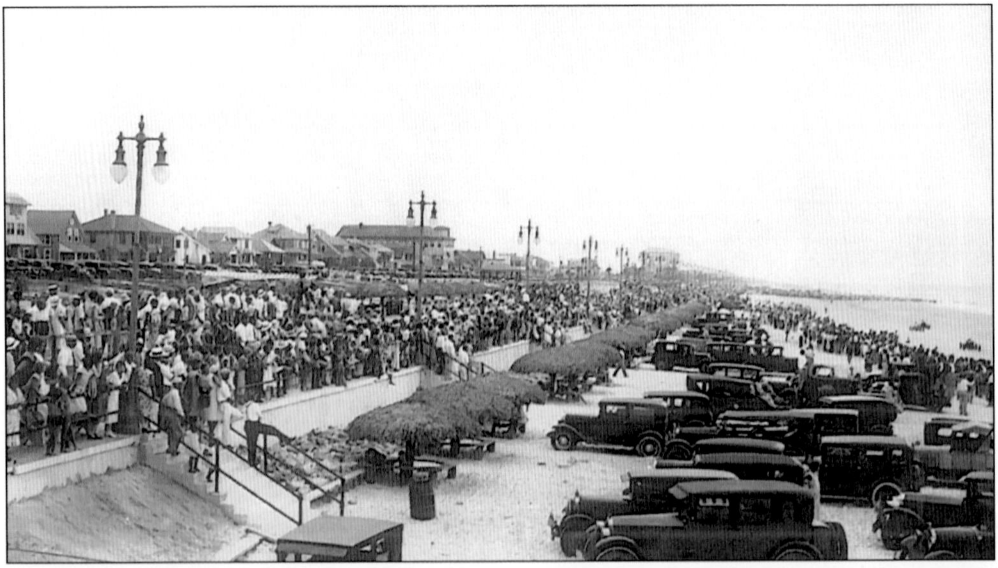

Beachfront, Before the Band Shell, c. 1935. In 1937, the famous Boardwalk and Band Shell was built by the Works Progress Administration (WPA). Sir Malcolm Campbell started his famous speed trial run from this area, heading south to approach the measured mile. (Courtesy of Halifax Historical Society.)

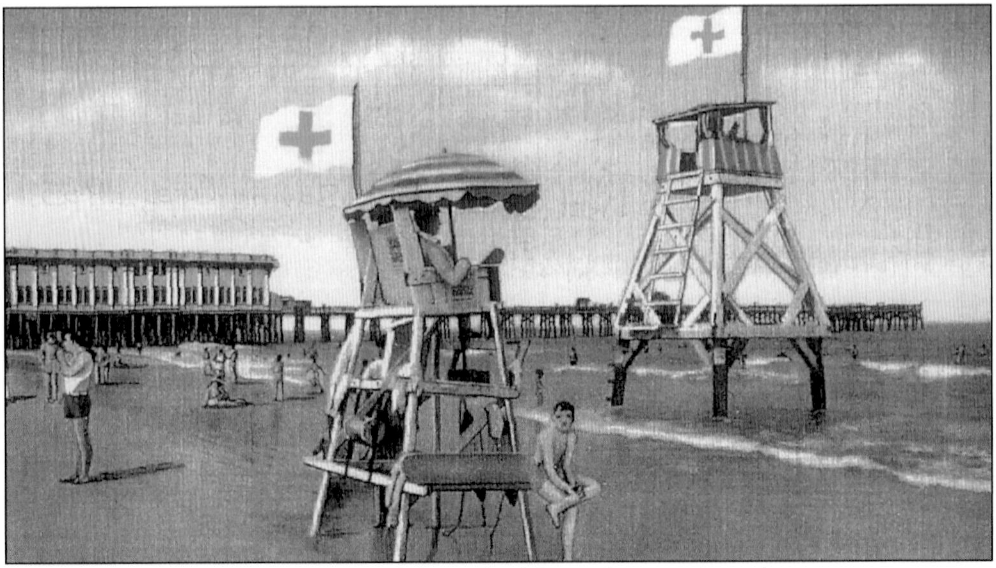

Red Cross Life Saving Corps, c. 1935. The lifeguards went through rigorous training to enable them to rescue bathers from the surf. Notice the vintage swimsuits that were, most often, made of wool. (Courtesy of Halifax Historical Society.)

Three

ROAD/BEACH COURSE FOR STOCK CARS AND MOTORCYCLES 1936–1947

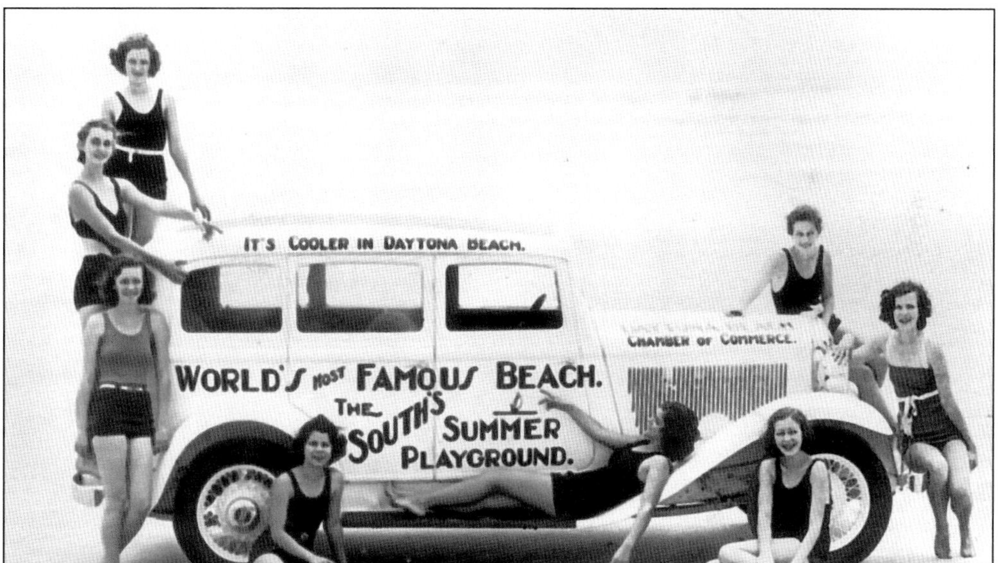

CHAMBER OF COMMERCE CAR AND GIRLS AT THE OPENING OF THE FIRST STOCK CAR RACE, MARCH 8, 1936. Businessmen of Daytona Beach realized that the ongoing Depression would have an impact on the tourist industry. After Sir Malcolm Campbell ended his speed trial runs on the beach, these leaders acted quickly to create new racing events. Jerome Burgman, a business leader, is credited with coining the phrase "World's Most Famous Beach." The racing saga continued through the creative efforts of these promoters. (Courtesy of John Gontner.)

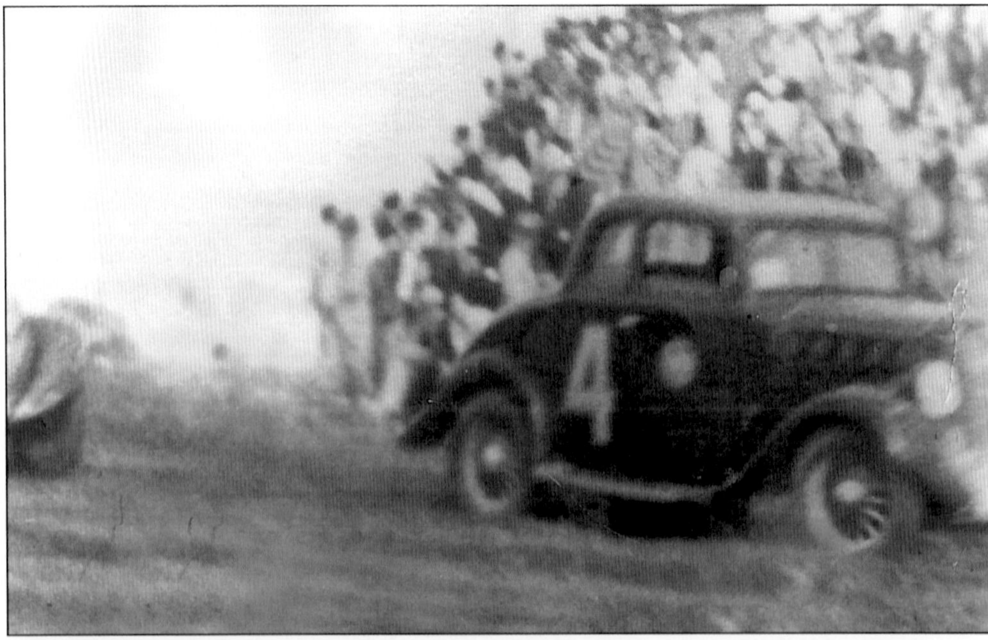

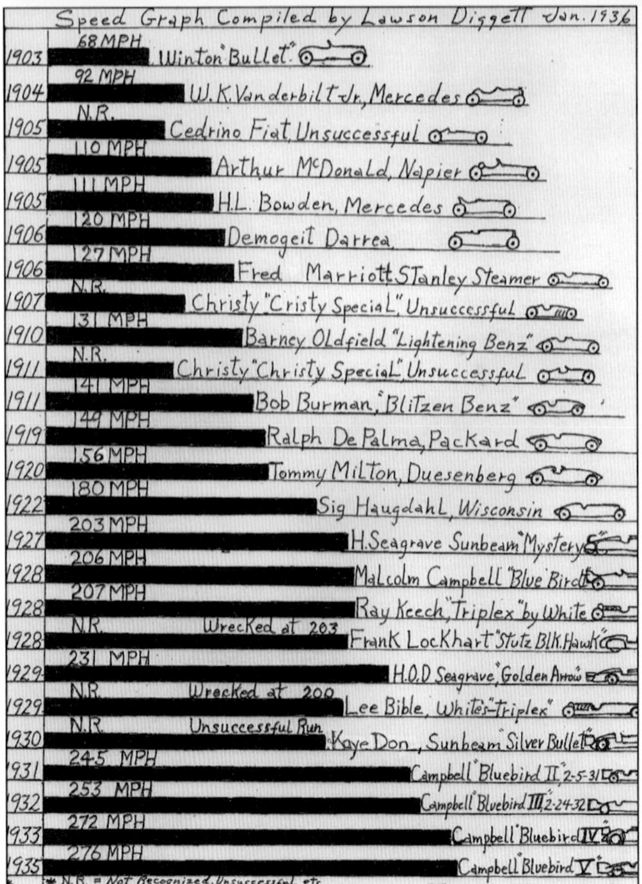

The Start of the First Stock Car Race, March 8, 1936. These cars are rounding the north turn from the beach, continuing their egress to the pavement heading south. The location of this turn today is just a point north of the Daytona Shores City Hall on Atlantic Avenue. Sig Haugdahl, former race driver, was credited with designing the layout for the first road/beach course, which was 3.2 miles around the track. The south turn was at present-day DeMotte Street, just south of Dunlawton Avenue. This encompassed the famous Measured Mile on the beach. (Courtesy of Halifax Historical Society.)

Speed Graph Compiled by Lawson Diggett, January, 1936. The Diggett collection of papers, models, and photographs is housed in the Halifax Historical Society Museum. (Courtesy of Halifax Historical Society.)

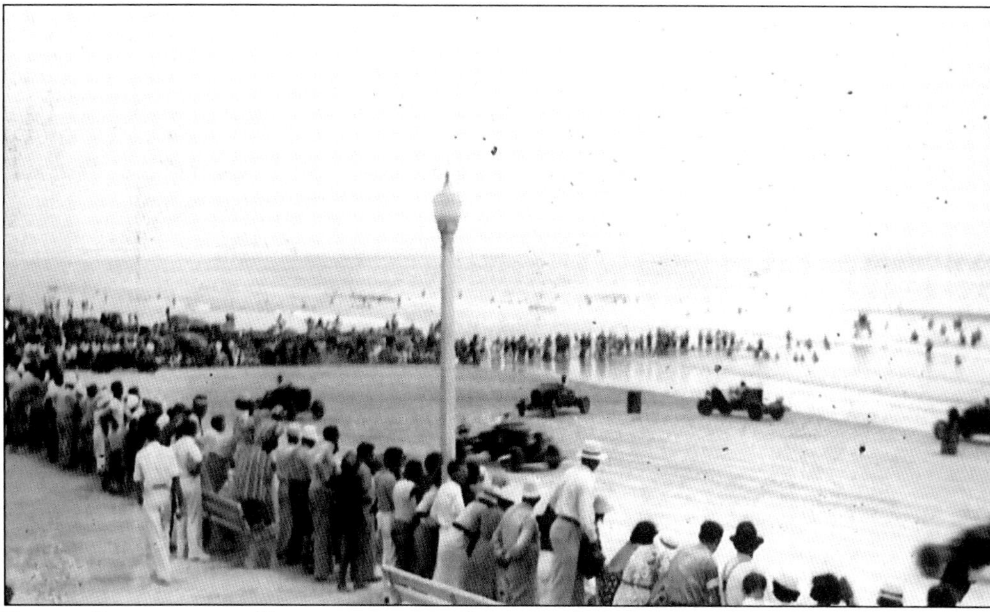

Barrel Races on the Beach, c. 1936. The City of Daytona Beach sponsored small racing events on the beach, just north of the pier, on special holidays like July 4th and Labor Day. These barrel races were an effort to boost the economy during the Depression years. (Courtesy of Halifax Historical Society.)

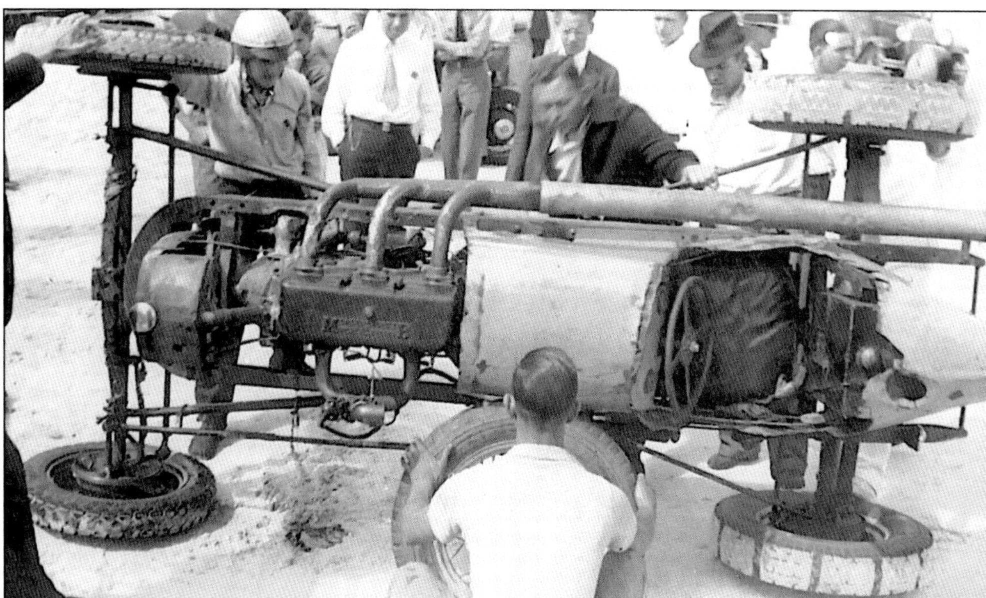

A New Method of Changing Tires, c. 1936. The special events gave thrills to visitors that came to the beach for the holidays. The unexpected always took place when the racers made the turns around the barrels. The cars would turn on their side, slide into each other, and sometimes drive into the edge of the surf. (Courtesy of Halifax Historical Society.)

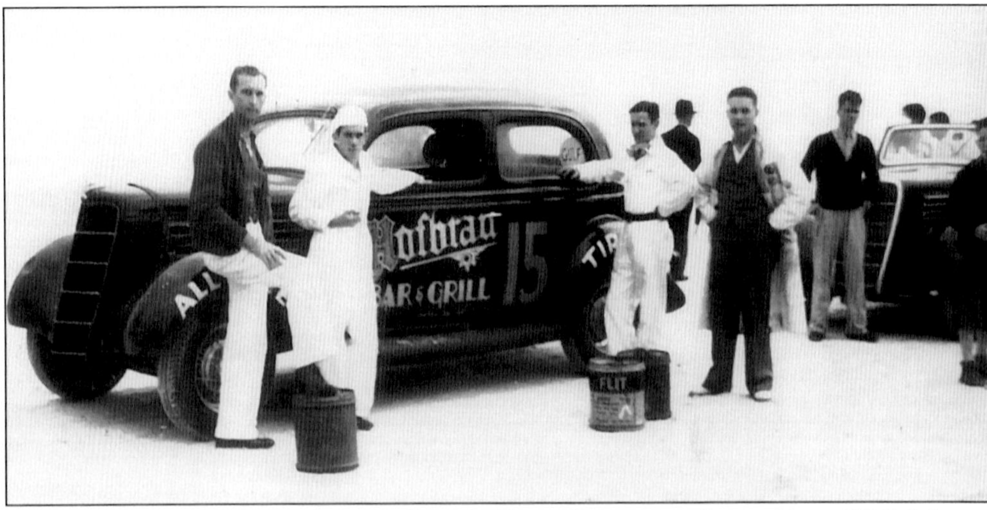

WALTER JOHNSON AND HIS HOFBRAU BAR & GRILL SPONSORED STOCK CAR, 1937. Johnson competed in the 51.2-mile Daytona Beach Race on September 5. Smokey Purser placed first in this event. (Courtesy of Halifax Historical Society.)

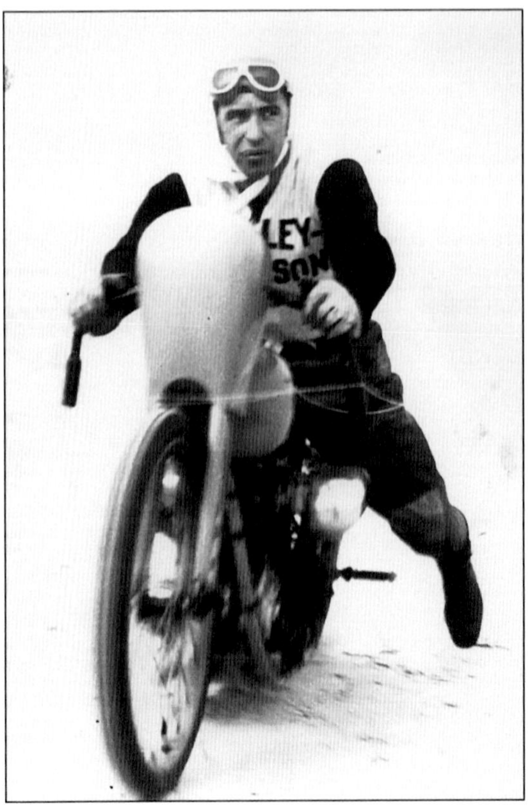

JOE PETRALI, 1937. Petrali's was the fastest bike to run on Daytona sand at 136.183 mph on March 13, 1937. The American Motorcycle Association sponsored cycle races each year from 1937 to 1958. The first racetrack, at Daytona Shores, was utilized from 1937 through 1947, and the second track, at the Ponce Inlet, from 1948 through 1958. (Courtesy of John Gontner.)

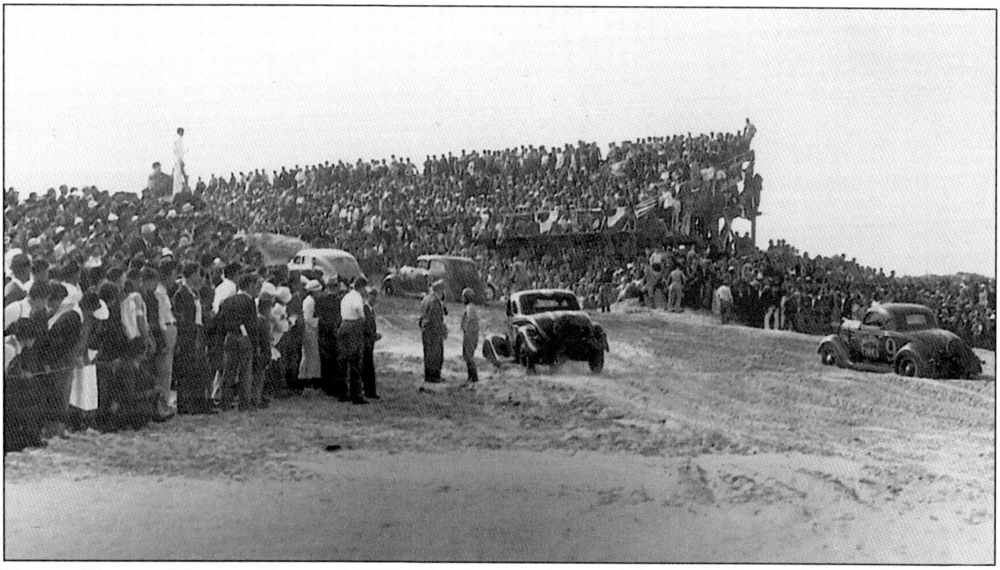

Beach Races, North Turn, 1937. The lessons learned from the 1936 race, on the north and south turns, was that the surface was improperly prepared causing it to become rutted and almost impassable. In 1937, a new method for preparing the surface was implemented by the County, using a white marl base with a thin coquina shell surface. This provided the necessary traction for the racers sliding sideways, braking, and negotiating the turns. This surfacing method was utilized through 1958. The old Measured Mile grandstand bleachers were resituated to accommodate race fans observing the north turn. (Courtesy of Halifax Historical Society.)

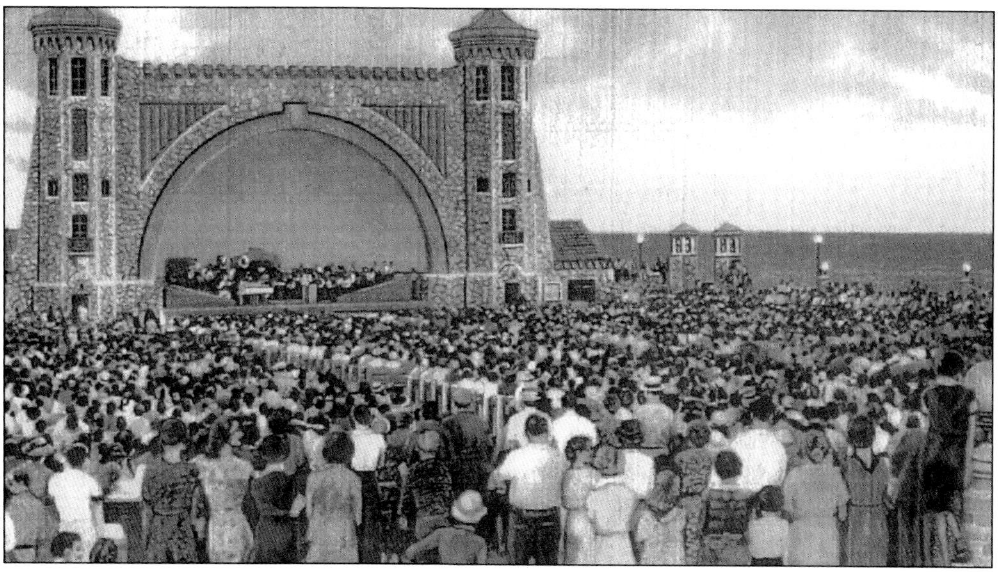

World's Largest Band Shell and Open-Air Theater, c. 1937–1938. This Mediterranean Revival–style structure accommodates thousands of visitors annually. The City of Daytona Beach sponsors many special programs each year—band concerts, beauty pageants, lectures, and sunrise church services on Easter morning. It was near this beachside landmark that Sir Malcolm Campbell, Maj. H.O.D. Segrave, and others began their attempts to break the World's Ground Speed Record to the south. (Courtesy of Midkiff Family Collection.)

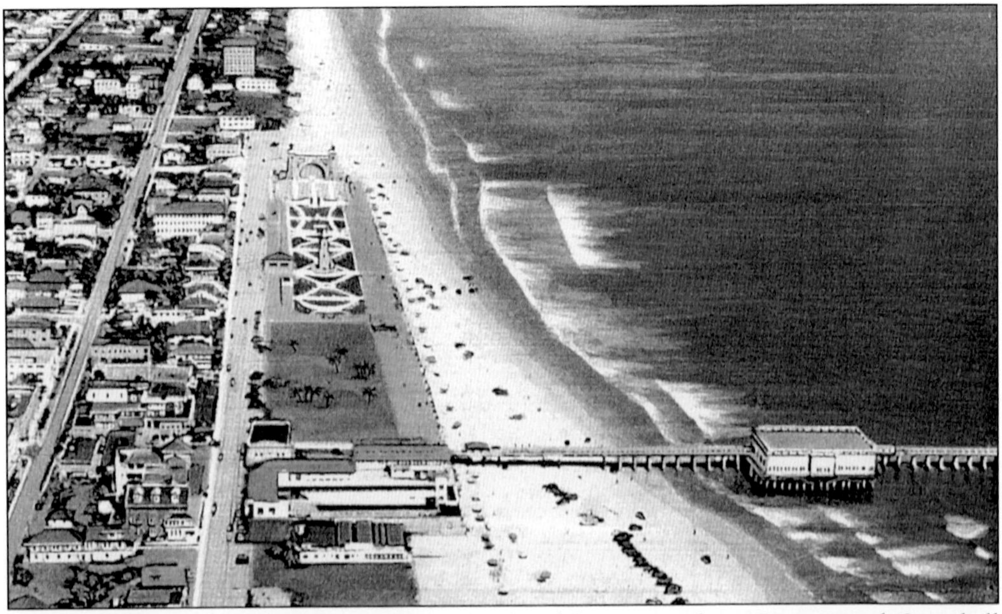

Aerial View of Boardwalk, c. 1938. This beachfront was where Segrave and Campbell started their time trials to break the world record. They raced south, under the pier, to enter the Measured Mile, with nine miles of beach to accelerate and decelerate. Segrave used a black line of oil down the beach and a gunsight mounted on the hood of his racer, while Campbell and others used flags to mark their course on the sand from 1927 to 1935. North of the boardwalk, on the beach, the famous Clarendon Hotel can be seen. (Courtesy of Halifax Historical Society.)

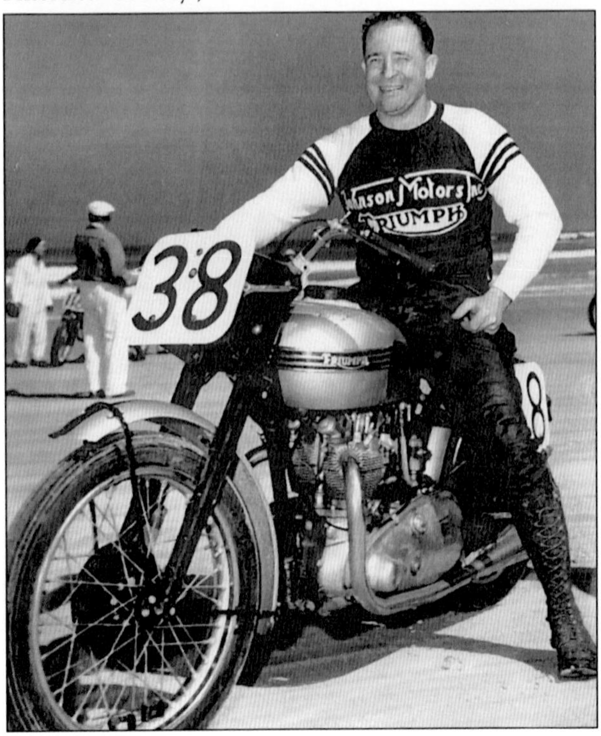

Ed Kretz Sr. and his Triumph #38, January 24, 1937. Kretz was the first Daytona 200 Mile Race winner on the Indian Sport Scout, sanctioned by the American Motorcycle Association (AMA). Second place went to Clark Trumbull on a Norton, with Ellis Pearce coming in third on a Harley-Davidson. Following his racing career, Ed Kretz became a motorcycle dealer in Pomona Park, California. (Courtesy of ISC Archives.)

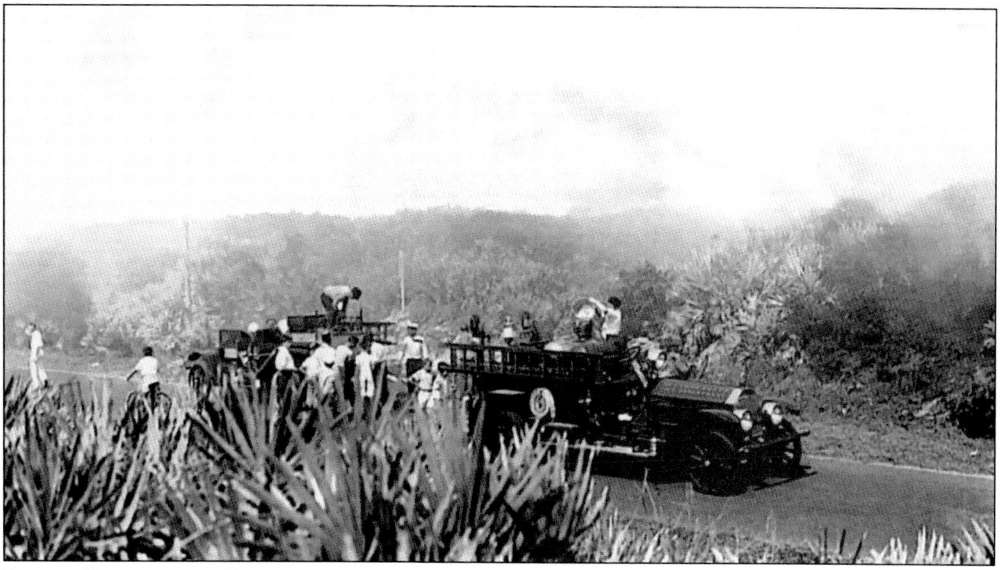

Brush Fire on the Backstretch, c. 1938–1939. Promoters were always fearful of a brush fire, especially with hundreds of spectators lining the beach area and automobiles parked along Atlantic Avenue and Peninsula Drive. These two roads were the only exit to safety and the only entrance for emergency vehicles. The beach was crowded with parked autos and the race barricaded access to the beach. Fortunately, there was never a fire that got out of control and firemen and law officers were able to keep the area safe for the race fans. (Courtesy of Halifax Historical Society.)

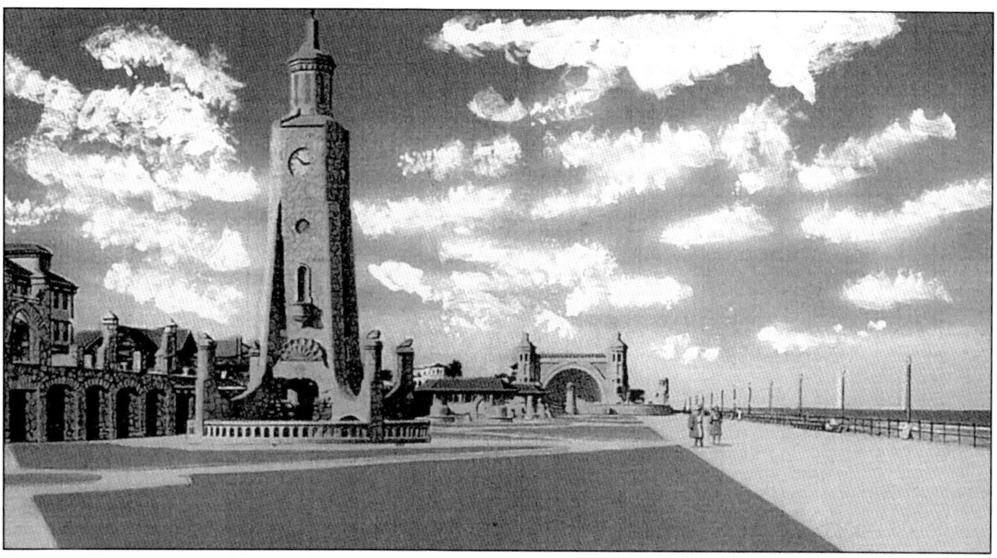

Clock Tower and Band Shell on the Boardwalk, c. 1938–1939. These structures were built by the Works Progress Administration during the Depression Era. Thousands of tourists come each year to enjoy the ocean beach and boardwalk area. (Courtesy of Cardwell Family Collection.)

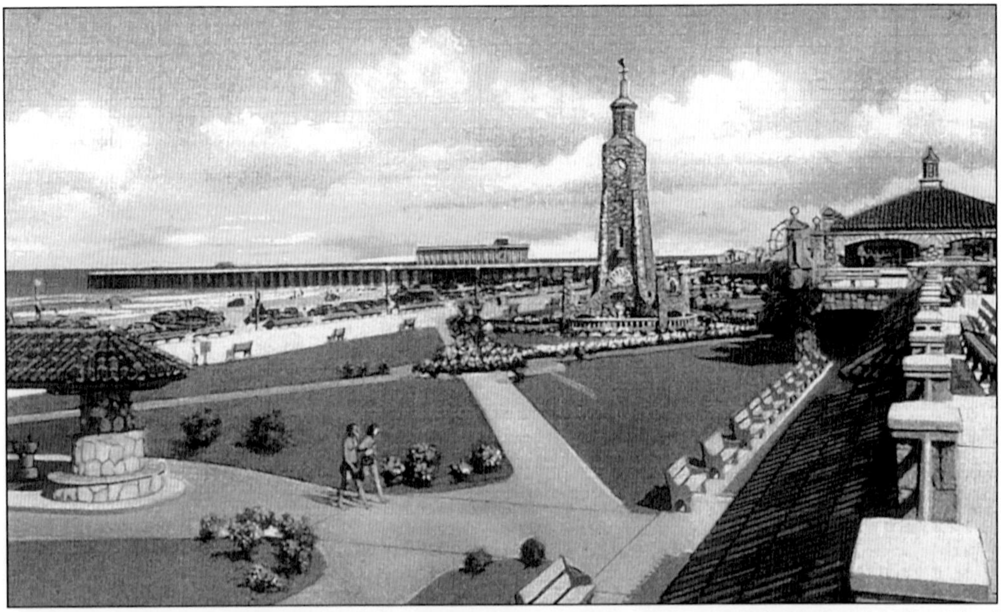

Overlooking Oceanfront Park and Boardwalk, 1939. This was a place that families liked to visit on vacation where they could get a "far-away" feeling. Many of these visitors were only a day's drive from their home. The oceanfront provided a peaceful and relaxing environment, which was ideal for vacationers. (Courtesy of Cardwell Family Collection.)

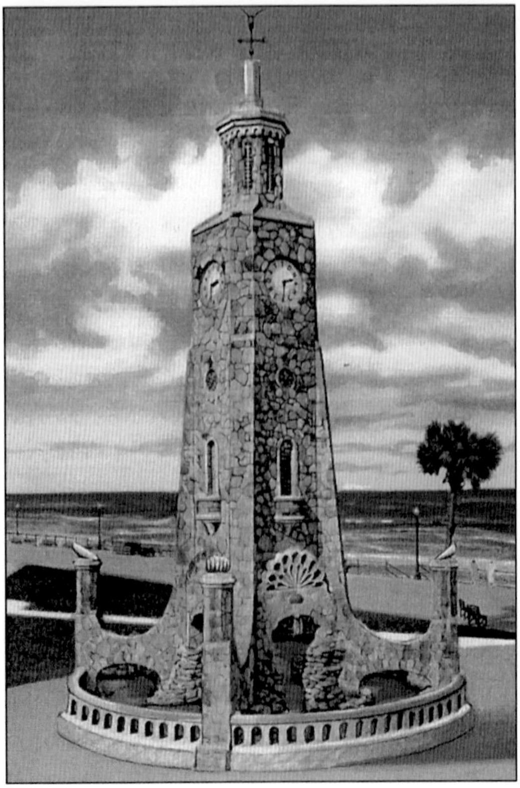

Clock Tower on the Boardwalk, 1939. This outstanding landmark was named the Sir Malcolm Campbell Clock Tower on January 4, 1994, by the Daytona Beach City Commission and the Daytona Beach Historic Preservation Board. This monument honors Campbell for his five World's Ground Speed Records starting on the beach, near this point, and heading south to enter the Measured Mile. (Courtesy of Cardwell Family Collection.)

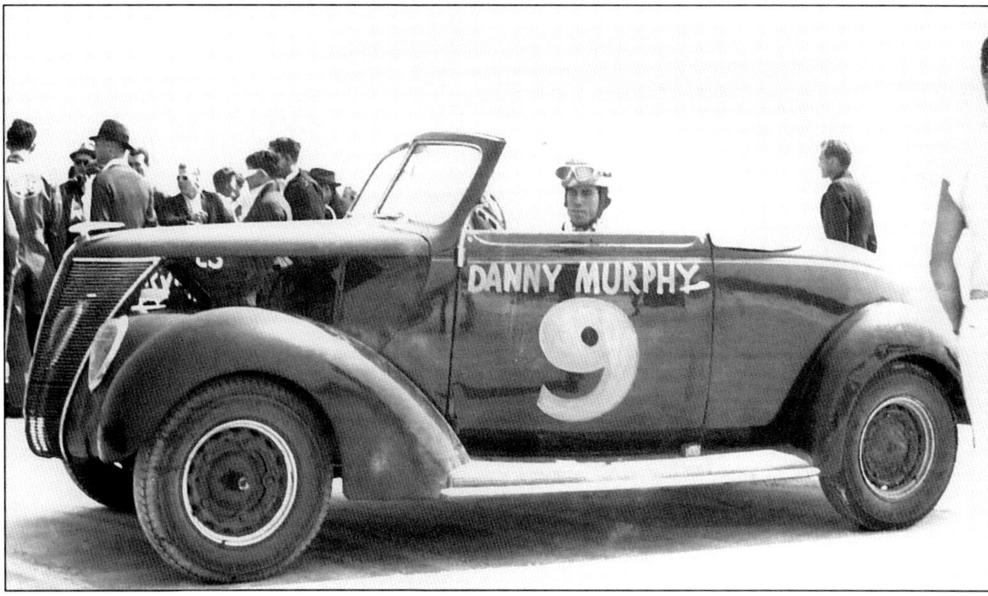

Danny Murphy, Beach/Road Race, March 19, 1939. Murphy was a favorite Daytona Beach race driver, having come in third in the September 5, 1937 race and first in the July 10, 1938 race. Unfortunately, he did not finish in the top ten in the 1939 race in his Ford V-8. (Courtesy of John Gontner.)

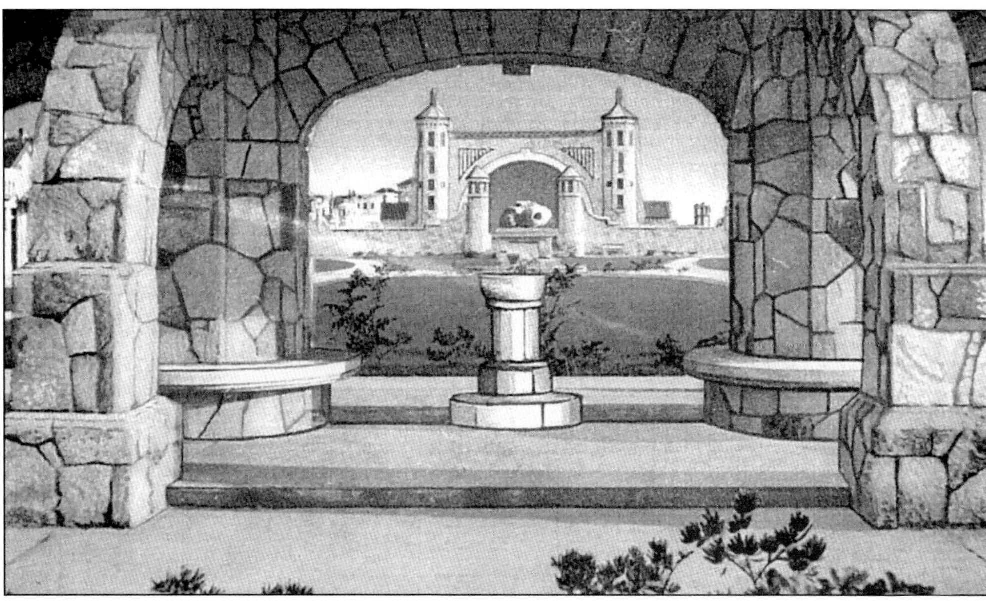

A View of the Band Shell through the Pavilion Archway, c. 1939–1940. This pavilion no longer stands as a park monument, however, the Band Shell remains and can seat up to 4,500 people. Race fans and their families came to Daytona to see both automobile and motorcycle races on the beach, and to enjoy the famous boardwalk and its attractions. (Courtesy of Midkiff Family Collection.)

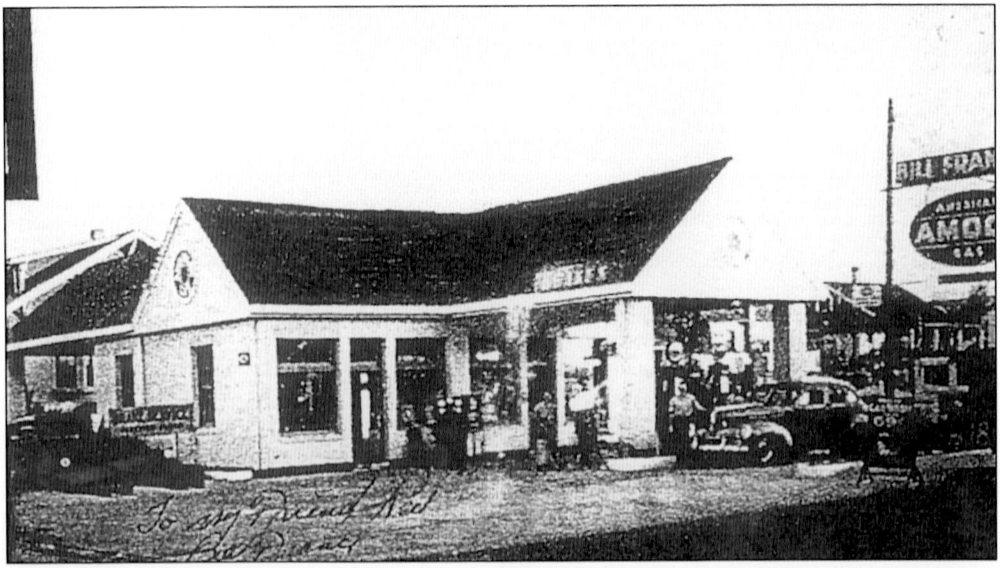

Bill France's Amoco Service Station, c. 1940. This filling station stood on the southwest corner of Main Street and Hollywood Avenue. There was always a hub of activity here before the racing events on the beach. France prepared his Graham Special and other race cars at this garage for the beach races. (Courtesy of Ron Edwards.)

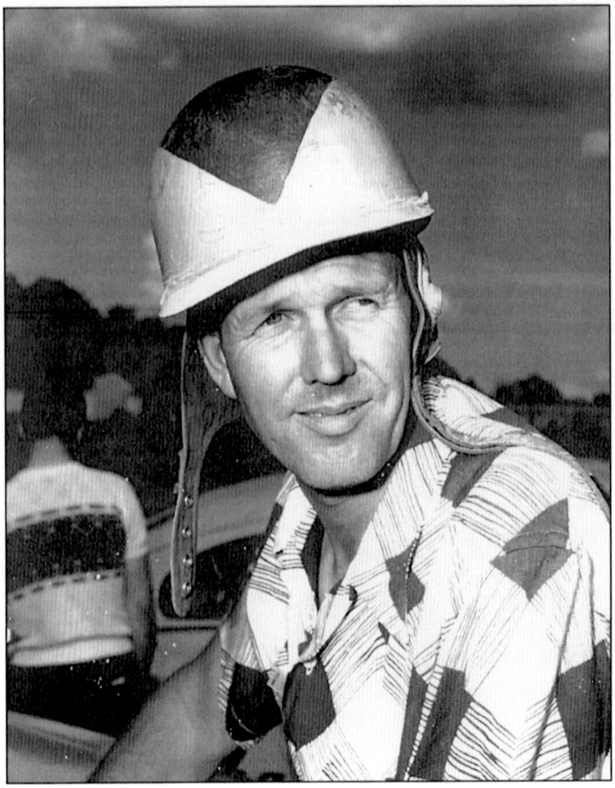

Bill France Sr., July 7, 1940. France went on to win this 160-mile Daytona Beach race in a 1939 Buick. France had an outstanding racing career from 1936 to 1946. He placed in each event with his first victory on September 5, 1938 in a 1937 Ford. There were no races from 1942 through 1945 due to World War II. (Courtesy of ISC Archives.)

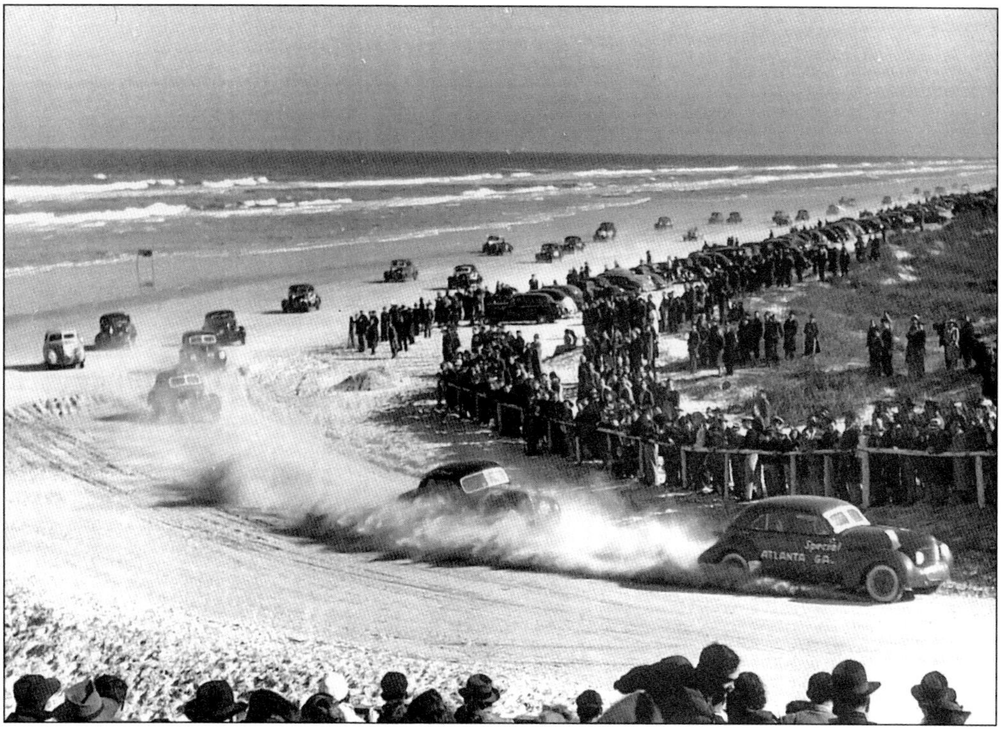

BILL FRANCE SR. Pictured here in the lead on the north turn in 1940, France was very skilled at controlling his car and entering the turns, even though he appeared to be sliding sideways. France stated that, of the many race cars he drove throughout the years, he liked and expected the most from the Graham Special. In 1947, he helped organize NASCAR, the world's largest stock car racing organization. (Courtesy of ISC Archives.)

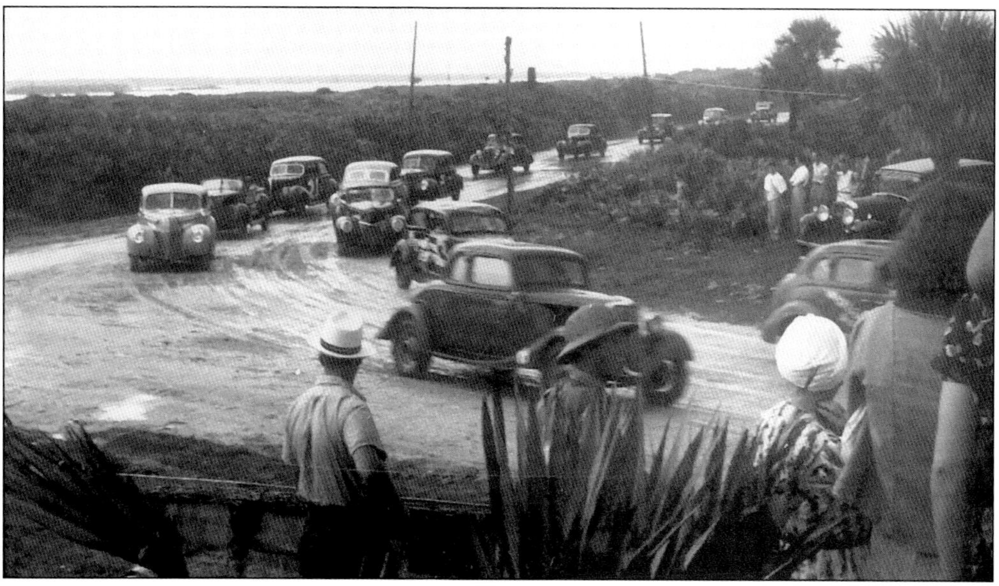

BEACH RACES, SOUTH TURN AT DEMOTTE STREET, 1940. Notice the Ford Coupe, a popular race car, rounding the south turn. The north turn was near where Daytona Beach Shores City Hall is located today. The first road/beach course was 3.2 miles. (Courtesy of John Gontner.)

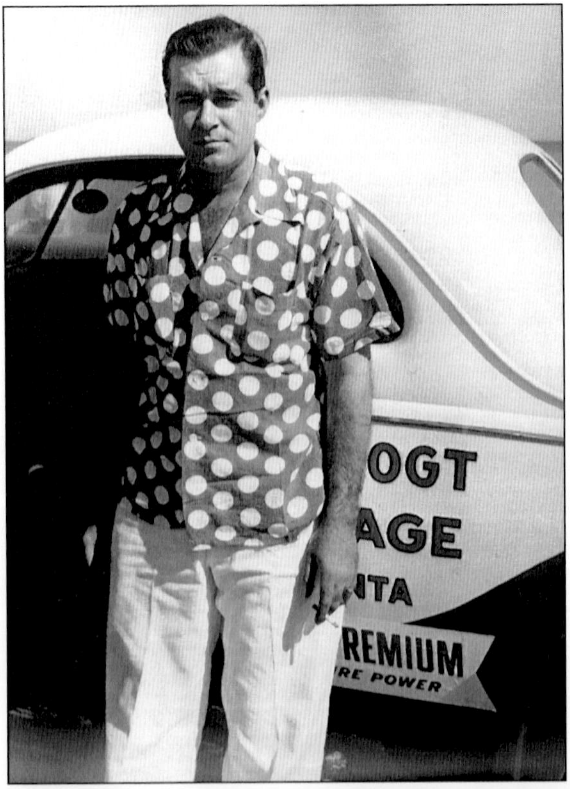

ROY HALL, C. 1940. It is alleged that young Roy gained his driving skills by hauling illicit whiskey from the mountains of north Georgia into the city of Atlanta. High speed driving was common in order to evade the law. Later, Roy put these skills to good use in his short racing career, winning the 160-mile Daytona Beach Race on March 10, 1940. (Courtesy of ISC Archives.)

AMBULANCE ON THE BEACH, C. 1940. Races were not without mishaps—accidents happened. Ambulances had to transport the injured to Halifax Hospital, just west of Daytona. The old wooden Port Orange Bridge fell into disrepair in 1932. The bridge was eventually rebuilt in 1951, which alleviated traffic problems. This new bridge was most important for emergency vehicles entering and leaving the racetrack on the peninsula. (Courtesy of Halifax Historical Society.)

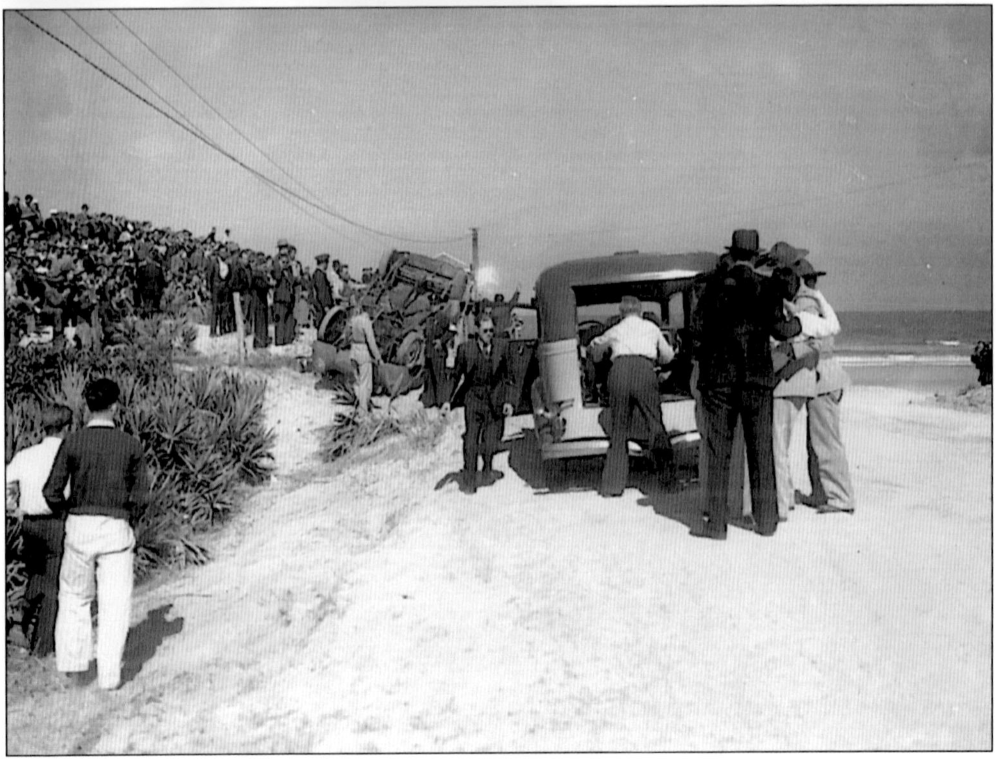

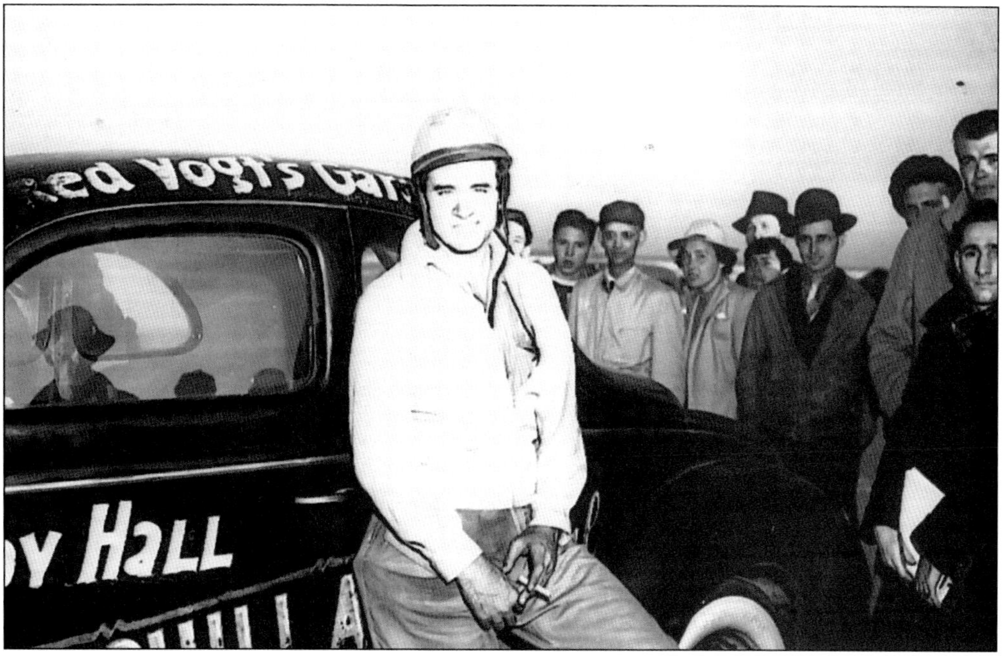

Roy Hall and his Ford Coupe, March 2, 1941. Hall came in first in this 160-mile Daytona Beach Race. Later, after the World War II hiatus, he won the 102.4-mile Daytona Beach Race on June 30, 1946, in a 1939 Ford. Roy Hall's name is remembered today among race enthusiasts for his competitive driving tactics. (Courtesy of Halifax Historical Society.)

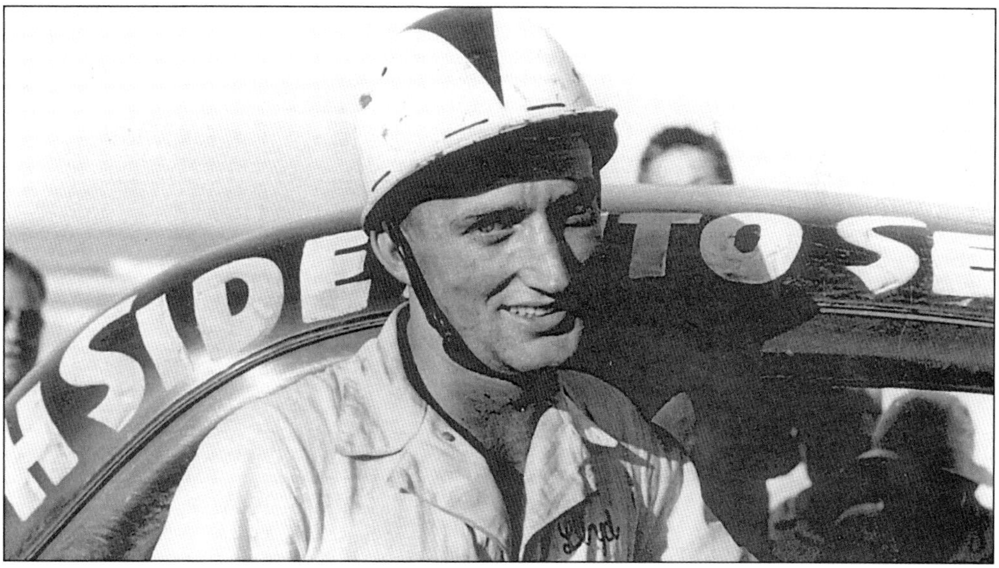

Lloyd Seay, 1941. This outstanding race car driver allegedly gained his skills from hauling illicit whiskey from Dawsonville, Georgia, to the Atlanta area also. He had a reputation for being the fastest driving transporter eluding the law. Lloyd won the 160-mile Daytona Beach Race on August 24, 1941 in a 1940 Ford. It was reported that Bill France said that, of the many race drivers that he has encountered throughout the years, Lloyd Seay was his favorite. Unfortunately, he was killed during an argument following a Labor Day Race in Atlanta, Georgia. (Courtesy of ISC Archives.)

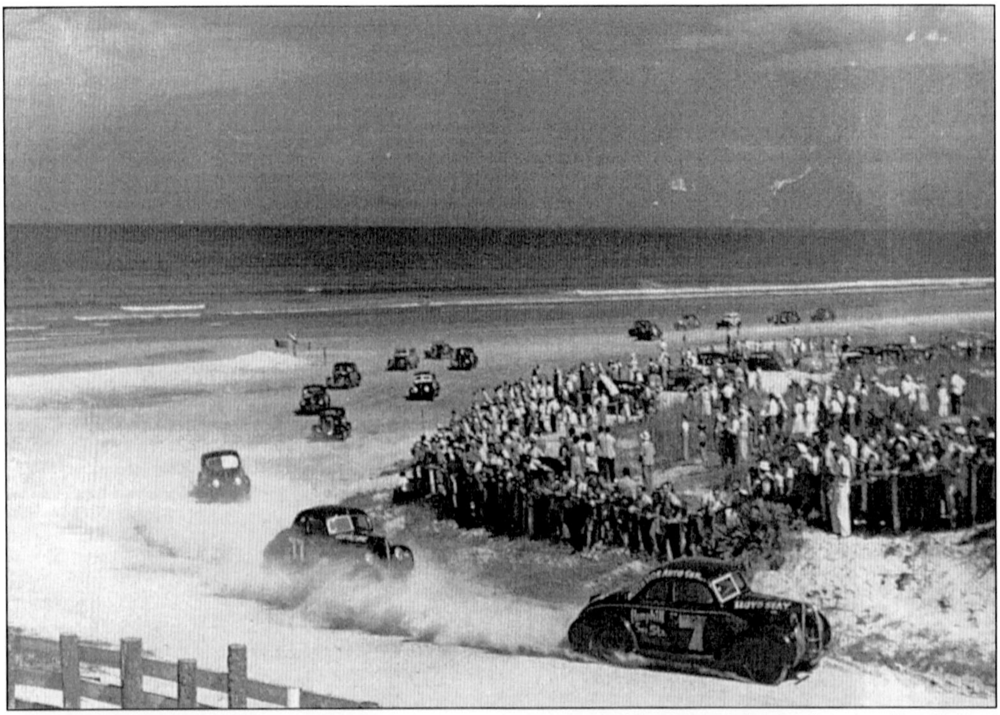

LLOYD SEAY (#7) LEADING THE PACK, AUGUST 24, 1941. He earned the nickname "Lightnin' Lloyd" because of his high speed and risky maneuvers on the beach. Seay came in first and Joe Littlejohn (#77) came in second. (Courtesy of Ron Edwards.)

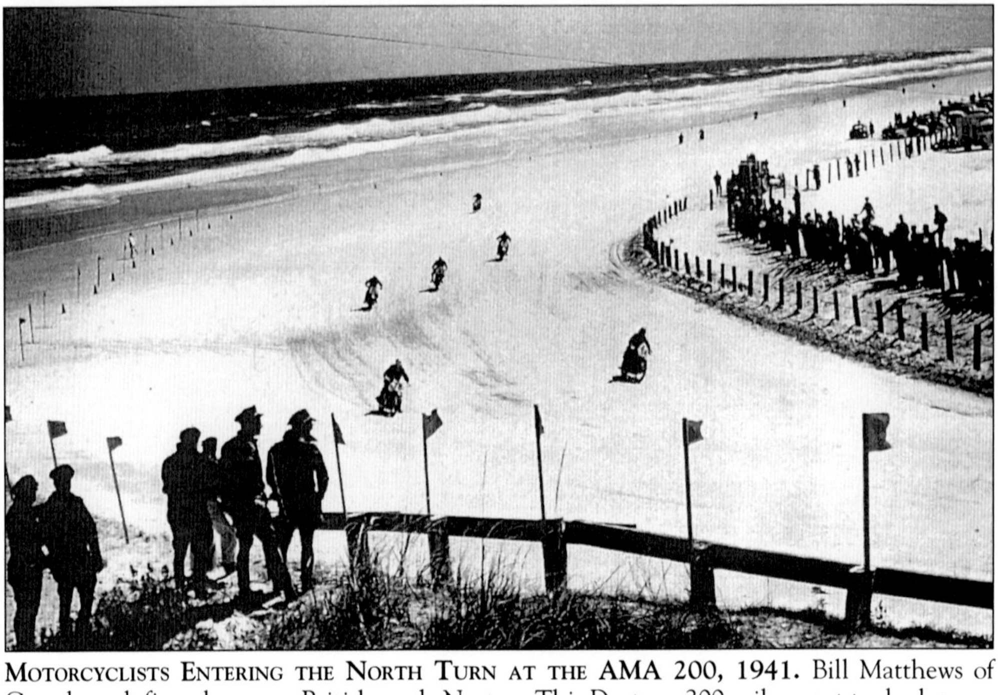

MOTORCYCLISTS ENTERING THE NORTH TURN AT THE AMA 200, 1941. Bill Matthews of Canada took first place on a British-made Norton. This Daytona 200-mile event took place on the 3.2-mile track, which is Daytona Shores today. (Courtesy of Ron Edwards.)

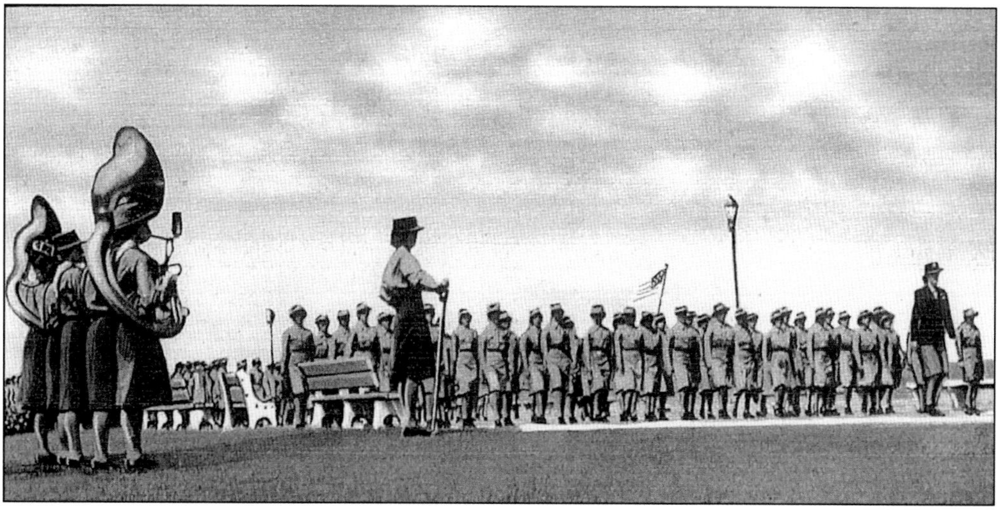

WORLD WAR II. Racing events were not held from 1942 to 1946 because of the war. Seen here are members of the Women's Army Corp (WAC) marching and training in parade dress on the Boardwalk, near the Band Shell and the Sir Malcolm Campbell clocktower. (Courtesy of Halifax Historical Society.)

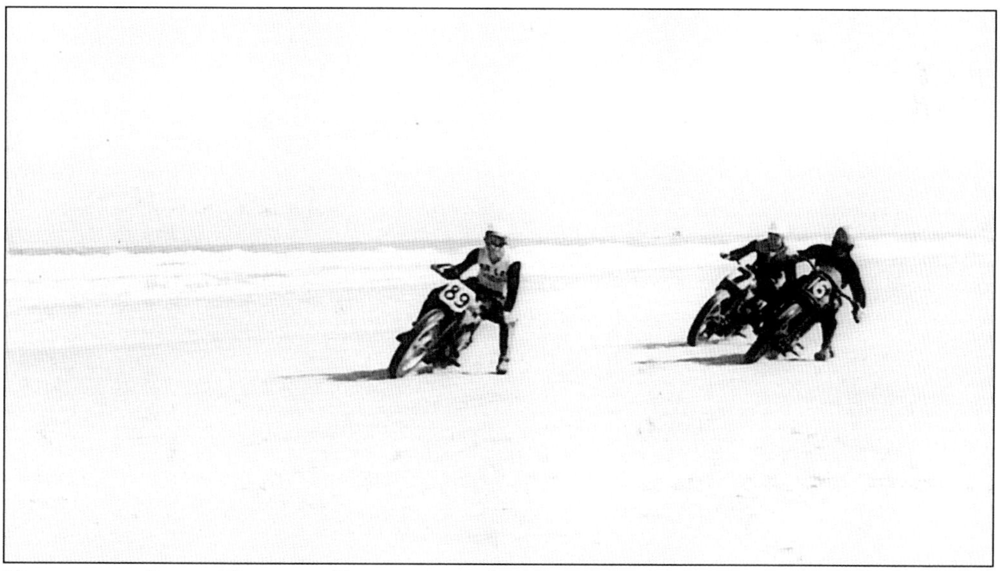

MOTORCYCLE RACES HEADING NORTH ON THE BEACH STRAIGHTAWAY, C. 1947. The American Motorcycle Association (AMA) sanctioned cycle races on the 3.2-mile road/beach course, which is Daytona Shores today. Riders came from all over the United States and abroad to participate in these outstanding beach events. (Courtesy of Halifax Historical Society.)

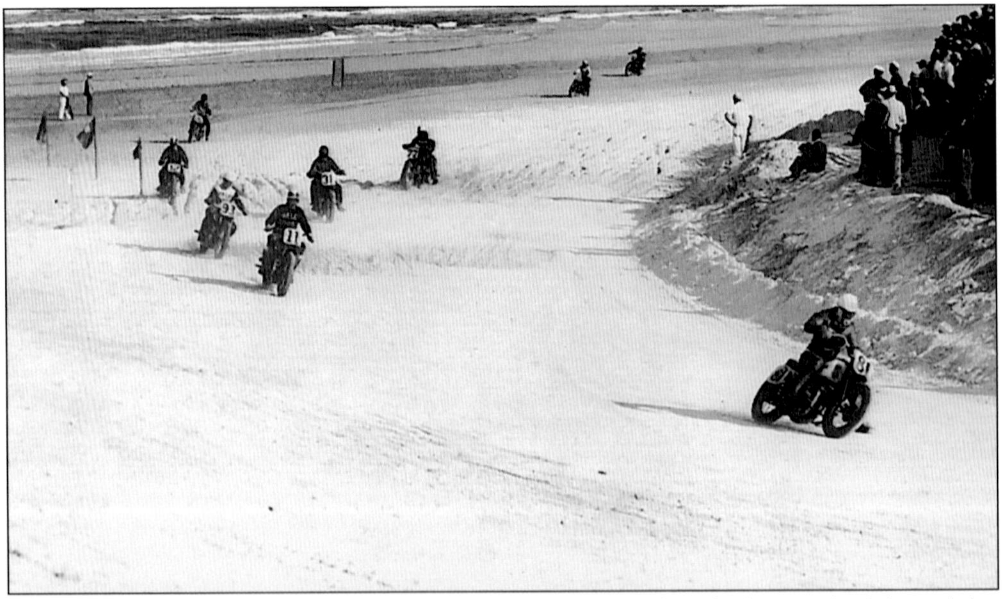

Motorcycles Entering the North Turn, c. 1947. Notice the rider bracing his bike with his left foot to avoid the rear wheel skidding beyond control. These riders were very skilled and had a steel plate, or "skate" attached to the bottom of their boot. This allowed them to negotiate the turns without laying down their bikes. (Courtesy of Halifax Historical Society.)

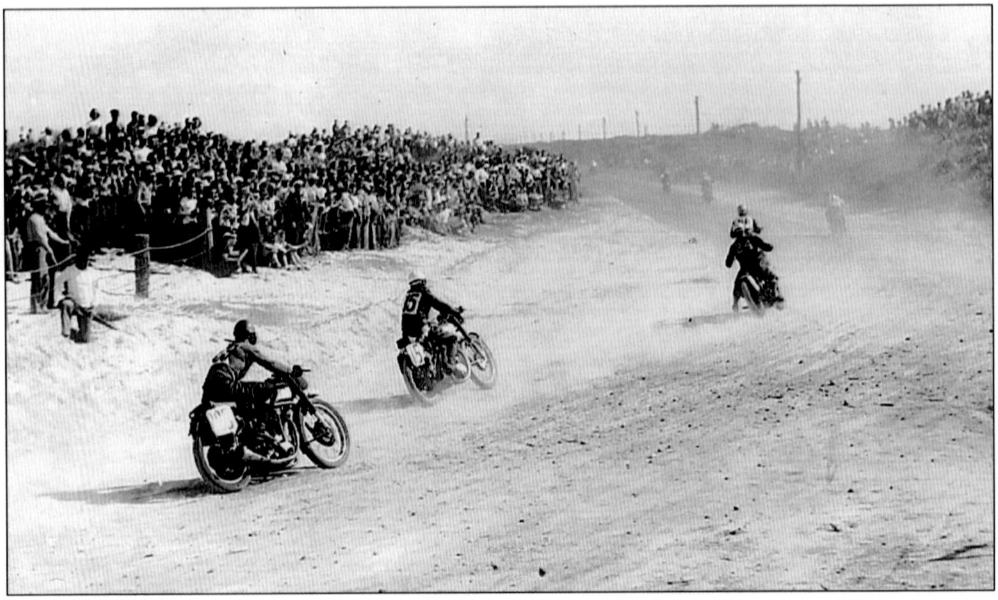

Motorcycles Heading South, c. 1947. Riders had to be alert to the fact that they were leaving the marl-shell surface and going onto the pavement. This was a tricky procedure, which meant you could win or lose the race at this point unless you had experience in throttling the bike to high speed heading south. (Courtesy of Halifax Historical Society.)

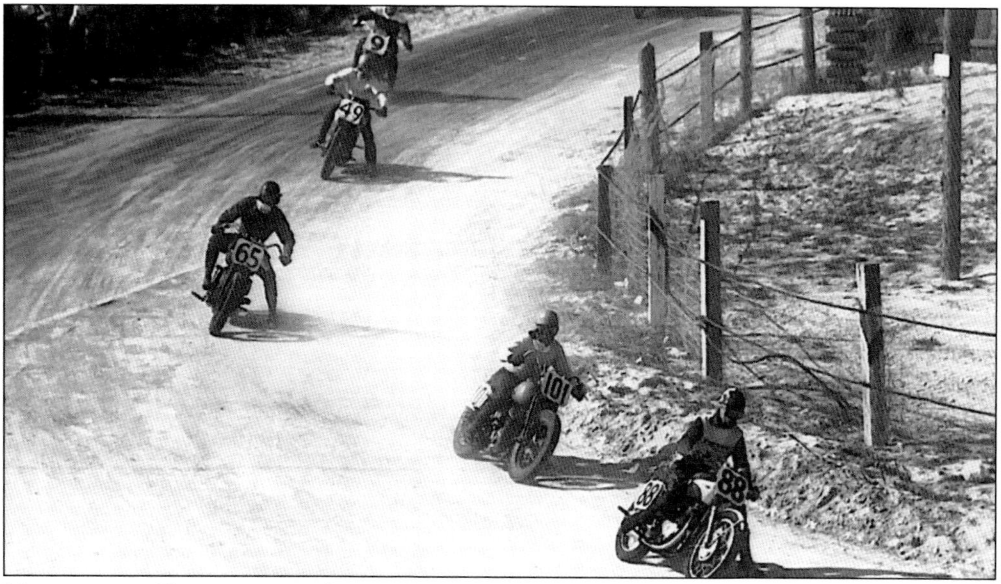

MOTORCYCLES ENTERING THE SOUTH TURN, C. 1947. The riders had to be very cautious and make split-second decisions on braking to enter the marl-shell surface of the south turn and the soft sand leading to the beach. A rider that was too high on the turn often went over the rim into the sand pit. If a rider decided that he was going too fast for the turn, there was an emergency escape route to spoil the speed of the cycle. This was the last year that motorcycle races were held at the 3.2-milerace course. Beginning in 1948, the cycle races were held further south on the beach at Ponce Inlet. (Courtesy of Halifax Historical Society.)

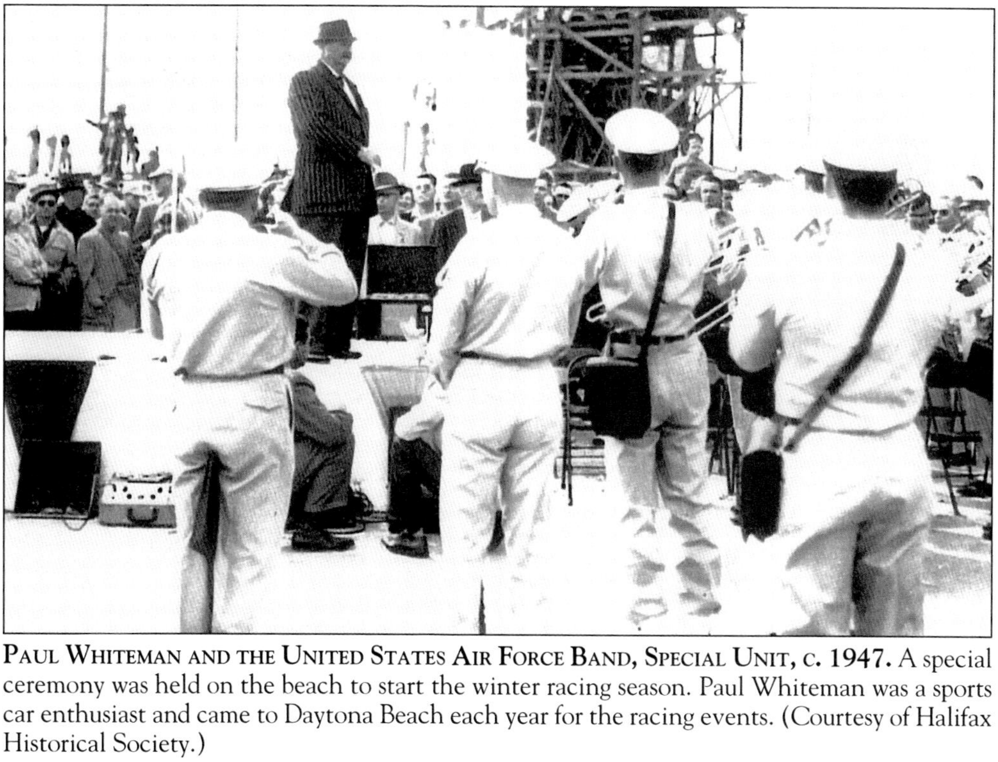

PAUL WHITEMAN AND THE UNITED STATES AIR FORCE BAND, SPECIAL UNIT, C. 1947. A special ceremony was held on the beach to start the winter racing season. Paul Whiteman was a sports car enthusiast and came to Daytona Beach each year for the racing events. (Courtesy of Halifax Historical Society.)

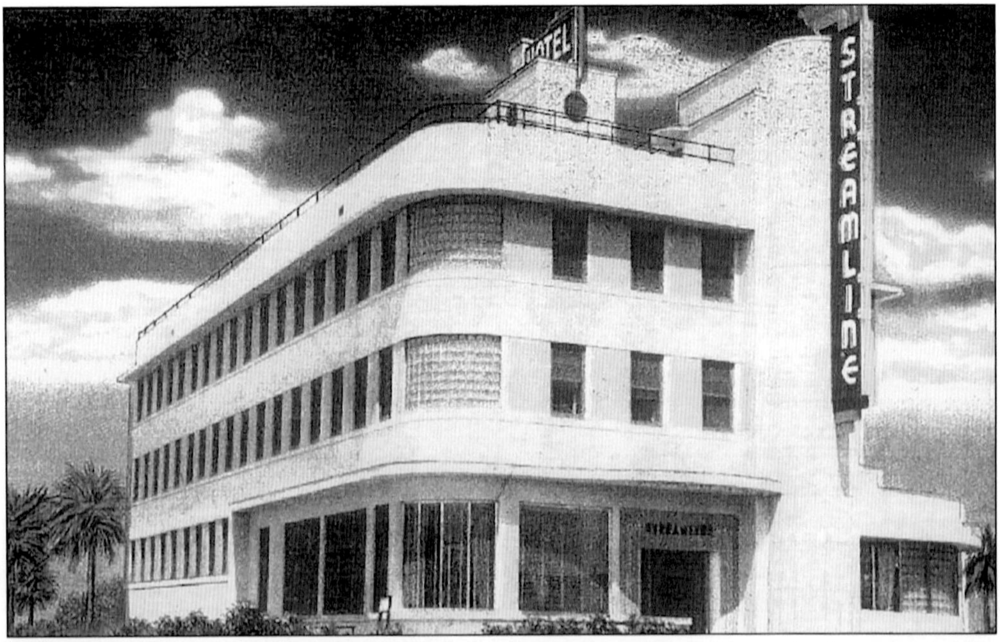

STREAMLINE HOTEL, 1947. This modern art deco style hotel on Atlantic Avenue was the birthplace of the National Association for Stock Car Auto Racing (NASCAR). On December 14, 1947, at 1 p.m., this new organization was formed. They met in the rooftop penthouse lounge. Bill France was elected president, Bill Tuthill was elected national secretary, and Erwin G. "Cannonball" Baker was elected national commissioner. There were more than 18 leaders representing stock car auto racing. "Red" Vogt was credited with naming the organization NASCAR. (Courtesy of Midkiff Family Collection.)

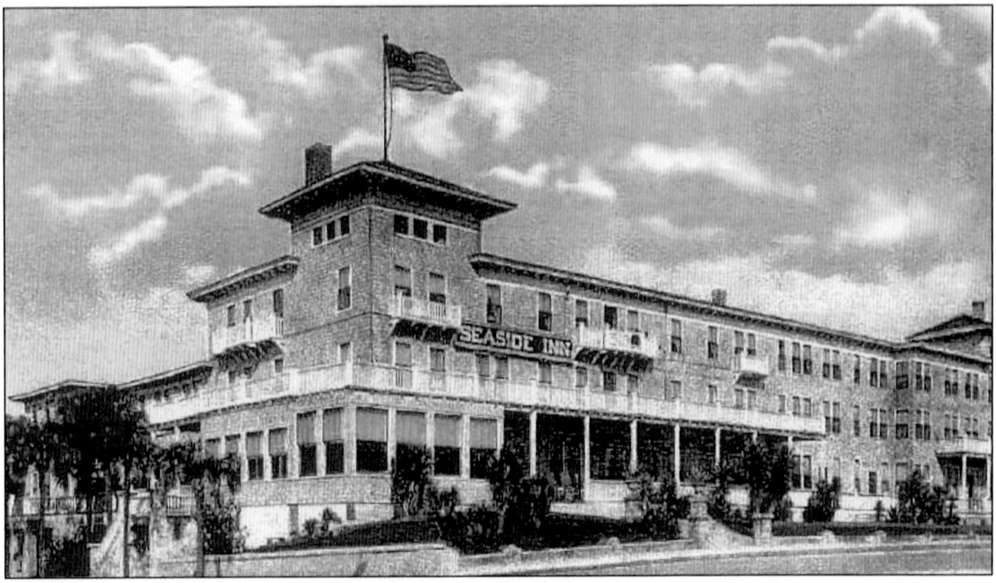

SEASIDE INN, CORNER OF OCEAN AVENUE AND MAIN STREET, c. 1947. This popular hotel was the place to see and to be seen when the racing events were held on the beach. Promoters and businessmen often advertised their products and services in the wide hallway and lobby of this grand old hotel. (Courtesy of Midkiff Family Collection.)

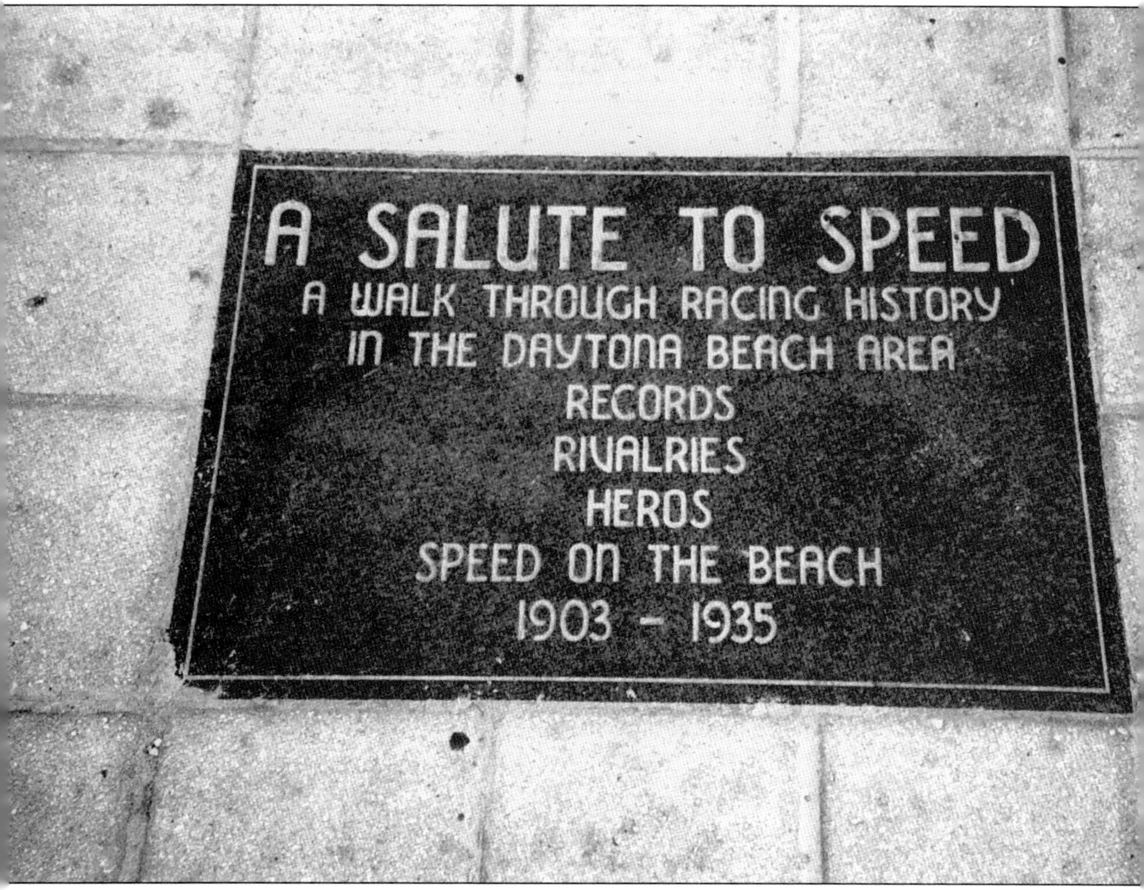

A Walk Through Racing History. The Daytona Beach City Commission and the Daytona Beach Historic Preservation Board Special Committee had these milestones placed in a section of the beachside boardwalk in 1997. (Courtesy of Cardwell Family Collection.)

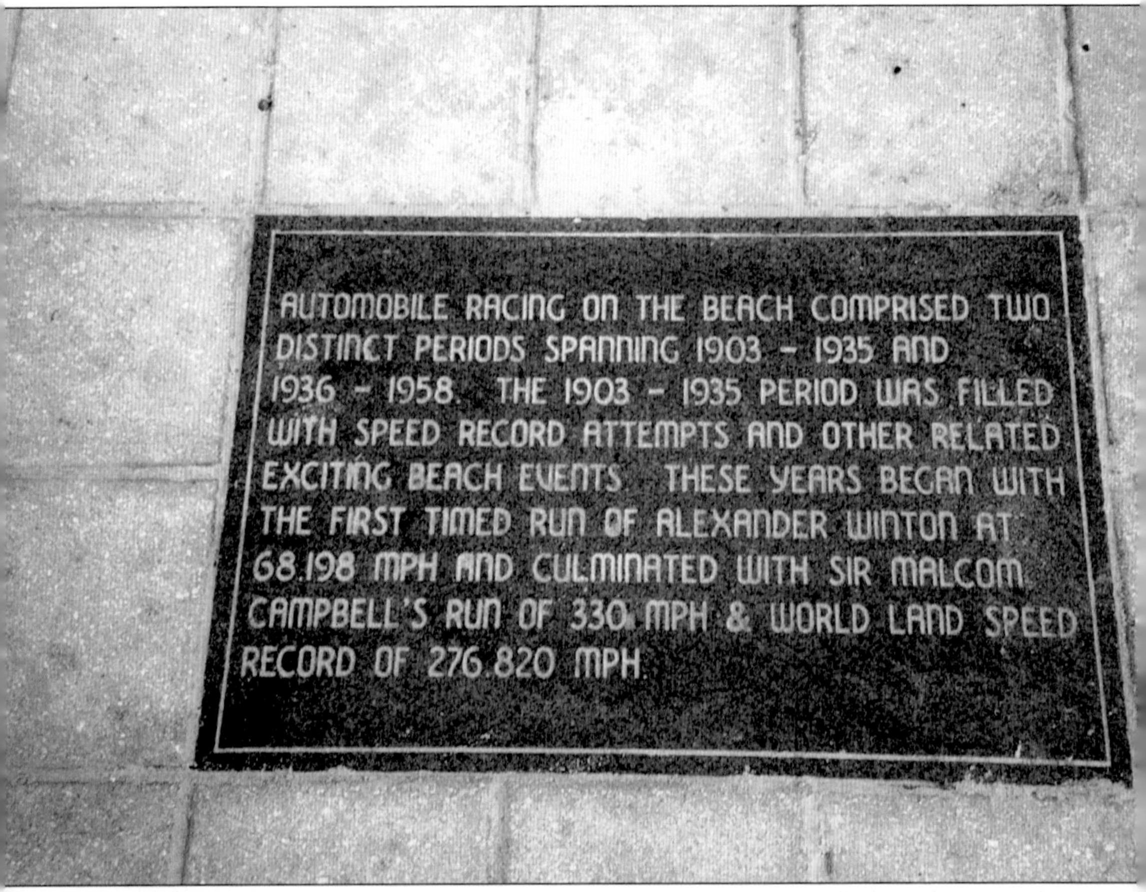

SPEED MILESTONES THROUGH TIME. A visitor can start in 1903 and walk the milestones of auto racing through 1958. They are located near the south end of the boardwalk where many of the major speed trials began on the beach. (Courtesy of Cardwell Family Collection.)

Four

BIDDING FAREWELL TO RACING ON THE BEACH

1948–1958

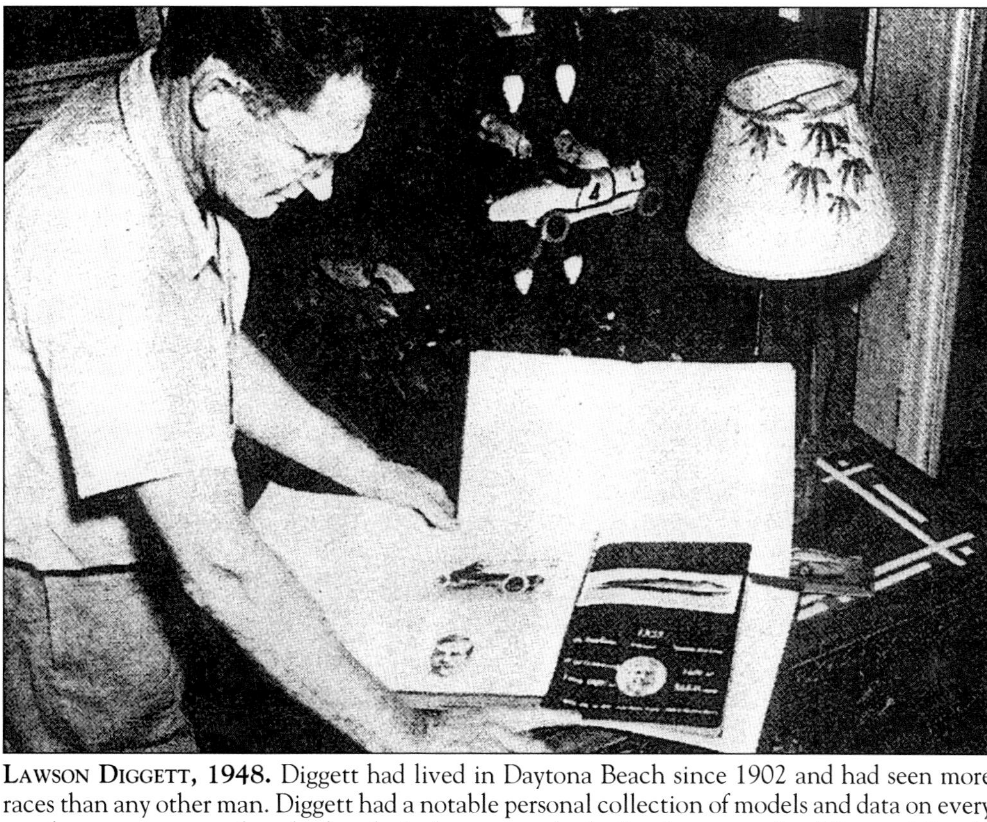

LAWSON DIGGETT, 1948. Diggett had lived in Daytona Beach since 1902 and had seen more races than any other man. Diggett had a notable personal collection of models and data on every car that ever competed at the beach. In later years, he built a home north of Ormond Beach. Upon his death on July 4, 1979, his entire estate was bequeathed to the Halifax Historical Society. (Courtesy of Halifax Historical Society.)

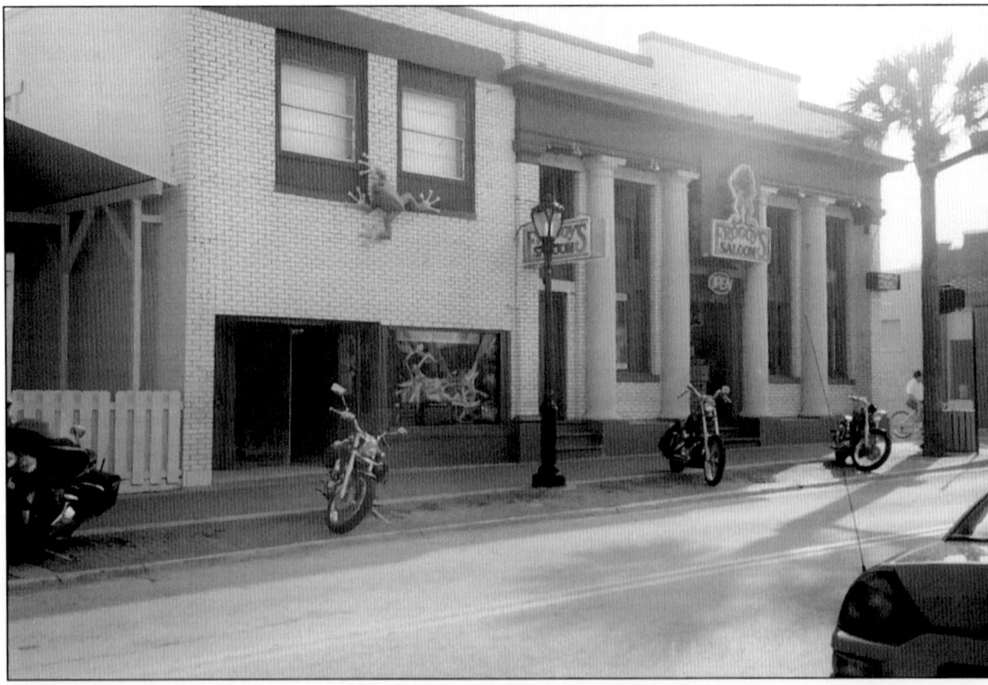

NASCAR Headquarters, 800 Main Street, Daytona Beach, 1948. This building was the former home of the East Coast Bank and the law office of Ray Selden. On the east side of the building there was a stairway leading to the small, second-floor NASCAR office where they promoted racing events and sold tickets. (Courtesy of Cardwell Family Collection.)

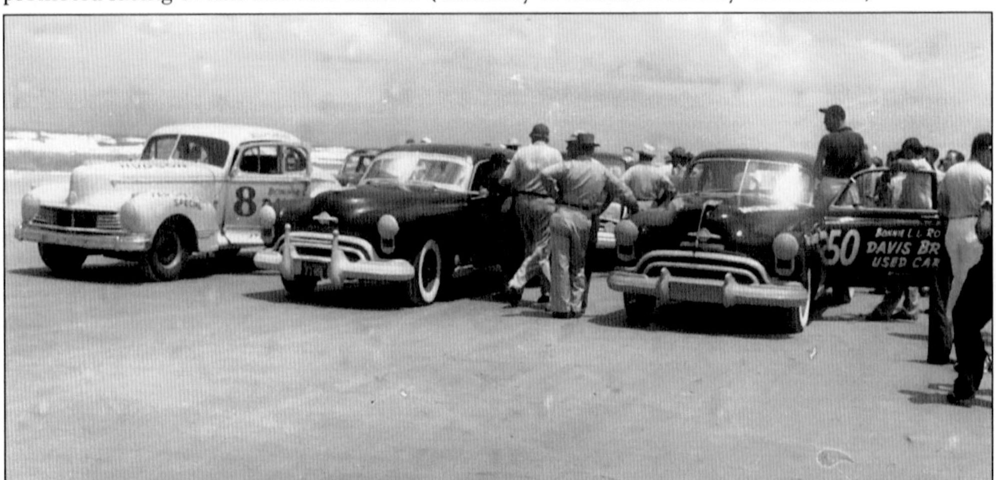

First Grand National Race, July 10, 1949. The new road/beach course, 4.1 miles long, was open at Ponce Inlet after moving from the 3.2-mile course at Daytona Beach (Daytona Shores today). Due to the building of homes and motels, the racing events had to be moved farther south. First place in the 166-mile "Strictly Stock" event went to Red Byron in his 1949 Oldsmobile, while Tim Flock took second place in his 1949 Oldsmobile. Among the many male drivers there were three women competing. Ethel Mobley finished 11th in a 1948 Cadillac, Sara Christian came in 18th in a 1949 Ford, and Louise Smith came in 20th in her 1947 Ford. (Courtesy of ISC Archives.)

ERWIN G. "CANNONBALL" BAKER, C. 1949. The colorful, well-respected "Cannonball" Baker left a legacy in racing. When NASCAR was organized, he was appointed commissioner and presided over many meetings. (Courtesy of ICS Archives.)

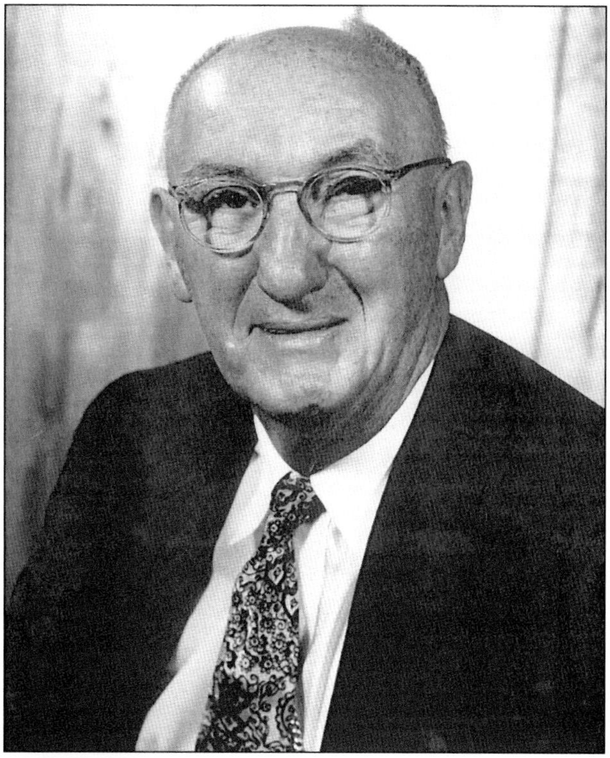

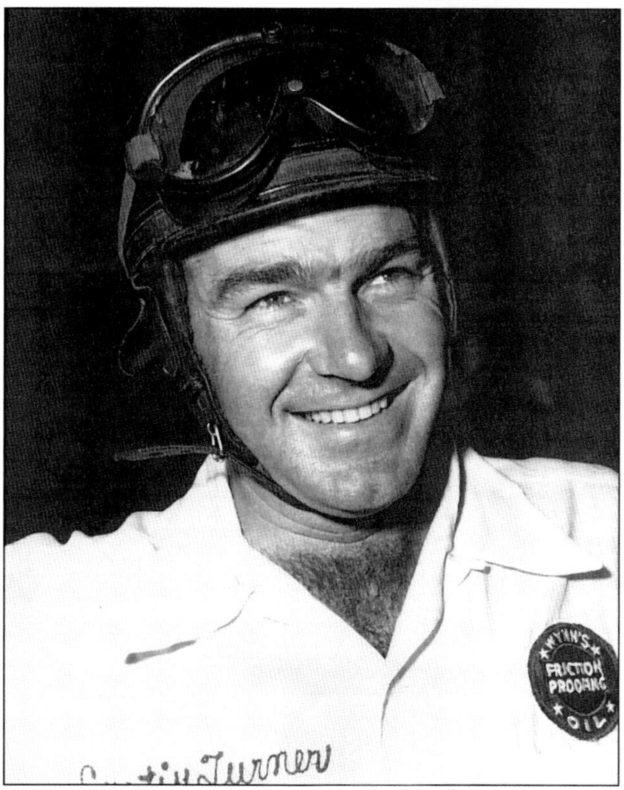

CURTIS TURNER, C. 1949. A skilled, fast, wild, and controversial race driver, Turner thrilled the crowds with his many races on the beach throughout the years. However, he finished in first place only twice, on February 25, 1956, and on February 22, 1958. Turner finished in second place in the February 15, 1957 race and again on February 23, 1958. (Courtesy of ISC Archives.)

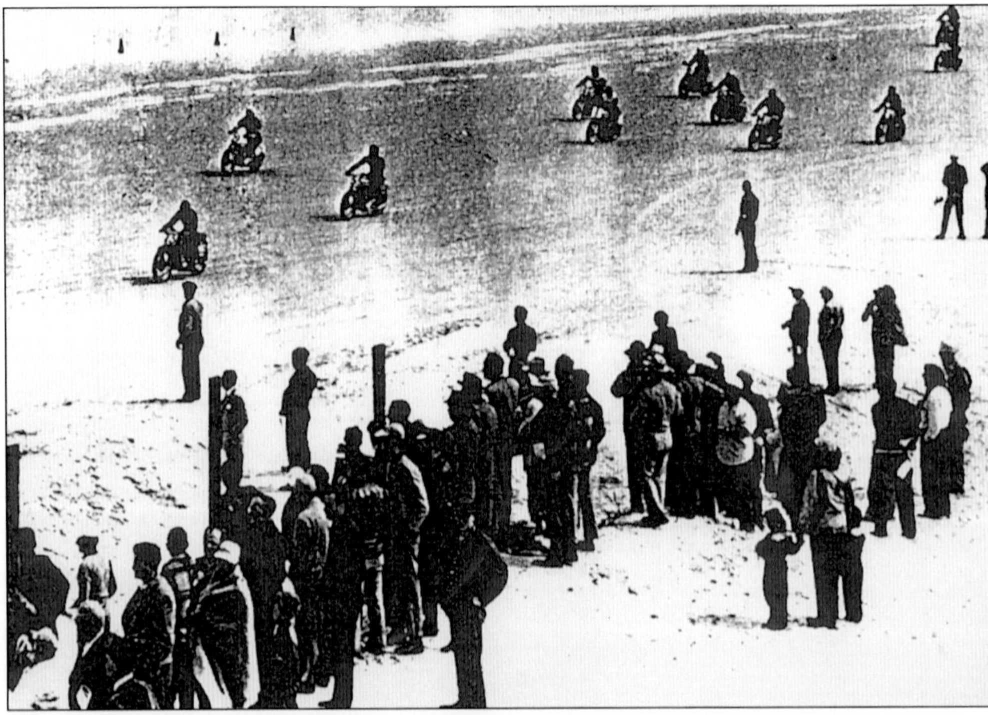

MOTORCYCLE RACES ON THE BEACH, 1950. The thrill of the cycles' roar and speed, heading north on the beach, and the smell of castor oil makes a scene on the World's Most Famous Beach that cannot be duplicated. (Courtesy of Halifax Historical Society.)

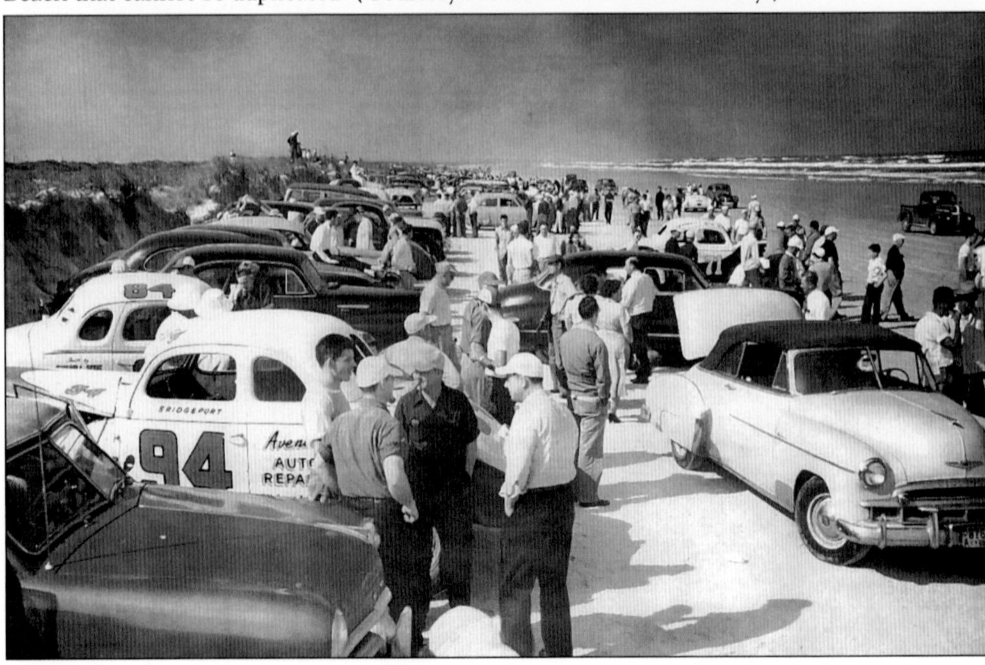

LOUISE SMITH'S (#94) 1949 FORD, 1950. Smith was an outstanding female driver who was a legend in her own time. She encountered car trouble in the first lap of this 196.8-mile Grand National Race and placed 41st in this event. (Courtesy of Halifax Historical Society.)

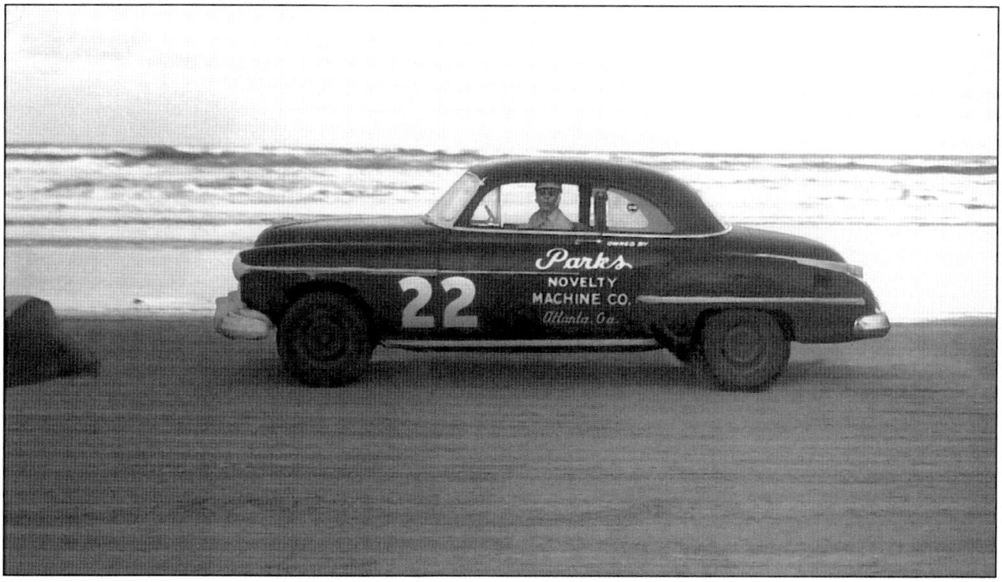

ROBERT "RED" BYRON, 1950. Byron came in second on February 5, in the 196.8-mile Grand National Race, in his 1950 Oldsmobile. He was the defending champion and a disabled war veteran. He won first place four times during his career on the beach—April 14, 1946 in a 1939 Ford; January 26, 1947 in a 1939 Ford; February 15, 1948 in a 1939 Ford; and July 10, 1949 in a 1949 Oldsmobile. The fans called him "The Boss of the Beach" because of his aggressive driving tactics. (Courtesy of Halifax Historical Society.)

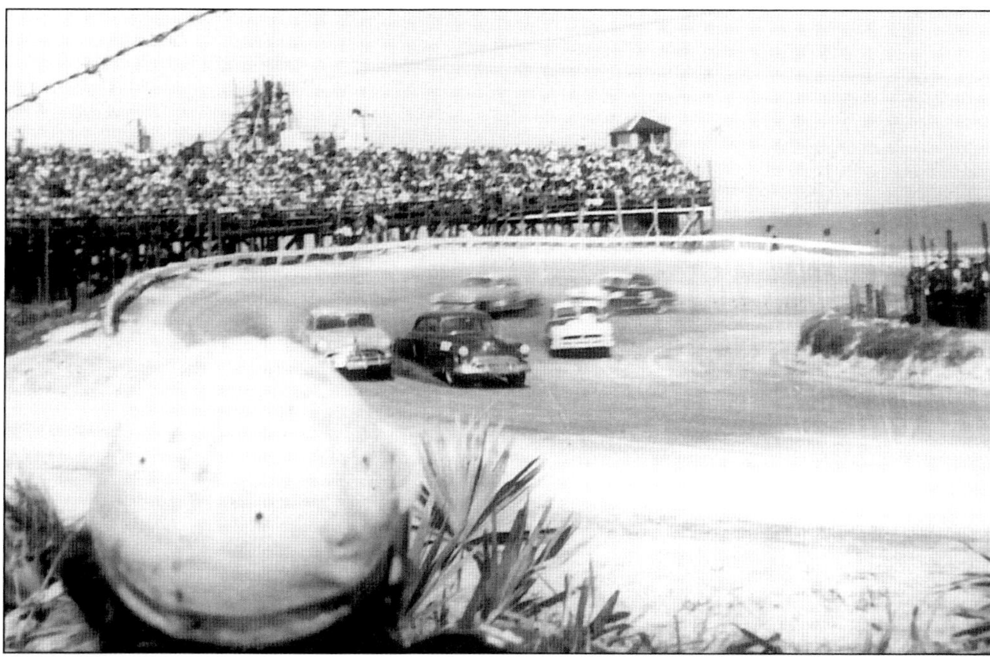

NORTH TURN, C. 1950. Pictured here are race cars approaching the backstretch after maneuvering the beach and the turn. Most fans favored the north turn to watch the cars go through the beach sand, marl, and onto the pavement. There were always spins, broadsides, and plenty of dust to please the crowd. (Courtesy of Halifax Historical Society.)

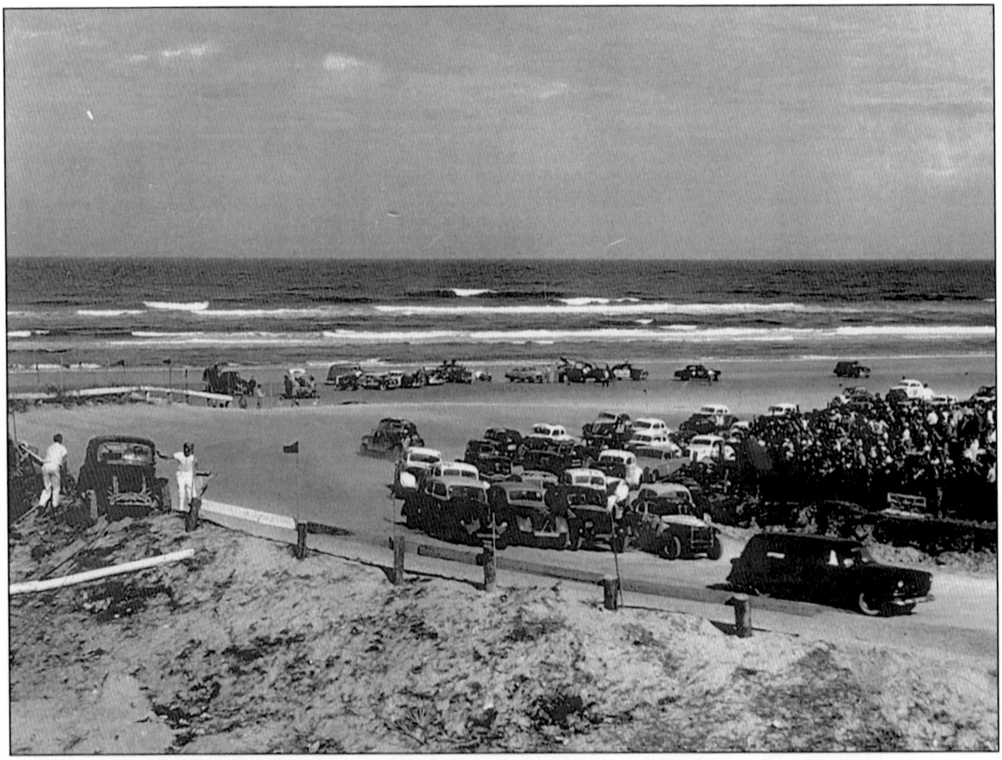

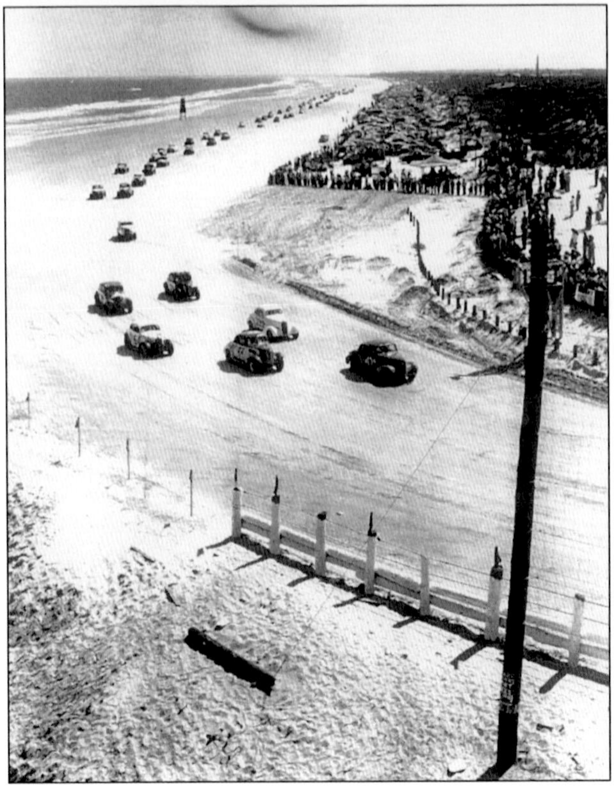

CRASH AT THE NORTH TURN, 1950. This Modified Sportsman's Race was interrupted by a racer running through the guardrail. A converted ambulance is taking the injured driver away to the hospital. Local funeral homes provided the ambulance service and often a hearse was utilized with a red light inside the windshield. Today this practice is obsolete. (Courtesy of ISC Archives.)

THE BEACH AND THE NORTH TURN, 1950. During the first lap, cars always needed to decelerate to enter the turn and accelerate on the pavement. This is where a driver won or lost a race. Their skills were demonstrated here while negotiating the turn. This separated the leaders from the pack. (Courtesy of Halifax Historical Society.)

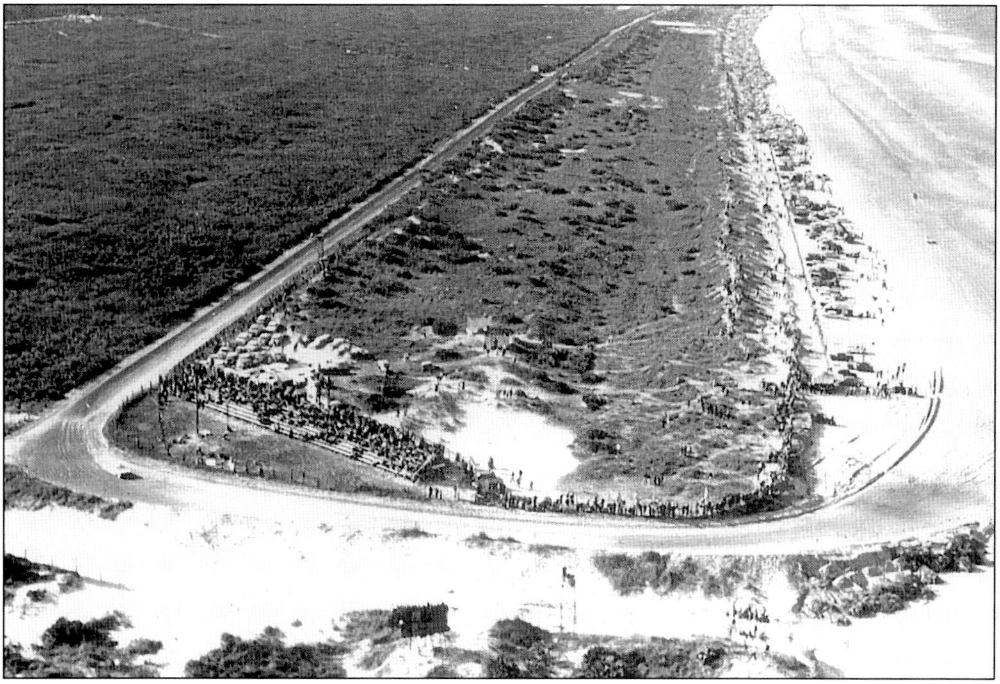

Aerial View of the South Turn, 1950. This is a far cry from the modern speedways of today and appears to be primitive. However, the thrills, chills, and suspense were all there as the cars braked, slid, and spun through the sand to enter the beach. Racing will never be quite like this again because of the paved speedways of today. (Courtesy of Halifax Historical Society.)

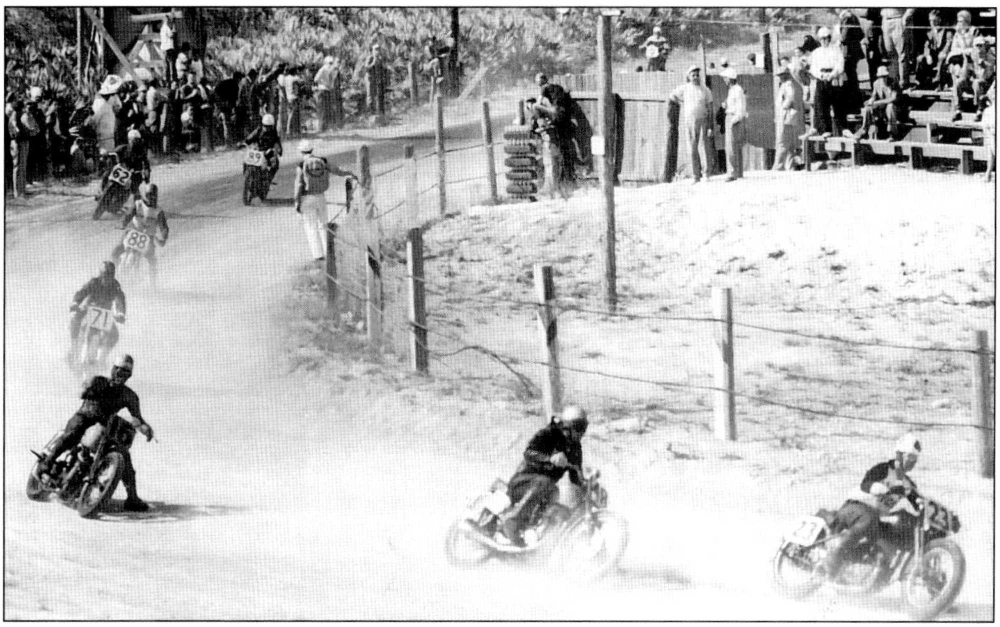

Motorcycle Race, South Turn, 1951. Dick Klamfoth rode to victory in the 200-mile, AMA-sanctioned race on a Norton Motorcycle. In the 100-mile Amateur Race this same year, Bob Michael also won on a Norton. The south turn was tricky because of having to brake and make the turn to ride through the sand onto the beach. (Courtesy of ISC Archives.)

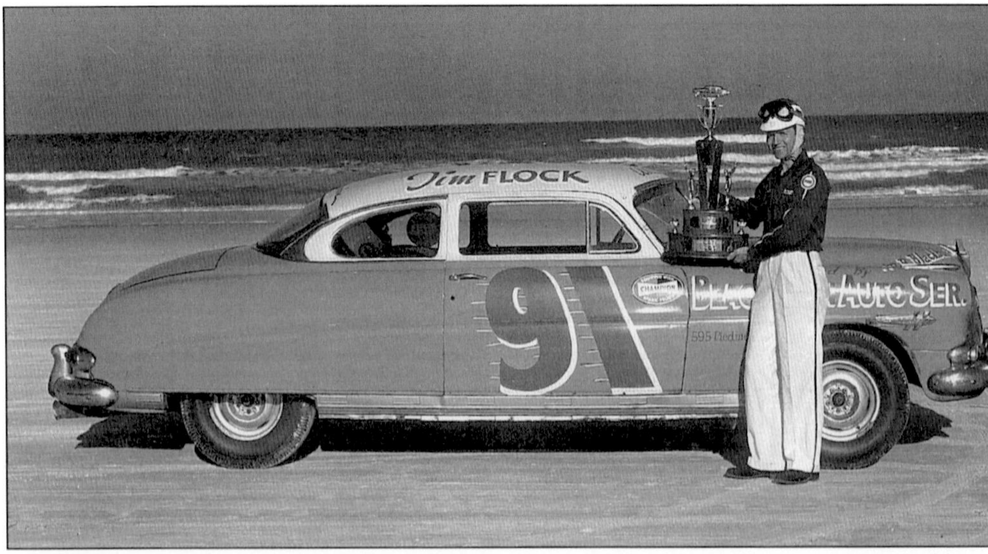

Tim Flock and His #91, 1951. Flock placed second in the 159.9-mile Grand National Race on February 11, 1951. He was one of the famed Flock brothers of stock car racing. Later, he won first place in four other racing events. (Courtesy of Halifax Historical Society.)

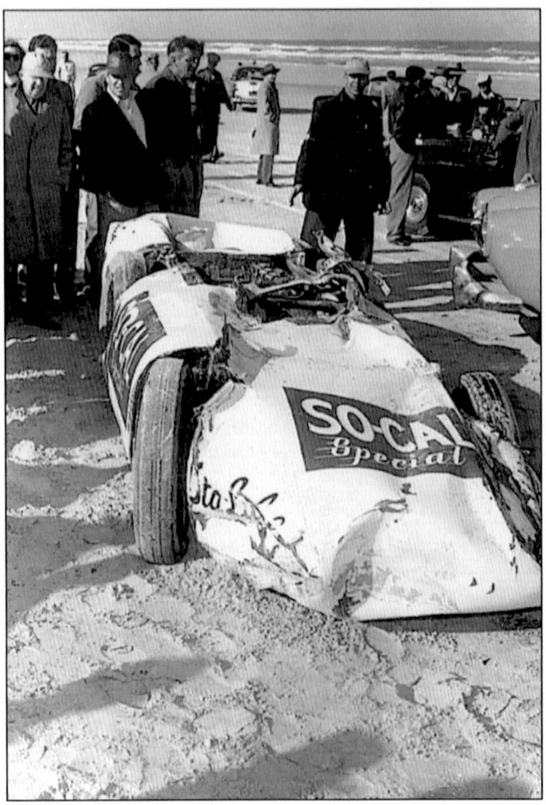

Don Bailey's Near-Fatal Crash, 1951. The So-Cal Special, a uniquely-designed car, wrecked when Bailey attempted to break a new speed record through the Measured Mile. He was going over 122 mph when he entered the Mile. He hit a soft spot on the beach, the car became airborne, and rolled end over end for 1,000 feet. He was badly injured but after a long convalescence, he did recover. This ended his speed trial on the beach. (Courtesy of Halifax Historical Society.)

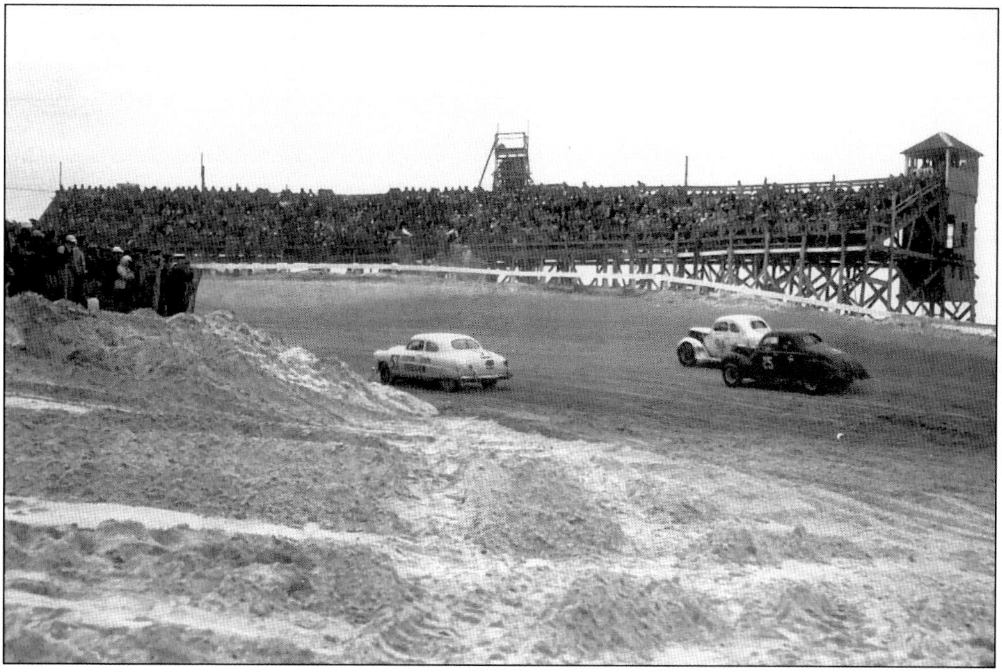

MODIFIED-SPORTSMAN RACE, FEBRUARY 9, 1952. Jack Smith was the winner of this race in a 1939 Ford-M. Making the turn are Tommy Moon (#57), Chuck Arnold (#94), and George Tidd (#25). All are driving modified Fords. (Courtesy of Halifax Historical Society.)

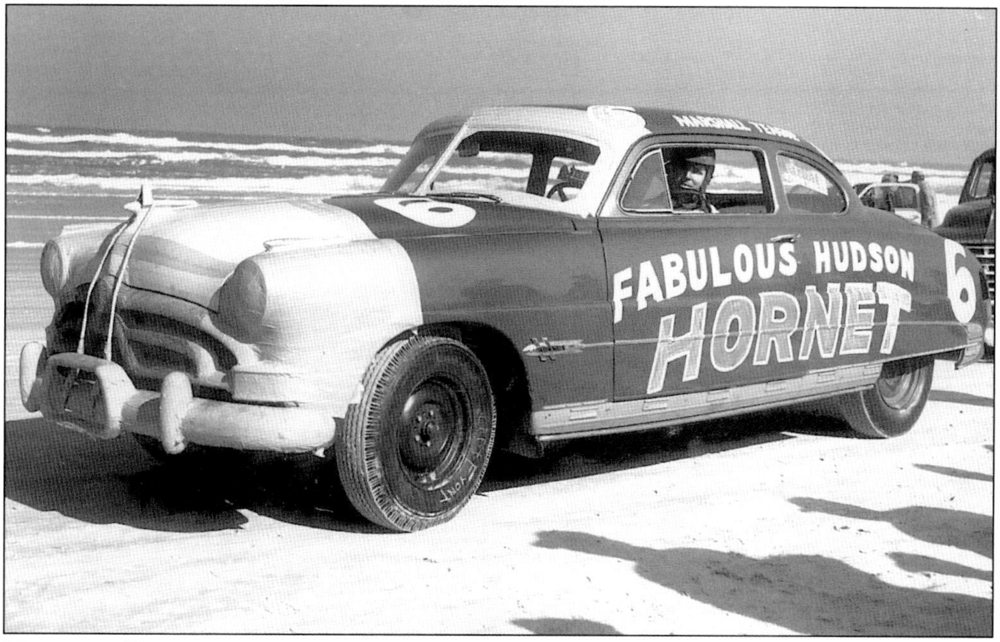

MARSHALL TEAGUE IN HIS FABULOUS HUDSON HORNET, 1952. This outstanding race driver from Daytona Beach was a garage and filling station owner. He won three times, first in 1949 in a 1939 Ford, in 1951 in a 1951 Hudson, and again in 1952 in a 1952 Hudson. Teague was a contender in many racing events and was a very skilled driver. However, after the opening of the new speedway, he was killed in an Indianapolis-styled race car. (Courtesy of ISC Archives.)

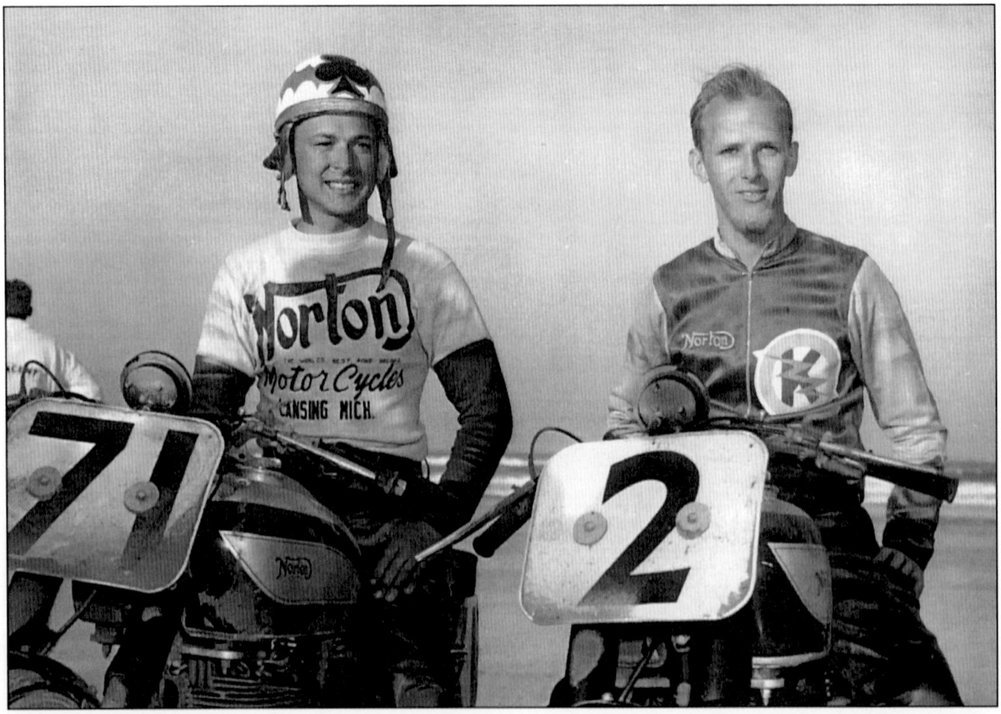

Bobby Hill and Dick Klamfoth, 1952. Both of these riders were top contenders for the 200-mile AMA Race. Hill won in 1954 on a BSA motorcycle, and in previous years was on the Norton Team. Klamfoth won in 1949, 1951, and 1952, all three times on a Norton. All races were held on the 4.1-mile road/beach course. (Courtesy of ISC Archives.)

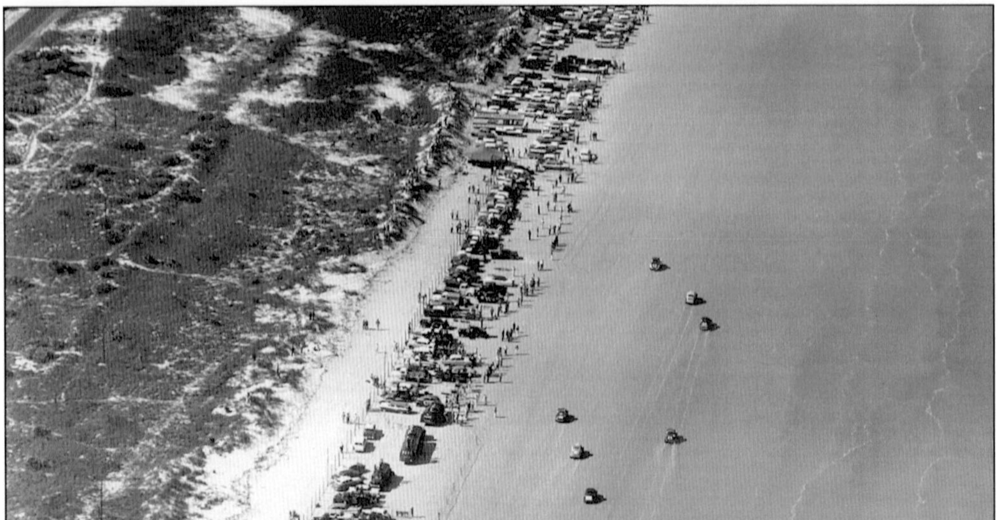

Grand National Race, February 10, 1952. This is an aerial view of the 4.1-mile race track. Lee Petty (#43) is leading the pack in his 1950 Lincoln. He finished in ninth place. Marshall Teague (#6) won this race in his 1952 Hudson. Herb Thomas (#92) came in second place in his 1952 Hudson. Lee Petty was the father of Richard and grandfather of Kyle, who later claimed racing fame in their own right. (Courtesy of Halifax Historical Society.)

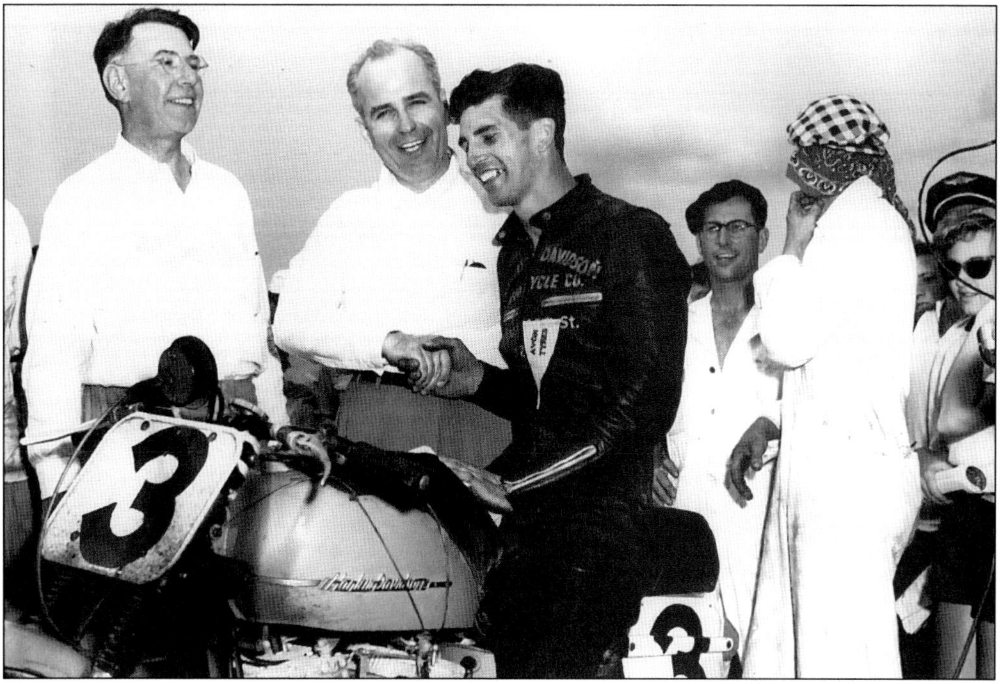

Paul Goldsmith, Winner of AMA 200-mile Race, 1953. He was an outstanding motorcycle racer and five years after this date, he won the 1958 Grand National Stock Car Race. He was the only two-time cycle and auto winner. (Courtesy of John Gontner.)

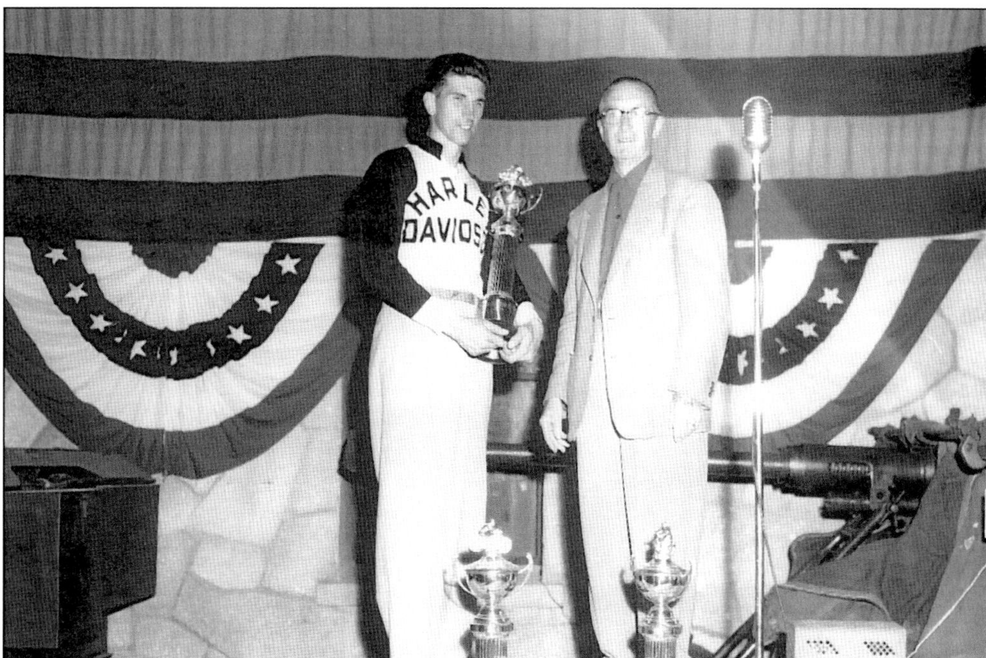

Paul Goldsmith, Winner of the AMA 200-mile Race, 1953. The AMA official presenting the trophy is unidentified. Goldsmith won this race, on a Harley-Davidson, at the 4.1-mile road/beach course. (Courtesy of ISC Archives.)

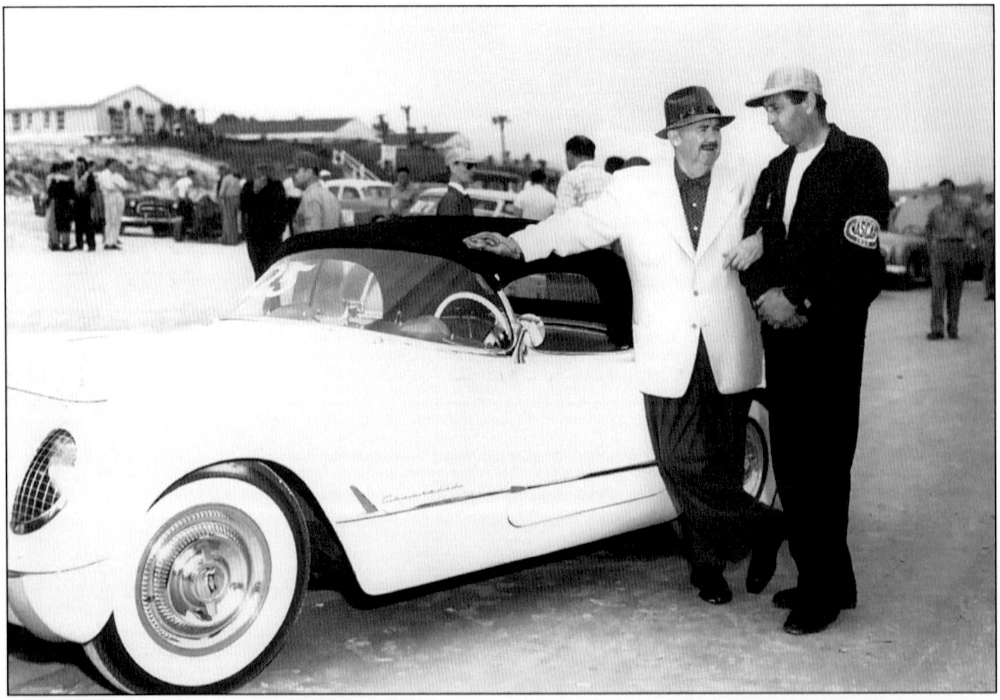

PAUL WHITEMAN AND BILL FRANCE SR. AT THE TIME TRIALS, FEBRUARY, 1954. Whiteman, a nationally known orchestra leader and a sportscar enthusiast, helped Bill with promoting races on the beach. (Courtesy of John Gontner.)

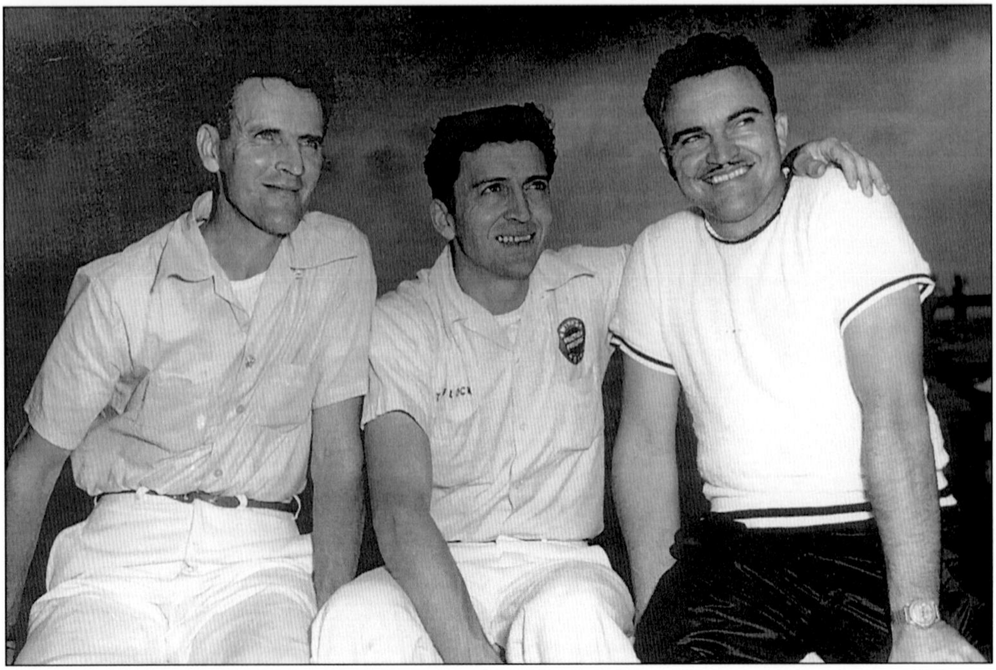

THE FLOCK BROTHERS, 1954. The Flock brothers, from left to right, are Bob, Tim, and Fonty. These three brothers were born to race and were a legacy in their own time. They were always contenders for the road/beach races at Daytona. (Courtesy of ISC Archives.)

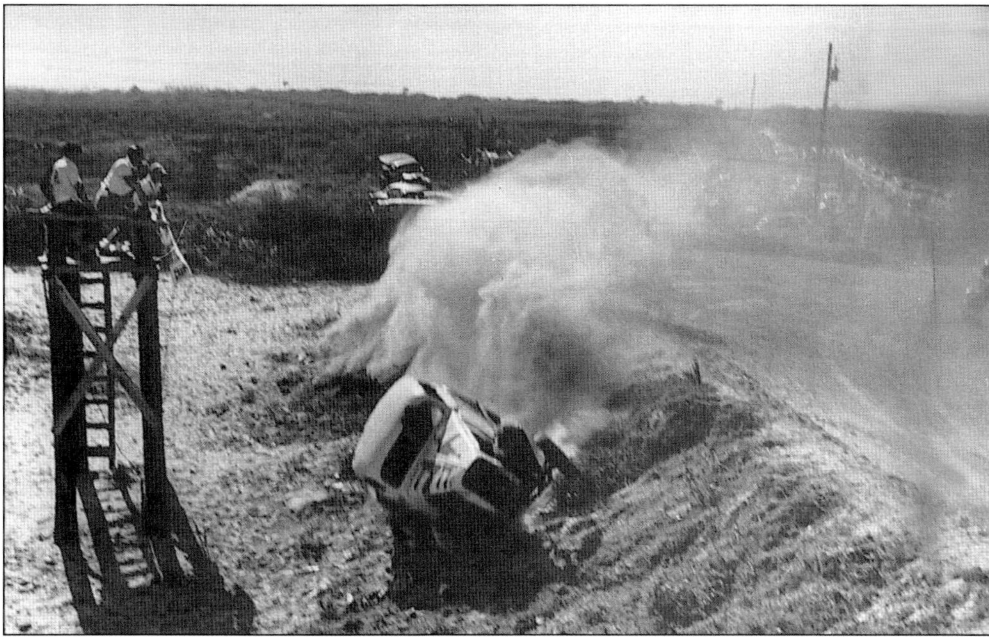

SOUTH TURN AT PONCE INLET, FEBRUARY 20, 1954. Jerry Ott failed to keep his car under control as he braked and entered the south turn. He rolled over the embankment and turned over. Notice the panic-stricken timekeepers on the platform. (Courtesy of Halifax Historical Society.)

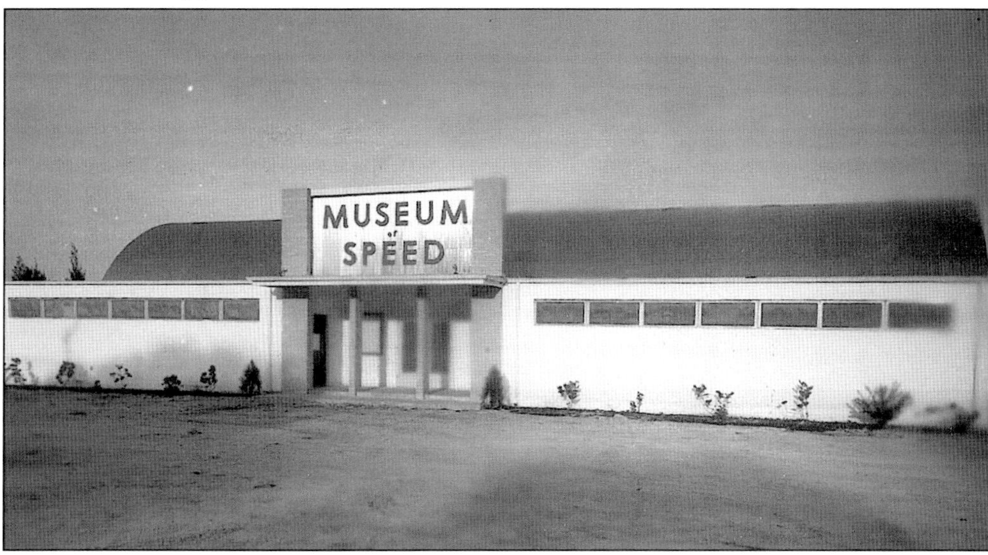

MUSEUM OF SPEED, SOUTH DAYTONA, 1954. William R. Tuthill established this museum of racing history in the early 1950s. He was appointed secretary of NASCAR in 1947 and actively engaged in the promotion of the road/beach races. Housed in the museum was the famous Campbell *Bluebird V*, as well as many other vehicles and exhibits. The museum closed in the late 1950s and all of the automobiles and exhibits were transferred to the Talladega Race Track Museum in Alabama. However, some of the printed materials and images were kept in Ormond Beach, Florida. Today, the *Bluebird V* has been restored and can be seen at Daytona USA on International Speedway Boulevard. (Courtesy of John Gontner.)

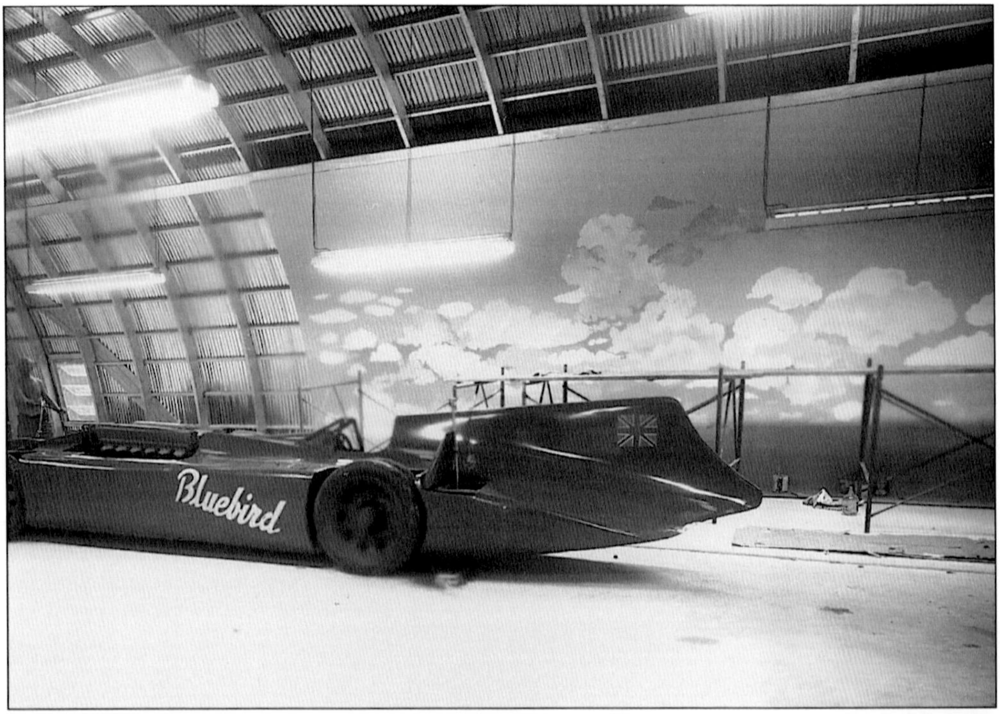

CAMPBELL'S *BLUEBIRD* V AT THE MUSEUM OF SPEED, 1954. This is the famous car that Sir Malcolm Campbell used to break ground speed records at Daytona Beach and at Bonneville Salt Flats. (Courtesy of John Gontner.)

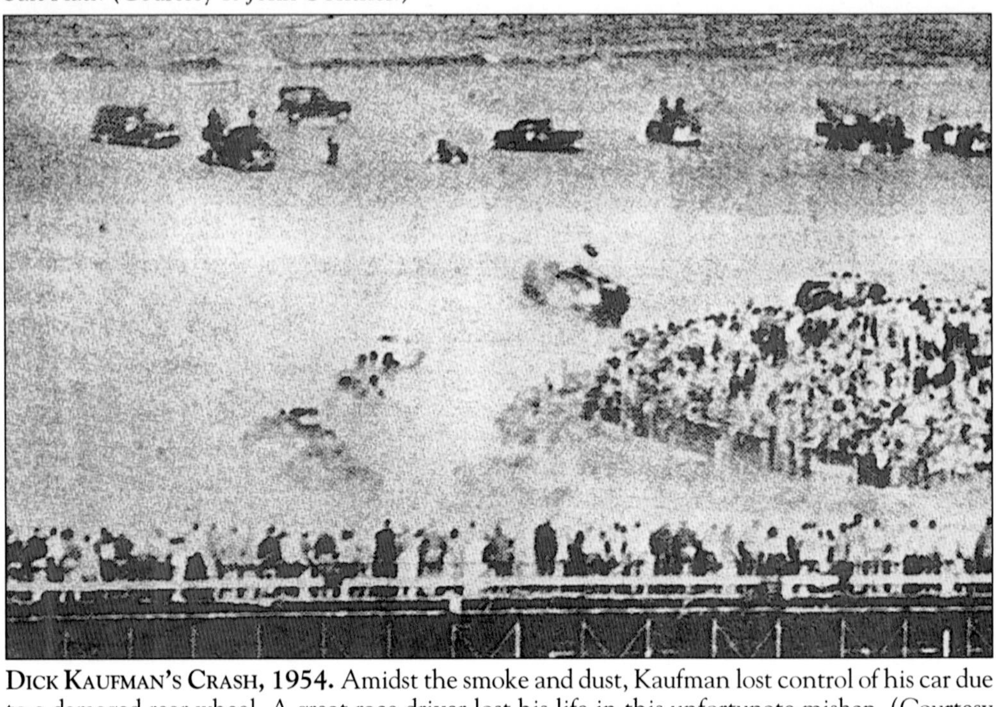

DICK KAUFMAN'S CRASH, 1954. Amidst the smoke and dust, Kaufman lost control of his car due to a damaged rear wheel. A great race driver lost his life in this unfortunate mishap. (Courtesy of Halifax Historical Society.)

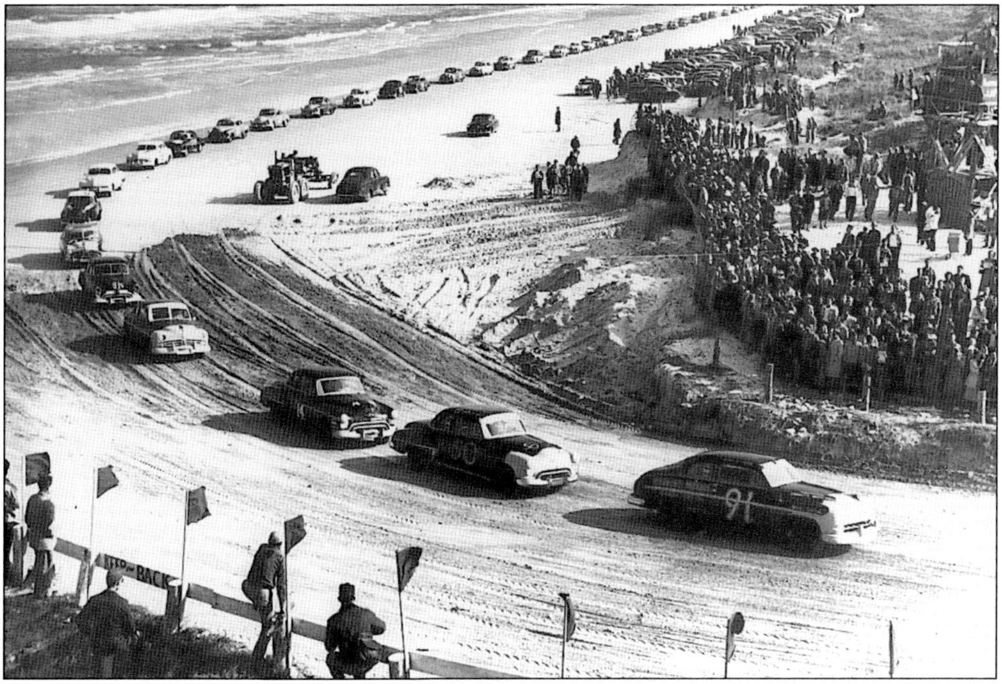

BEACH RACES, NORTH TURN, 1955. This is the first parade lap before getting the starting flag on February 26, 1955. (Courtesy of John Gontner.)

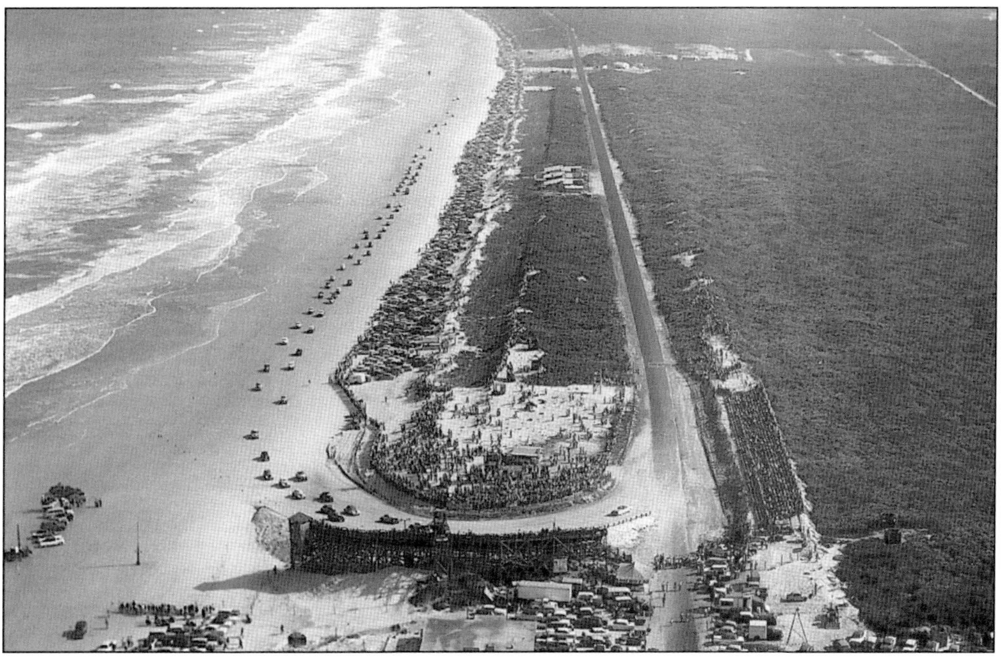

AERIAL VIEW OF THE MODIFIED-SPORTSMAN RACE, FEBRUARY 26, 1955. Cars heading north on the beach and the lead cars can be seen entering the north turn. Banjo Matthews won this race in his 1940 Ford-M, while Earl Moss came in second in his 1940 Ford-M. These Modified Sportsman Races were always held before the Grand National Races. (Courtesy of ISC Archives.)

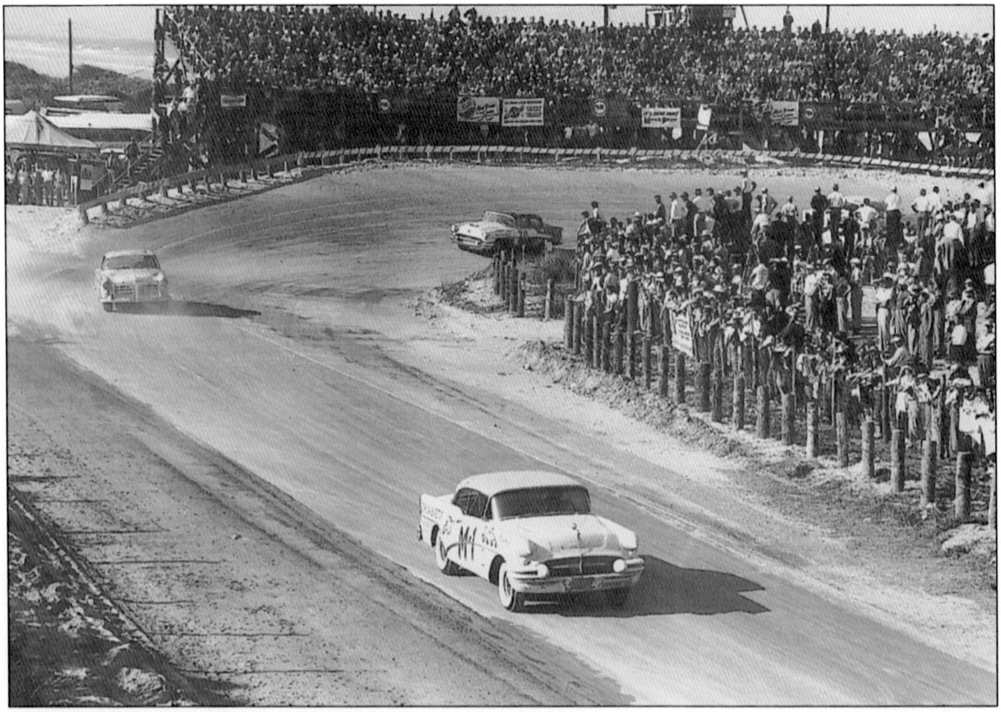

GLENN EDWARD "FIREBALL" ROBERTS IN THE LEAD AT THE FEBRUARY 26, 1955 GRAND NATIONAL RACE. Roberts in his M-1 1955 Buick was disqualified. Tim Flock in his #300 1955 Chrysler came in second and was later declared the winner. The #78 car, seen here in third place, was a 1955 Oldsmobile driven by Jim Paschal who ended up in 26th place by the end of the race. (Courtesy of Halifax Historical Society.)

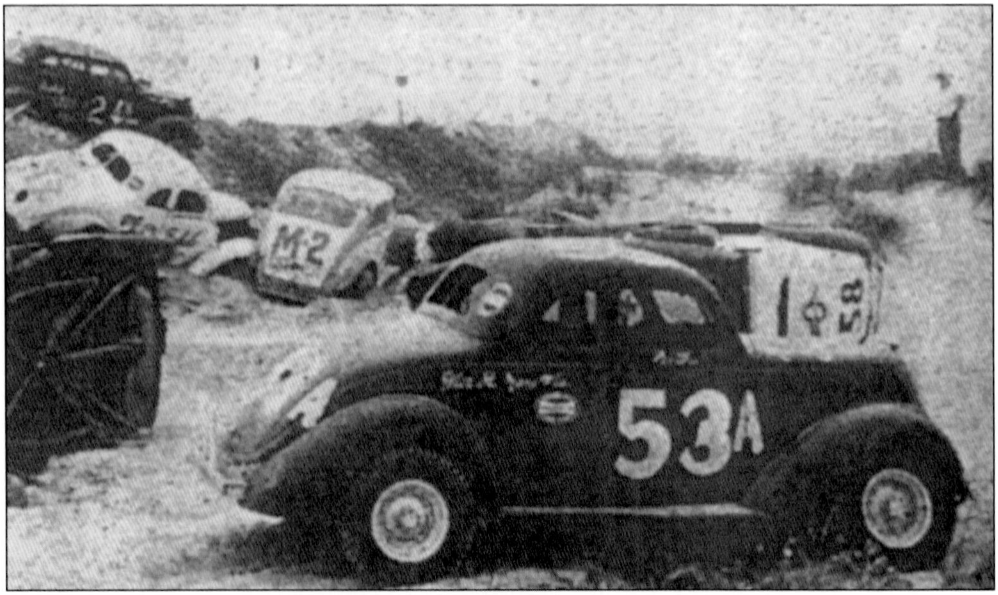

PILE-UP ON THE SOUTH TURN, FEBRUARY 26, 1955. Fans were thrilled with this kind of action, and scenes like this were common during the Modified-Sportsman Race. (Courtesy of Halifax Historical Society.)

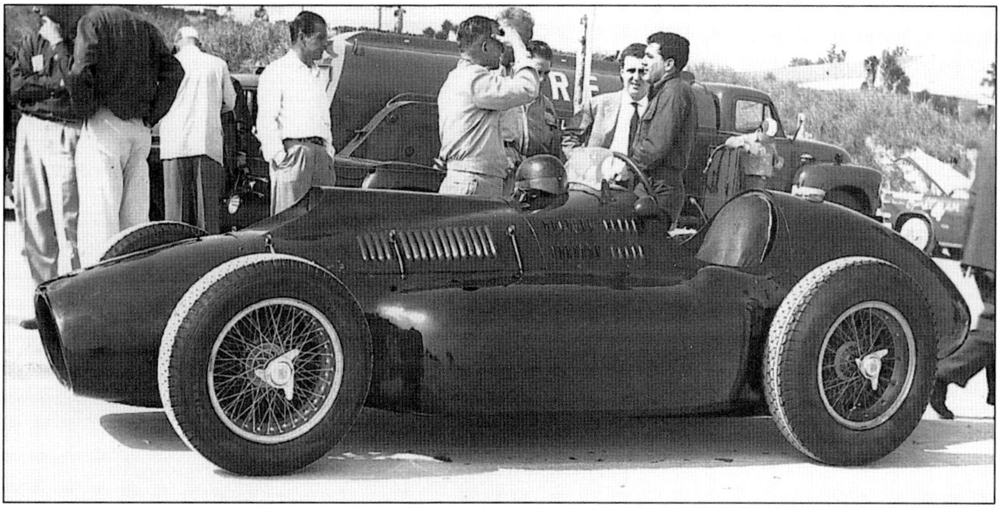

ONE-MILE SPEED TRIALS ON THE BEACH, 1955. These special events were held during the winter for experimental cars. The results of these speed trials yielded new achievements for the automotive industry. The Dodge Daytona was one of the earliest cars to gain recognition from these trials. (Courtesy of John Gontner.)

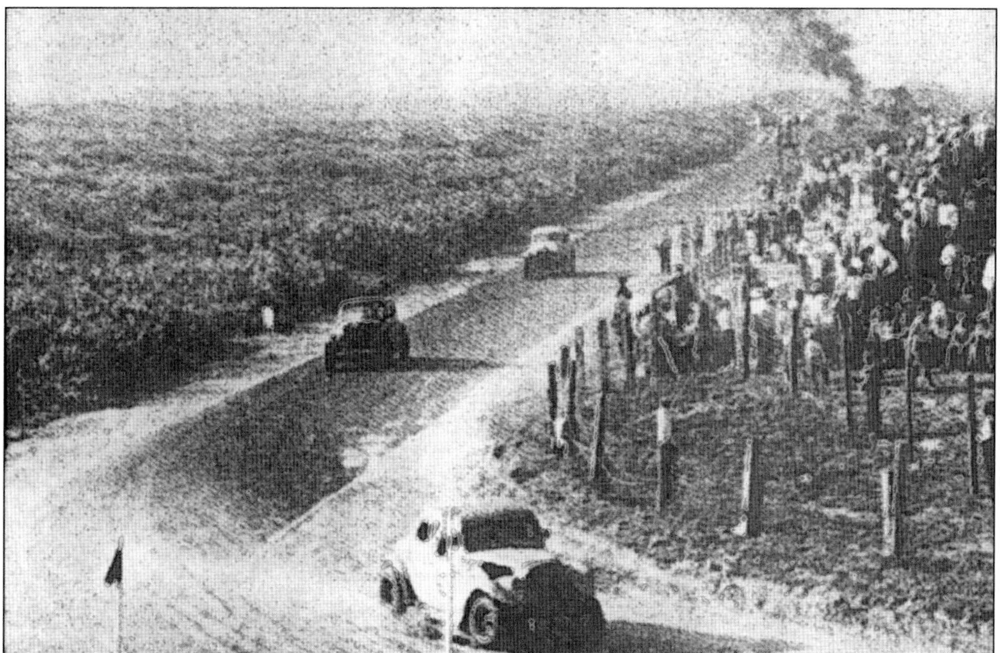

A DREADED FATAL CRASH ON THE BACKSTRETCH, 1955. This was the most feared of all pile-ups. Al Briggs died in this crash after losing control of his vehicle. The danger of vehicles igniting brush fires made these situations most vulnerable. Rescue and fire trucks were posted at each turn. (Courtesy of Halifax Historical Society.)

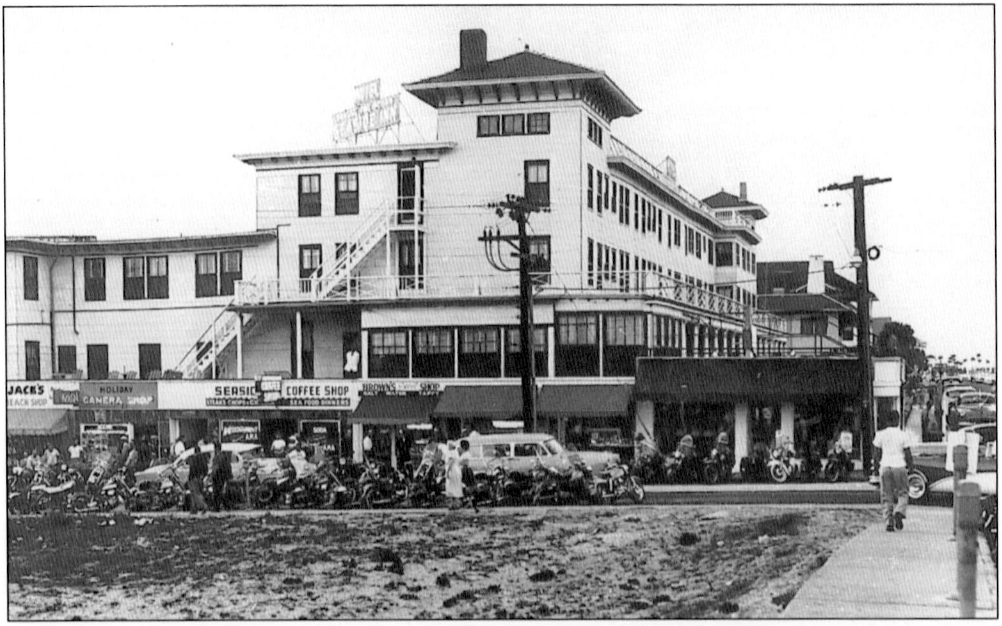

BIKE WEEK, MAIN STREET AND OCEAN AVENUE, FEBRUARY 12, 1955. Hundreds of cycles line the sidewalks around Seaside Inn. This has been a favorite gathering place for motorcycle enthusiasts since 1937, returning each year for the AMA Races. (Courtesy of John Gontner.)

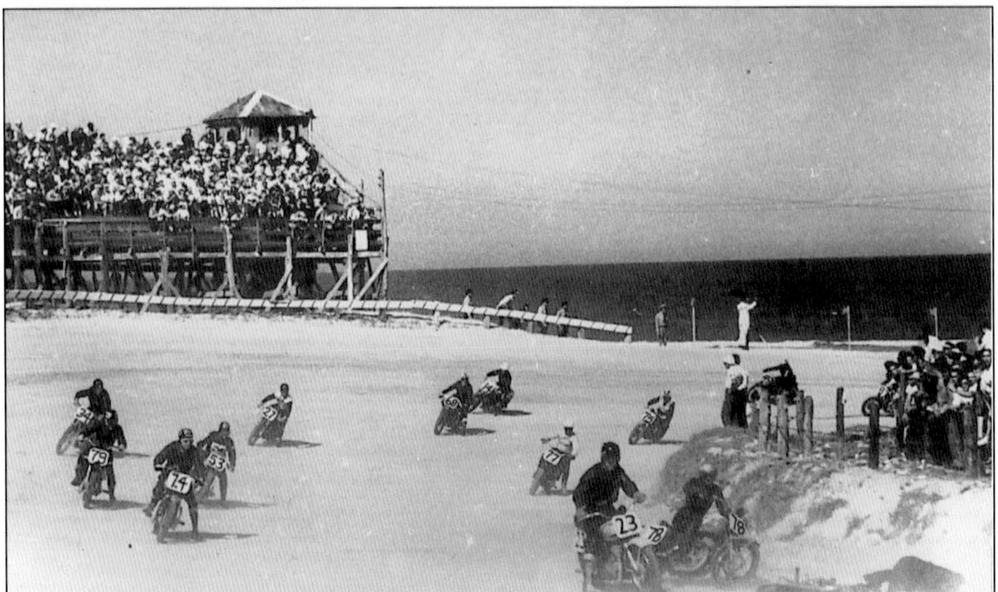

DAYTONA 200, NORTH TURN, FEBRUARY 13, 1955. The cyclists entering the north turn in this photo are #23 Charles Berg, #78 Ralph Nelson, #74 Ray Mahoad, #79 Jon Lewis, #34 Charley West, #27 Milton Lassiter, #68 Walter Grimm, #77 Rodger Sanderstorm, and #45 James Gregory. However, riders #53, #14, #75, and #9 are unidentified. Notice the riders are using their left legs and a steel plate on their boots to stabilize their machines while banking through the north turn. The downed rider, with nowhere to go, is narrowly missed by two of his competitors. (Courtesy of John Gontner.)

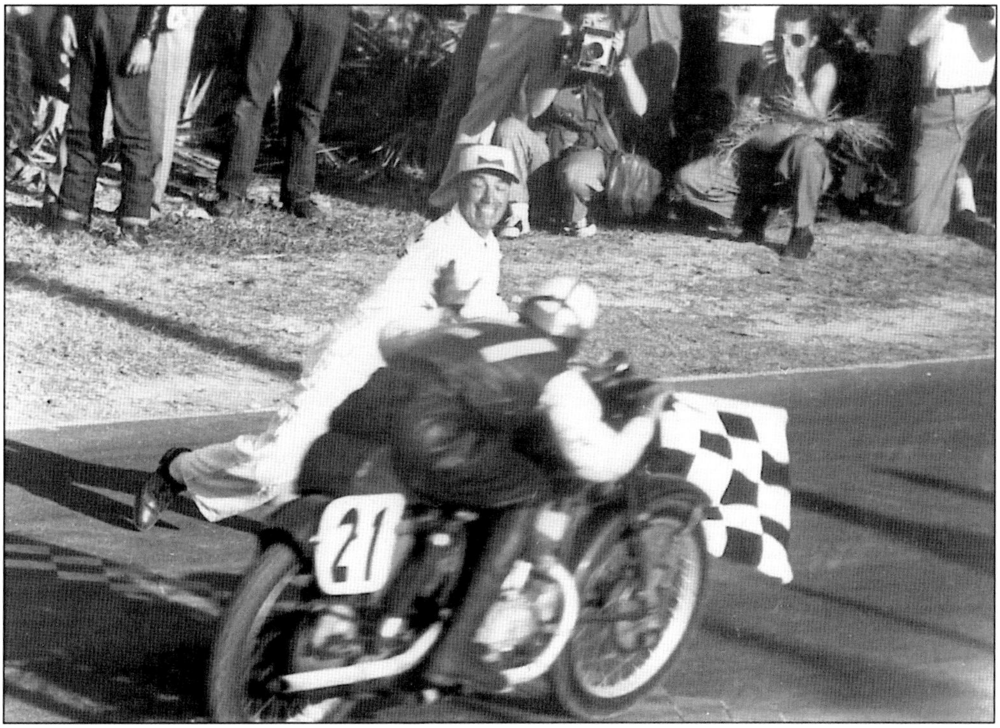

Daytona 200 Beach Races, February 13, 1955. Bradley Andres, #21, wins the AMA Race after receiving the checkered flag on the beach. Andres hailed from San Diego, California, and rode a Harley-Davidson, winning this race with an average speed of 94.57 mph. (Courtesy of John Gontner.)

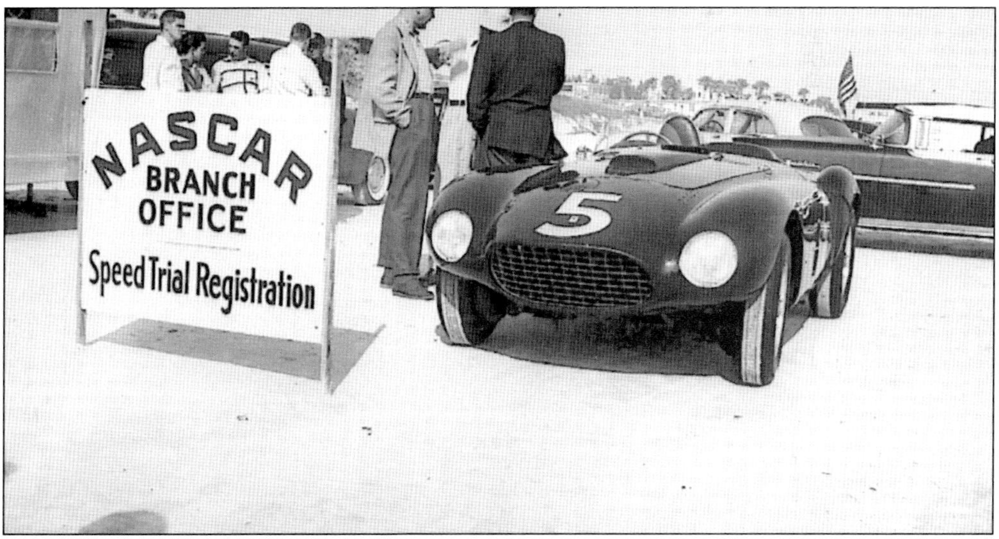

Ferrari Pace Car, #5, Outside the NASCAR Speed Trial Registration Office, 1955. Race drivers were required to register and go through a rigid inspection by a NASCAR team of mechanics. The top cars were scrutinized closely at the end of the race to avoid violations of the rules. (Courtesy of Halifax Historical Society.)

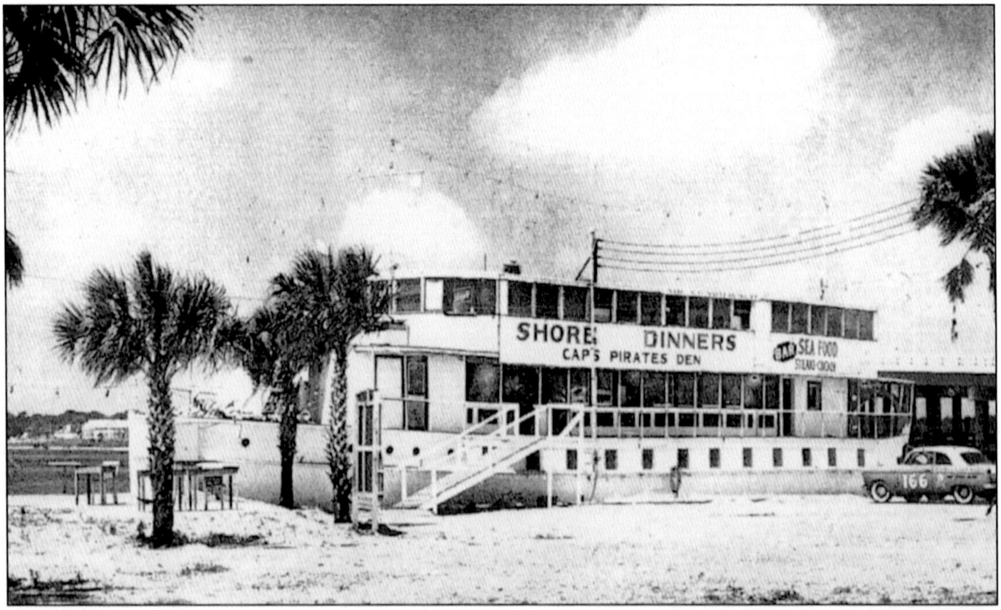

Cap's Pirates Den, 1955. This popular nightspot was originally built for a gambling ship. After World War II, the ship was docked at the east end of the Port Orange Bridge. Later, it was permanently anchored on the south side of the causeway. Bud Palmer's 1955 Dodge race car, #166, is parked in front of the restaurant. (Courtesy of Midkiff Family Collection.)

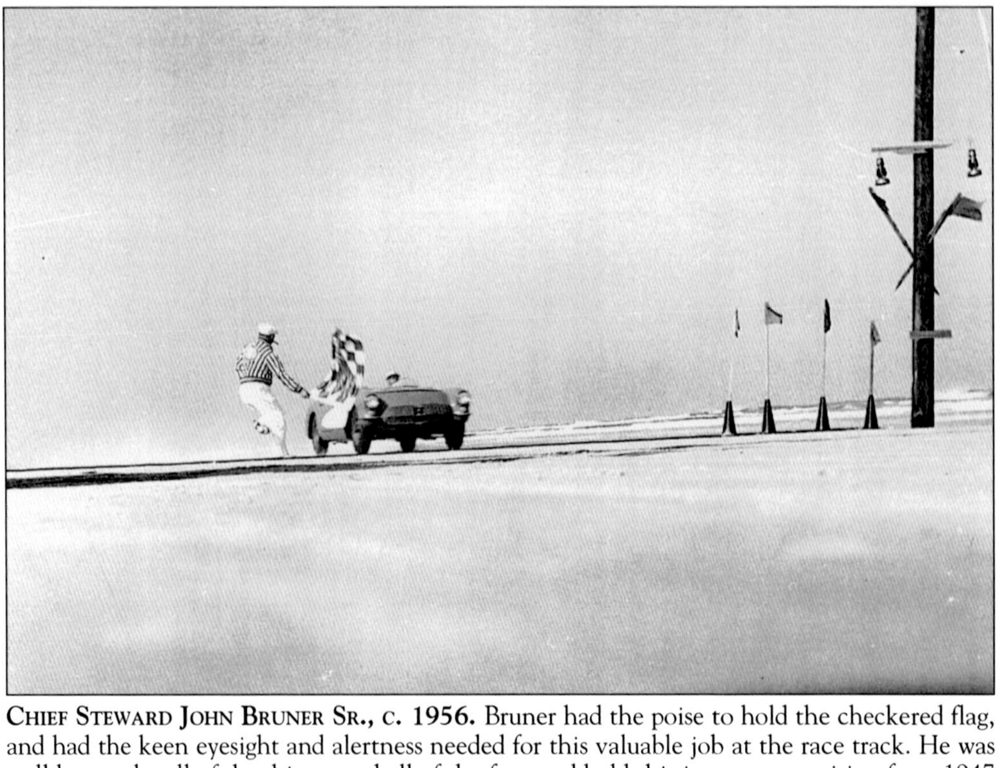

Chief Steward John Bruner Sr., c. 1956. Bruner had the poise to hold the checkered flag, and had the keen eyesight and alertness needed for this valuable job at the race track. He was well known by all of the drivers and all of the fans and held this important position from 1947 until his retirement in 1975. (Courtesy of ISC Archives.)

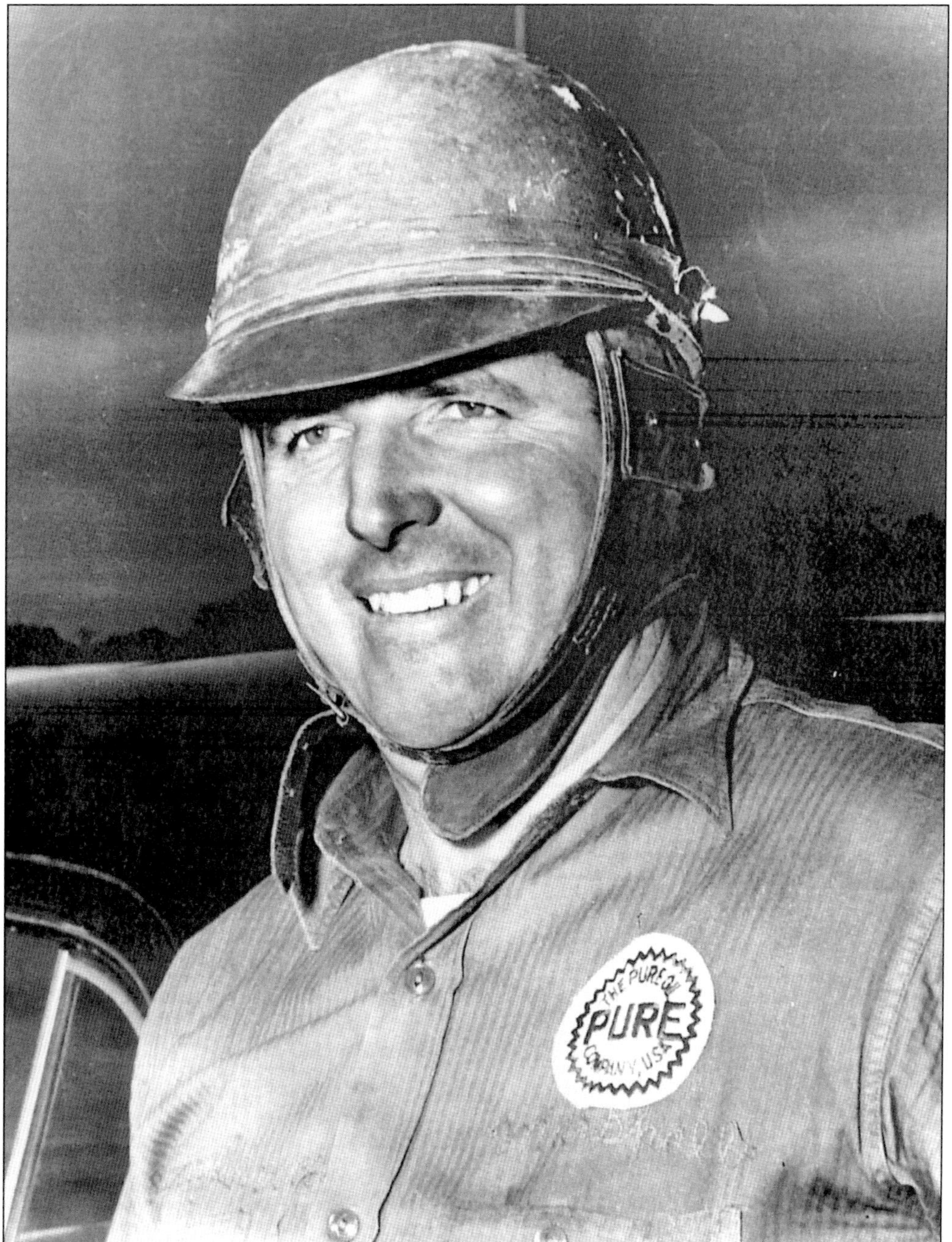

MARSHALL TEAGUE, 1956. Teague was one of the most talented and skilled drivers ever to race on the road/beach race courses. A local garage owner, he collaborated with the Hudson Factory and prepared several *Hudson Hornets* for the road-beach races. He entered in the Mexican Road Race and had two entries in the Indianapolis 500. He was killed in an Indianapolis-style race car while making an experimental practice run at the new Daytona Beach International Speedway in 1959. (Courtesy of ISC Archives.)

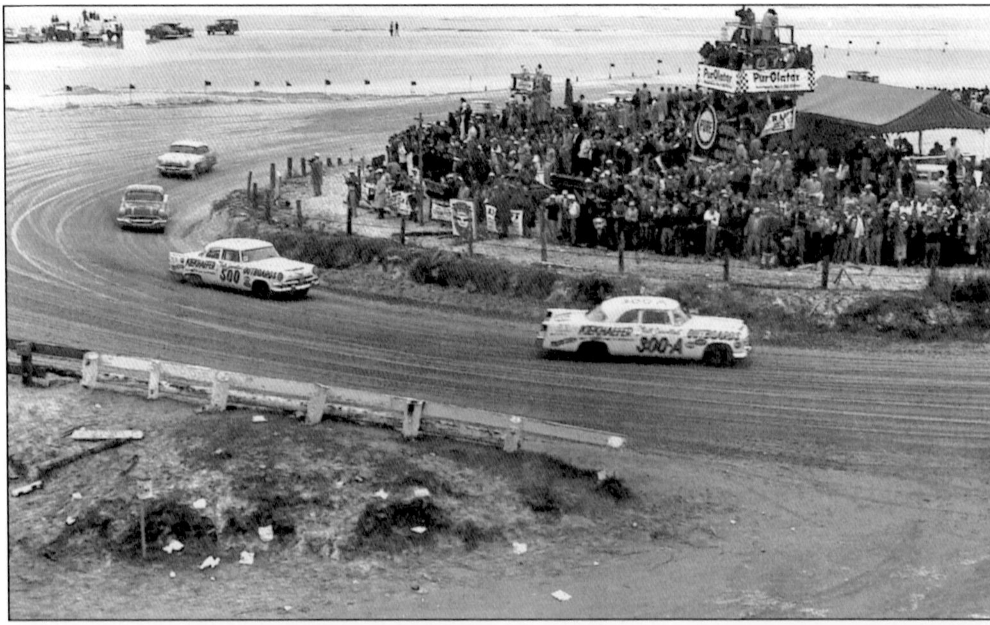

GRAND NATIONAL RACE, FEBRUARY 26, 1956. Tim Flock, in his #300-A 1956 Chrysler enters the north turn in the lead with Speedy Thompson, in his #500 1956 Dodge in hot pursuit. The other two racers are unidentified. Notice the lead car is slightly "fishtailing" in the turn. Tim Flock was the winner while Billy Myers took second place in his 1956 Mercury. (Courtesy of Halifax Historical Society.)

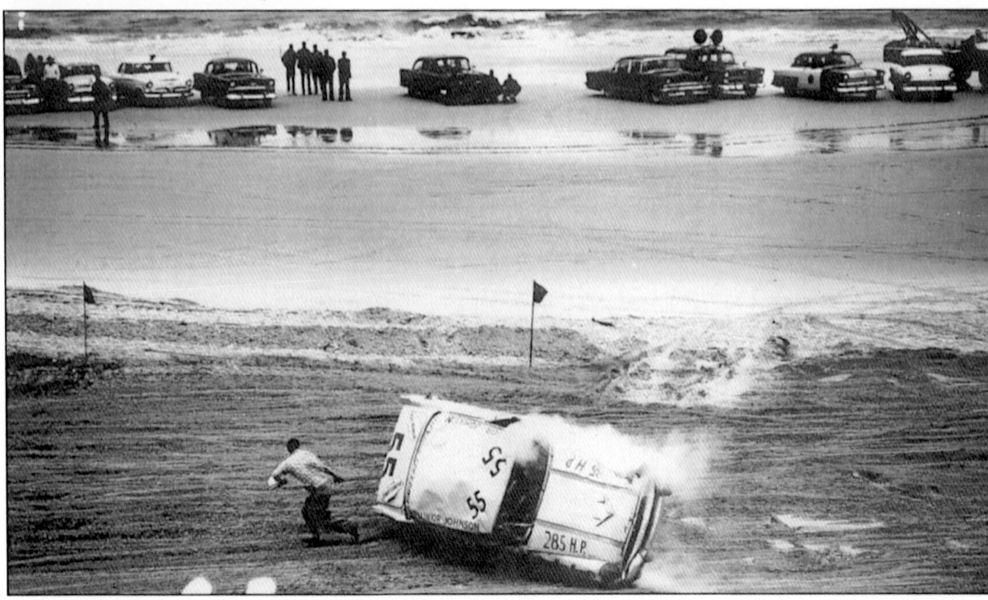

GRAND NATIONAL RACE, FEBRUARY 26, 1956. Robert Glen "Junior" Johnson (#55) is pictured here escaping from his 1956 Pontiac race car after it rolled over near the north turn. He ended up placing 40th, despite this exciting incident. It was also alleged that he gained his driving skills in his early days, while hauling illicit whiskey in North Carolina. Later, he became a poultry farmer and was one of the most popular race car drivers of the 1950s and 1960s. (Courtesy of ISC Archives.)

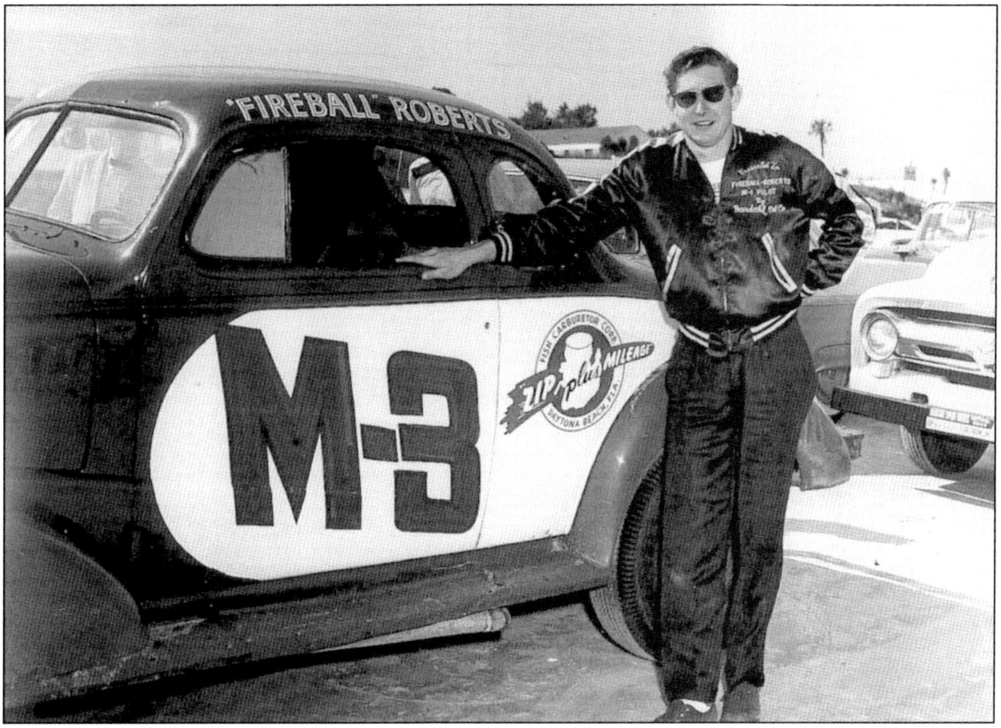

GLENN E. "FIREBALL" ROBERTS, MODIFIED-SPORTSMAN RACE, FEBRUARY 24, 1956. Roberts raced in all three races. On the 24th, he placed 73rd in his #M-3 1938 Chevrolet-M; on the 25th, he placed 2nd in his #22 1956 Ford; and on the 26th, in his #22 1956 Ford, he placed 59th in the Grand National Race. Roberts claimed he was jinxed, and couldn't win at Daytona. (Courtesy of Halifax Historical Society.)

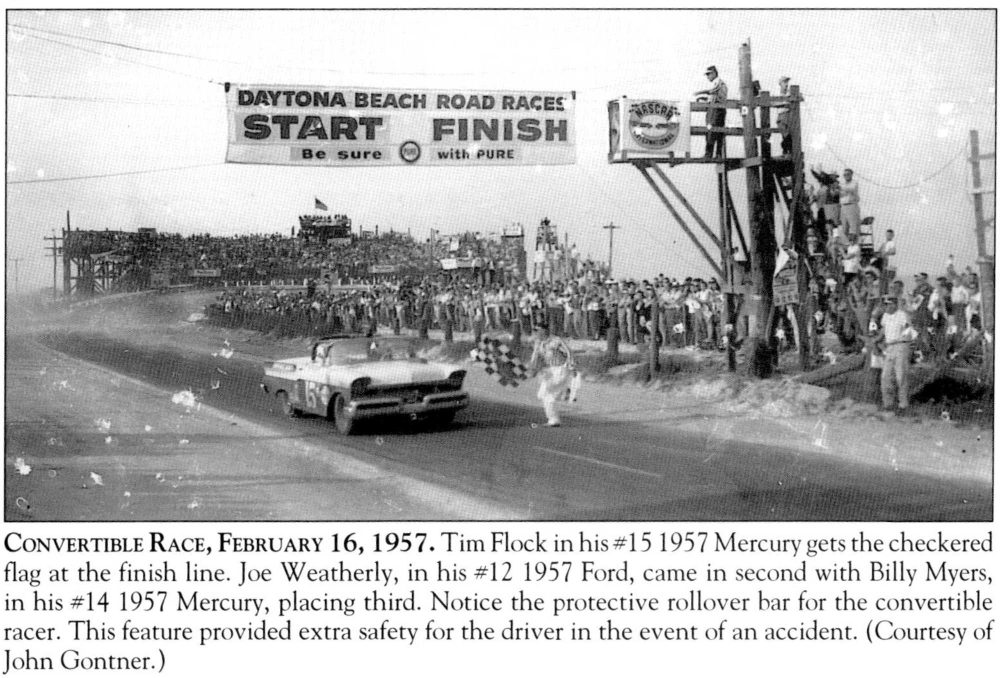

CONVERTIBLE RACE, FEBRUARY 16, 1957. Tim Flock in his #15 1957 Mercury gets the checkered flag at the finish line. Joe Weatherly, in his #12 1957 Ford, came in second with Billy Myers, in his #14 1957 Mercury, placing third. Notice the protective rollover bar for the convertible racer. This feature provided extra safety for the driver in the event of an accident. (Courtesy of John Gontner.)

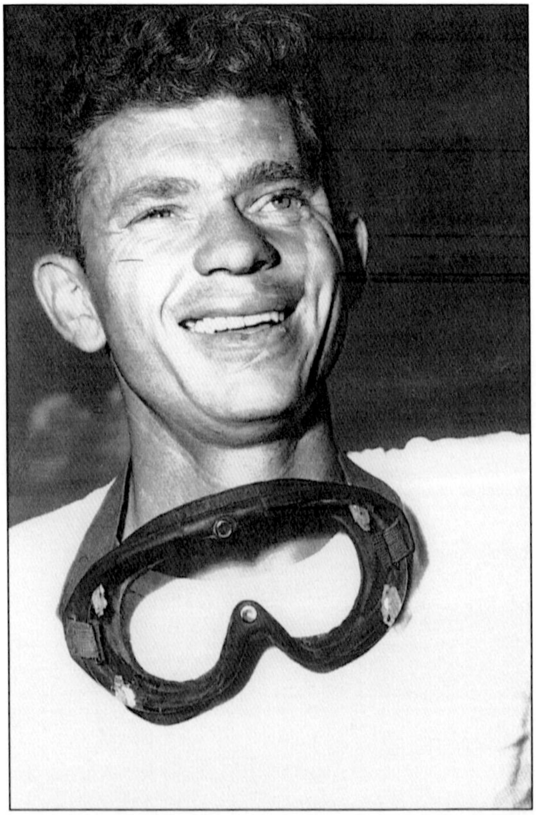

Joe Weatherly, 1957. Weatherly was a popular modified-sports-car race driver throughout a period of eight years. He won second place on February 16, 1957 and came in third in the convertible races on February 22, 1958, with other lower standings on other modified races. In addition, he placed fourth in the 1958 Grand National Race on February 23 in his #12 1958 Ford. Later, he continued his racing career on the new International Speedway. (Courtesy of ISC Archives.)

Grand National Race, February 17, 1957. Jim Russell (#118) in his 1957 Ford edges ahead of Joe Lee Johnson (#310) in his 1956 Dodge as they head down the paved backstretch of the 4.1-mile road/beach course. The winner was Cotton Owens (#6) in his 1957 Pontiac, second place went to Johnny Beauchamp (#50) in his 1957 Chevrolet, and third place went to Fonty Flock (#18) in his 1957 Mercury. (Courtesy of ISC Archives.)

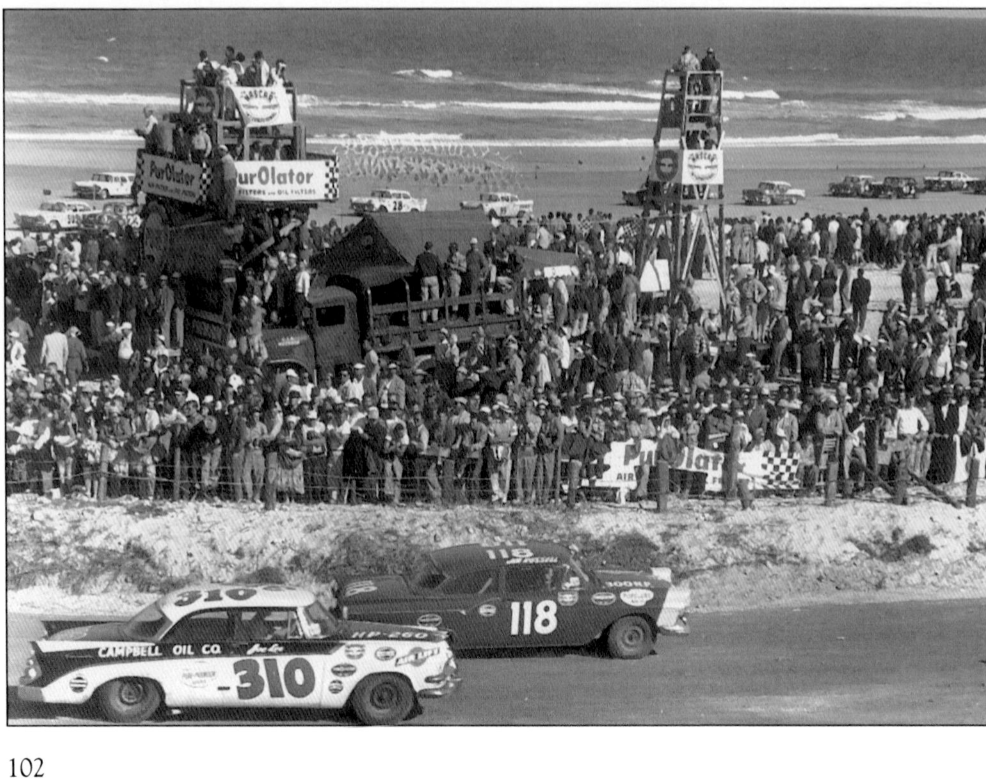

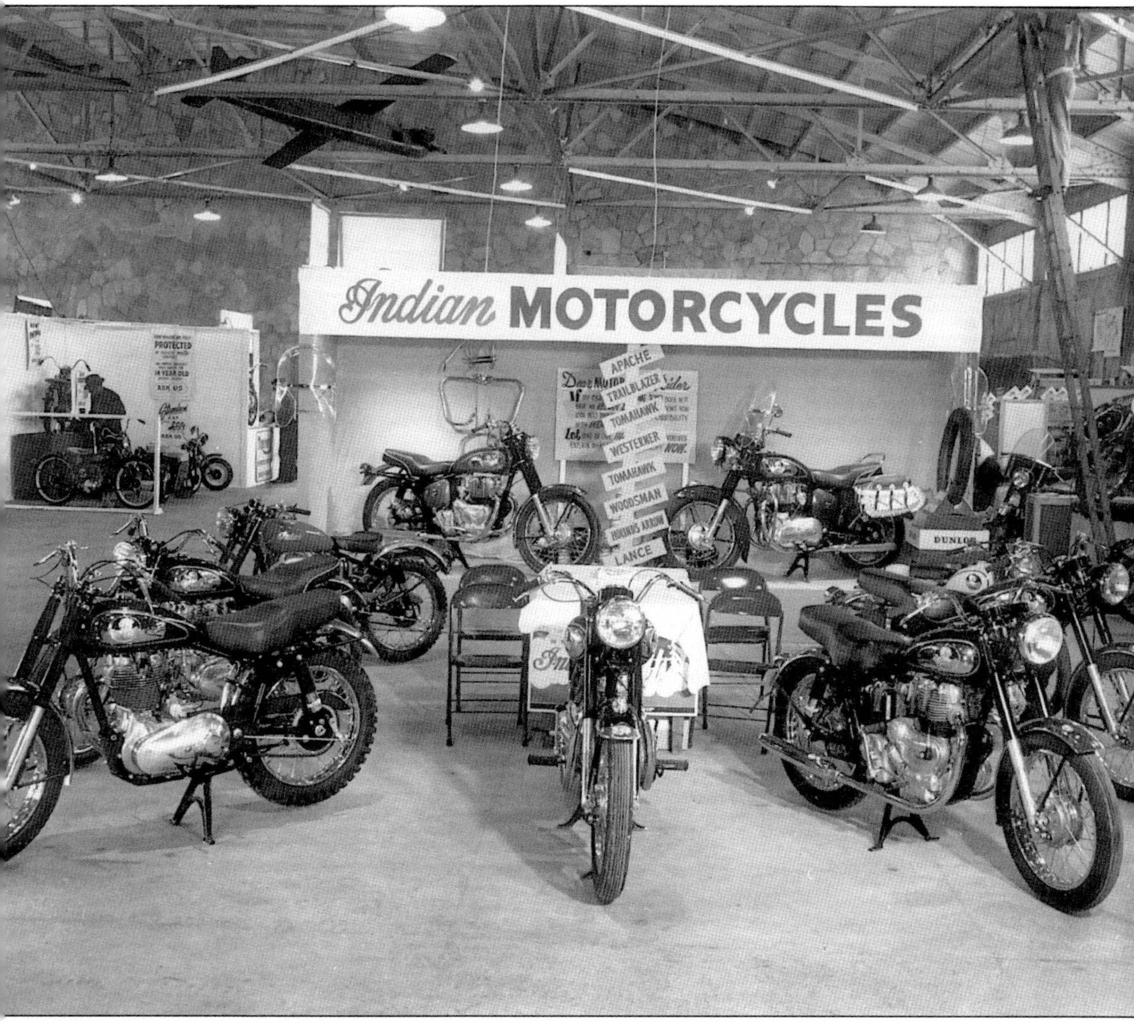

Indian Motorcycle Exhibit at the Daytona Beach Armory, 1958. Each year, there are pleasure and racing motorcycles on exhibit to entertain the thousands of fans that come to Daytona for the Bike Week festivities. The last AMA Daytona 200 was held on the 4.1-mile course in 1958, when Joe Leonard of San Jose, California, won on a Harley-Davidson. The 1958 100-Mile Amateur race was won by Larry Shafer of Sarasota, Florida, also on a Harley-Davidson. This ended the era of motorcycle beach racing. (Courtesy of John Gontner.)

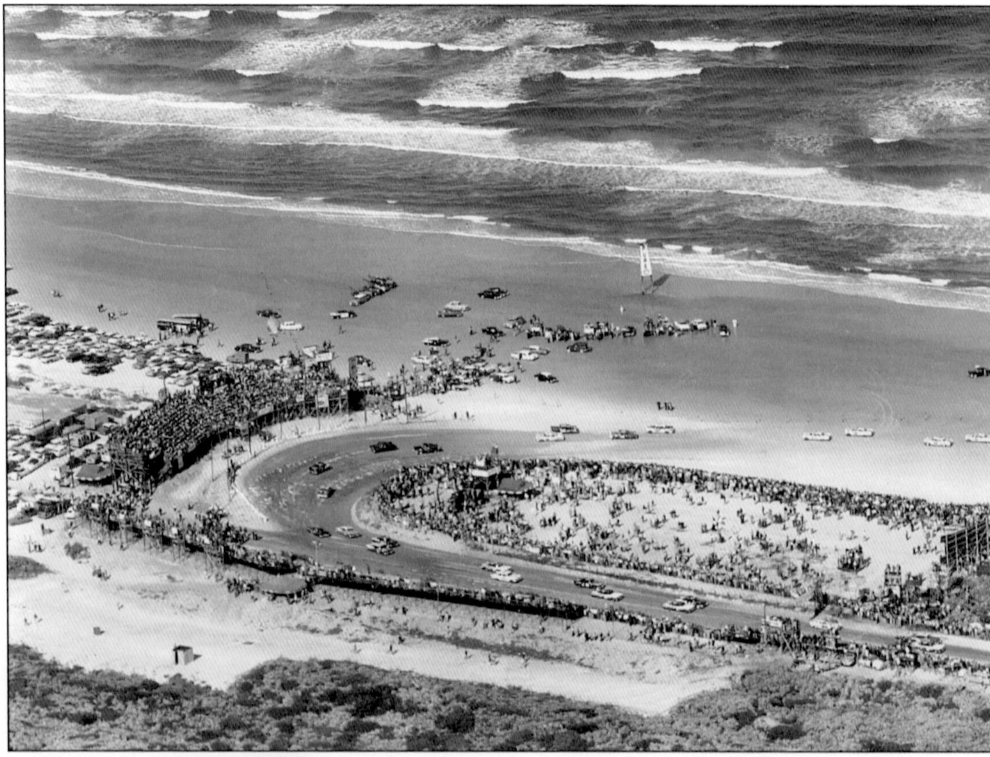

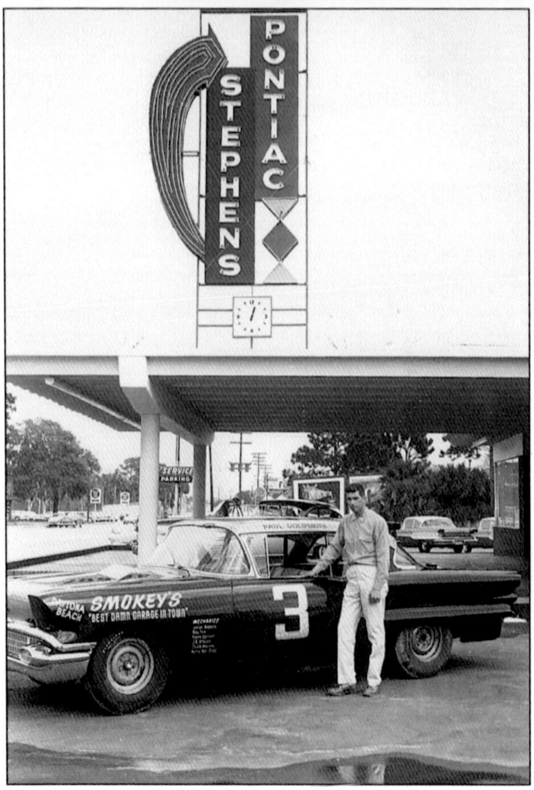

Aerial View of the Last Modified-Sportsman Race on the Beach, February 21, 1958. Banjo Matthews was the winner of this final event on the beach in his #M-4 1955 Ford-M. Jimmy Thompson came in second in his #50 1949 Ford-M. Today, in the new millennium, luxurious condominiums now stand where fans once gathered for these 4.1-mile races. (Courtesy of ISC Archives.)

Paul Goldsmith, Winner of the February 23, 1958 Grand National Race. Goldsmith, who hailed from St. Clair Shores, Michigan, was the only driver to win first place in both motorcycle and automobile racing events. Goldsmith is seen here standing next to his #3 1958 Pontiac in front of Stephens Pontiac Dealership in Daytona. This was the last Grand National Race to be held on the road/beach course. In 1953, he won the AMA Daytona 200 on a Harley-Davidson. (Courtesy of John Gontner.)

Five

The Daytona International Speedway 1959–2003

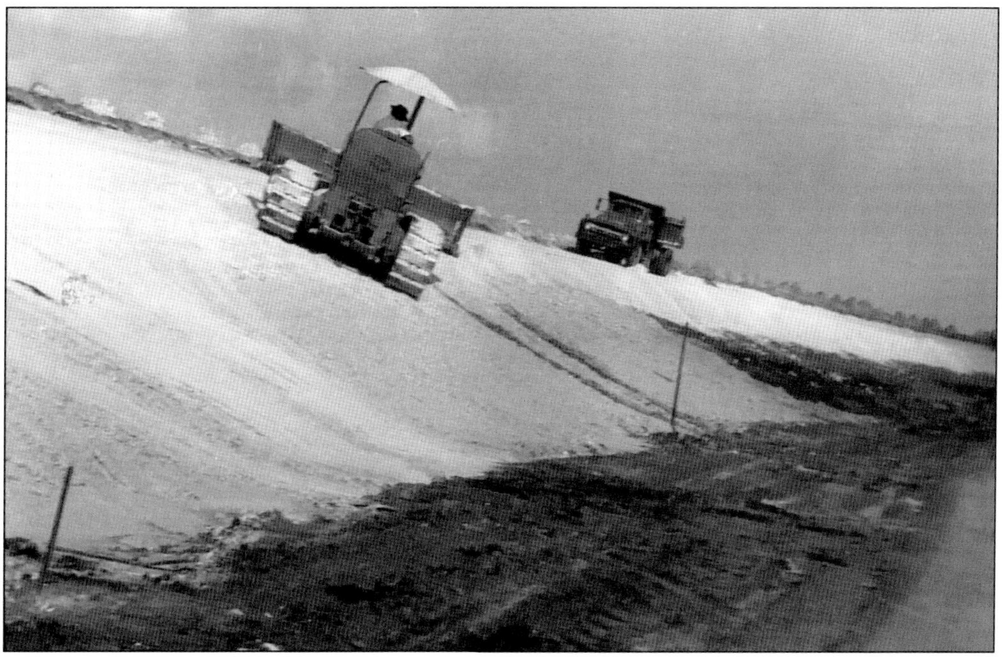

Construction of the High Bank Grade at the New Speedway, November 17, 1958. The area that was cleared for the speedway consisted of cypress ponds, flat pine land, and ridges. When the track was cleared, a large lake was created in the center, which later was named Lake Lloyd. The soil and sand that was excavated was utilized to shape the high sloping banks and the straightaways of the track into the shape of a capital "D." This project was closely supervised by Bill France Sr. and his oldest son, Bill. (Courtesy of John Gontner.)

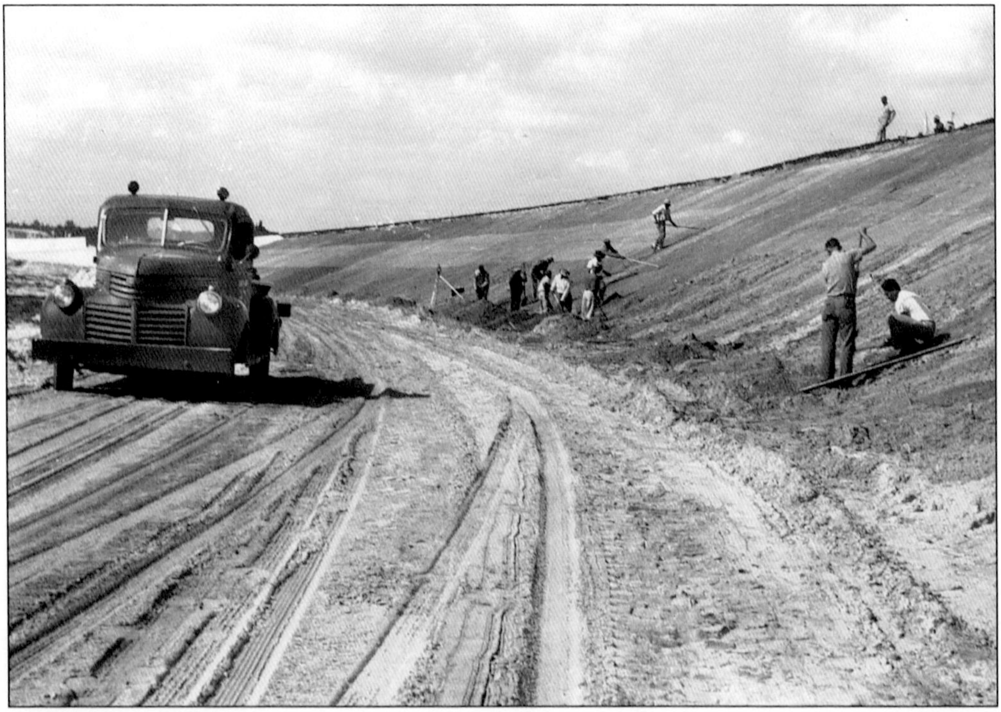

INTERNATIONAL SPEEDWAY UNDER CONSTRUCTION, NOVEMBER 17, 1958. The speedway was constructed at an approximate cost of $3 million. The land the speedway was built on was owned by Volusia County and a separate corporation was formed—The Daytona Beach Racing and Recreation Facilities District. This enabled Bill France to construct a 2.5-mile speedway with banked turns in the shape of a capital "D." This facility would qualify for international status. (Courtesy of John Gontner.)

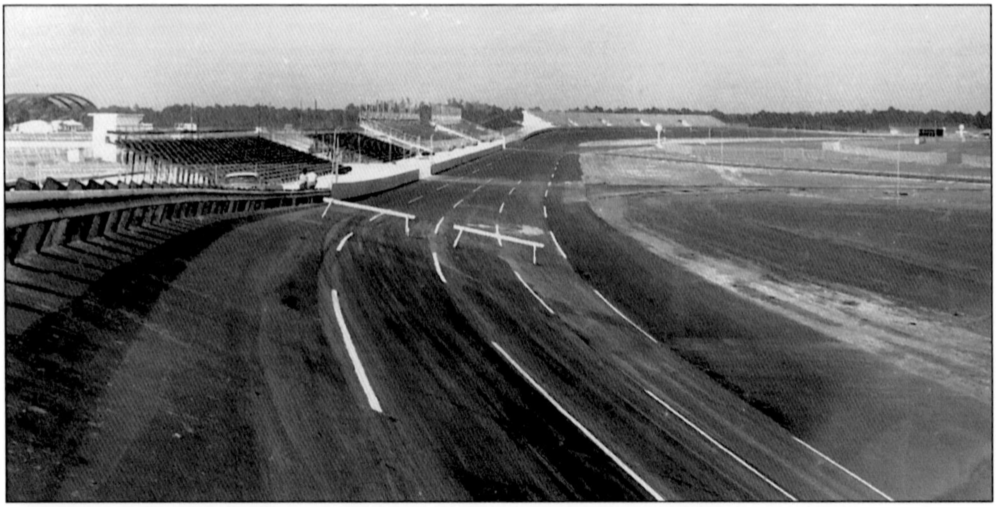

PREPARING FOR THE GRAND OPENING OF THE SPEEDWAY, FEBRUARY 1959. Charles H. Moneypenny engineered the grades on the turns and straightaways to allow for speeds of more than 180 mph. This engineering feat gave him international recognition and wide acclaim by his colleagues. The raceway was a monument to France and Moneypenny. (Courtesy of John Gontner.)

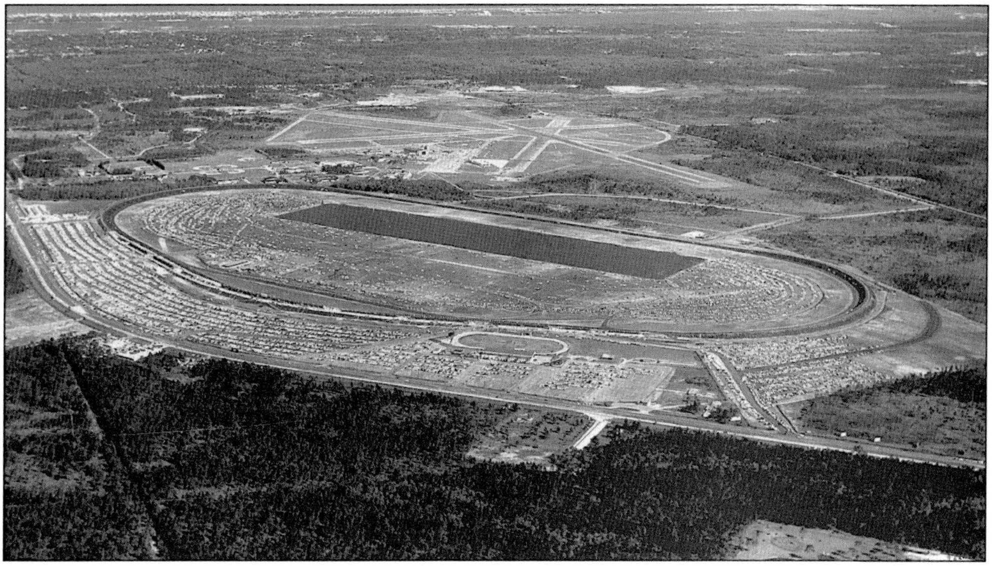

New Daytona Speedway, Aerial View, February 22, 1959. This is the grand opening of the first Daytona 500 Race. On this opening day, safety measures had been implemented with concrete walls topped by a 10-foot chain-link fence and steel guardrails, amid other safety measures. There was adequate parking for 35,000 vehicles and enough viewing area to accommodate the fans. There were originally five grandstands and each section was named for the five championship notables—Campbell, Segrave. Oldfield, DePalma, and Keech. (Courtesy of John Gontner.)

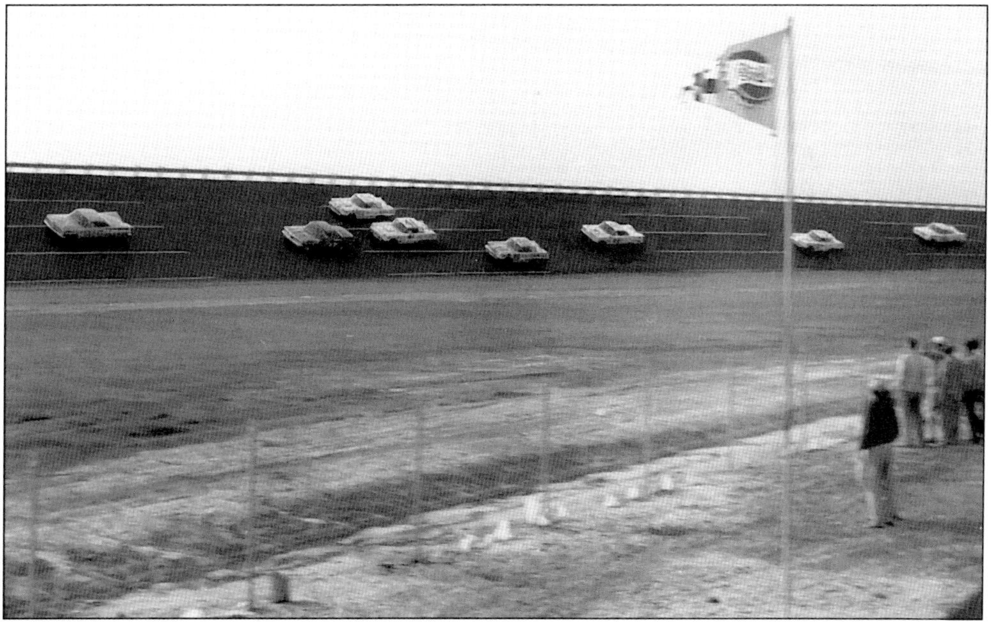

First Daytona 500 at the New Track, February 22, 1959. The cars are coming off turn two onto the backstretch. Lee Petty (father of Richard Petty) won the race in his Oldsmobile 200, with Johnny Beauchamp coming in second and Jack Griffith in third. This race ushered in a new era of racing and the old road/beach courses were now outdated. Fans were saddened by the thought that beach races had ended. (Courtesy of John Gontner.)

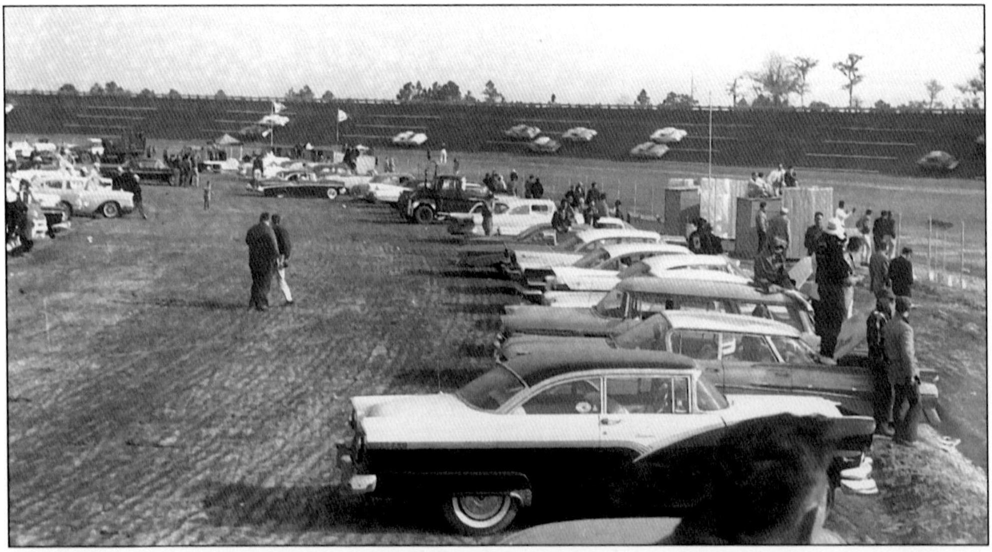

THE INFIELD AT THE SPEEDWAY, C. 1960. To gain access to the infield, vehicles must go through a 250-foot long tunnel to reach designated areas inside the infield. To exit, you must leave through the outlet tunnel to reach the outside. Many fans prefer the infield rather than the grandstands because it allows them greater freedom to move around and the ability to use their vehicles as a viewing point. (Courtesy of Halifax Historical Society.)

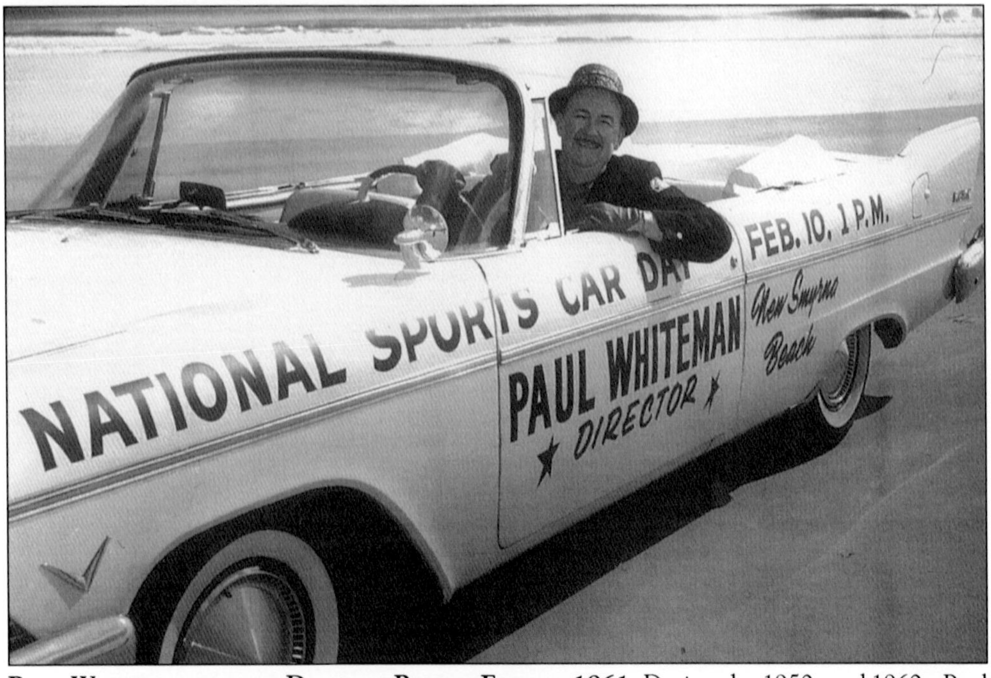

PAUL WHITEMAN AND THE DAYTONA RACING EVENTS, 1961. During the 1950s and 1960s, Paul Whiteman was a great orchestra leader who helped promote racing events. He was a member of the board of directors at the Daytona International Speedway and served as director of Sports Car Racing Activities. Whiteman was known all over the world as a sports car racing enthusiast. The first Paul Whiteman Trophy Race was inaugurated in Daytona Beach in 1961. He died in 1967 at the age of 77. (Courtesy of ISC Archives.)

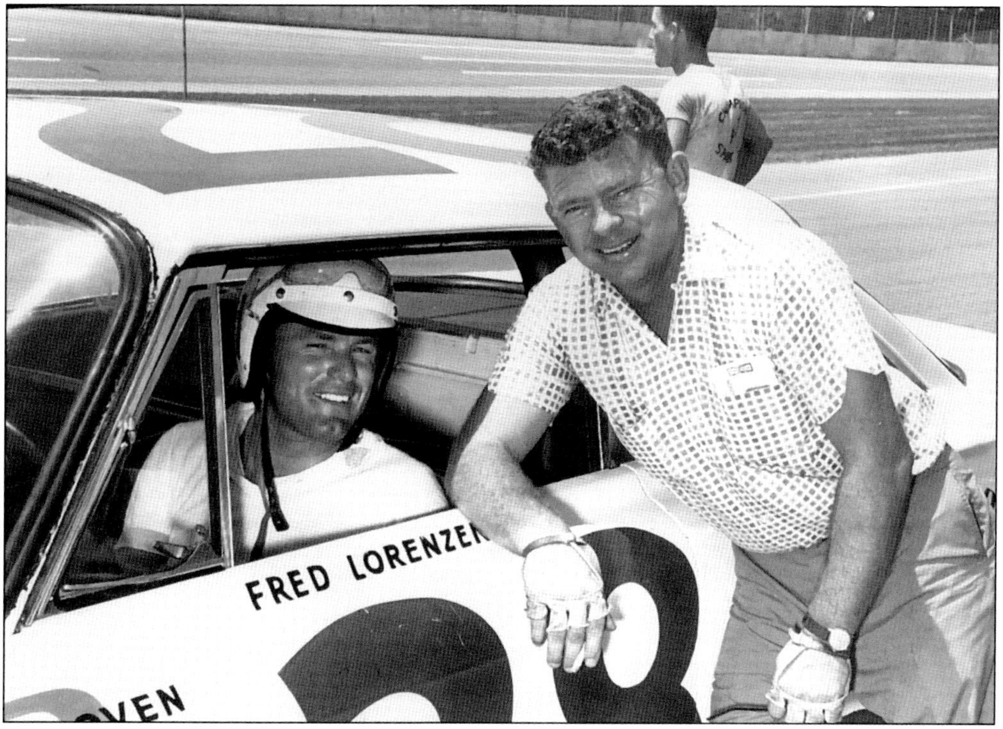

Daytona 500 Race, 1961. Pictured here are two well-known race drivers—Fred Lorenzen (in car) and Joe Weatherly talking on the pit road before the race. Marvin Panch won the race in his Pontiac 200 with Joe Weatherly coming in second, Paul Goldsmith in third, and Fred Lorenzen in fourth. (Courtesy of John Gontner.)

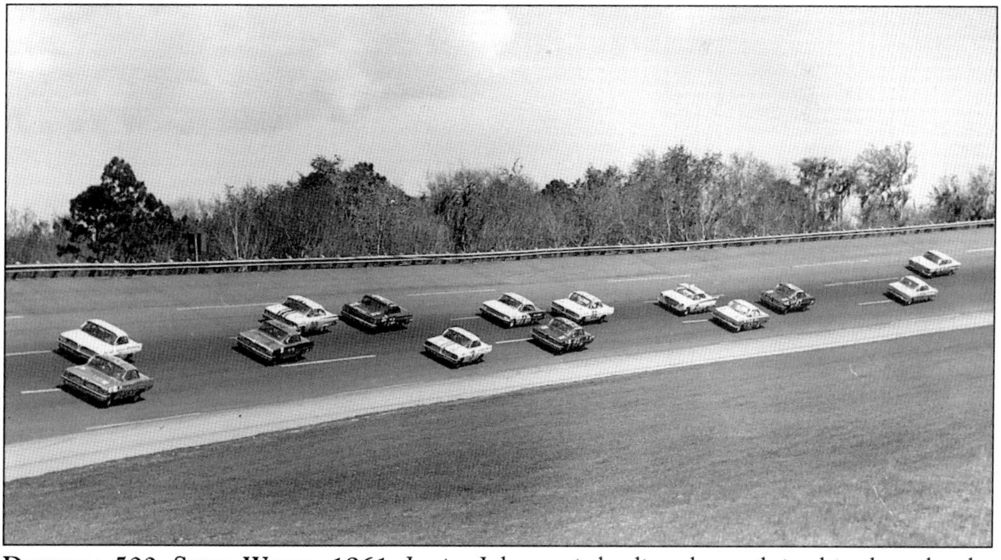

Daytona 500, Speed Weeks, 1961. Junior Johnson is leading the pack in this photo but he does not win this race. This driver, a legend in his own time, won the 1960 Daytona 500. He was the first driver to master the art of "drafting," which helped him win over other challengers by continually using this method. "Drafting" is a technique of using the slipstream off of faster vehicles to make another racer's car more competitive. (Courtesy of ISC Archives.)

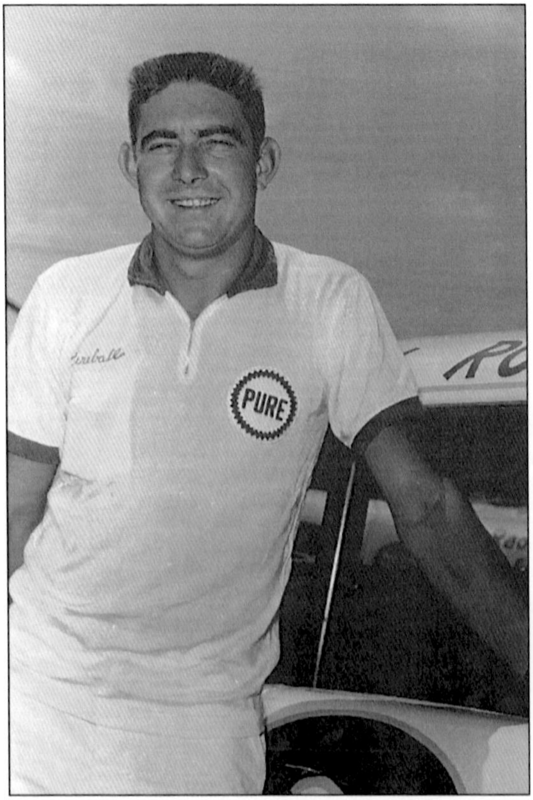

GLENN EDWARD "FIREBALL" ROBERTS, 1962. One of the most renowned drivers of all the Daytona Beach racers received the nickname "Fireball," which was given to him while playing baseball at Seabreeze High School and the University of Florida. Ironically, the name "Fireball" stayed with him during his racing career and he died from his injuries in a fiery crash on July 2, 1964, following the Charlotte 600 Race on May 24. Roberts won his first 500-mile race on February 18, 1962. He had entered many beach races before his victory at the speedway. (Courtesy of ISC Archives.)

"FIREBALL" ROBERTS (LEFT) AND BILL FRANCE SR., FEBRUARY 10, 1963. Roberts and France are photographed while discussing the Speed Weeks leading up to the Daytona 500. Roberts was a favorite among the fans at all racing events. He was proud to call Daytona Beach his home. (Courtesy of John Gontner.)

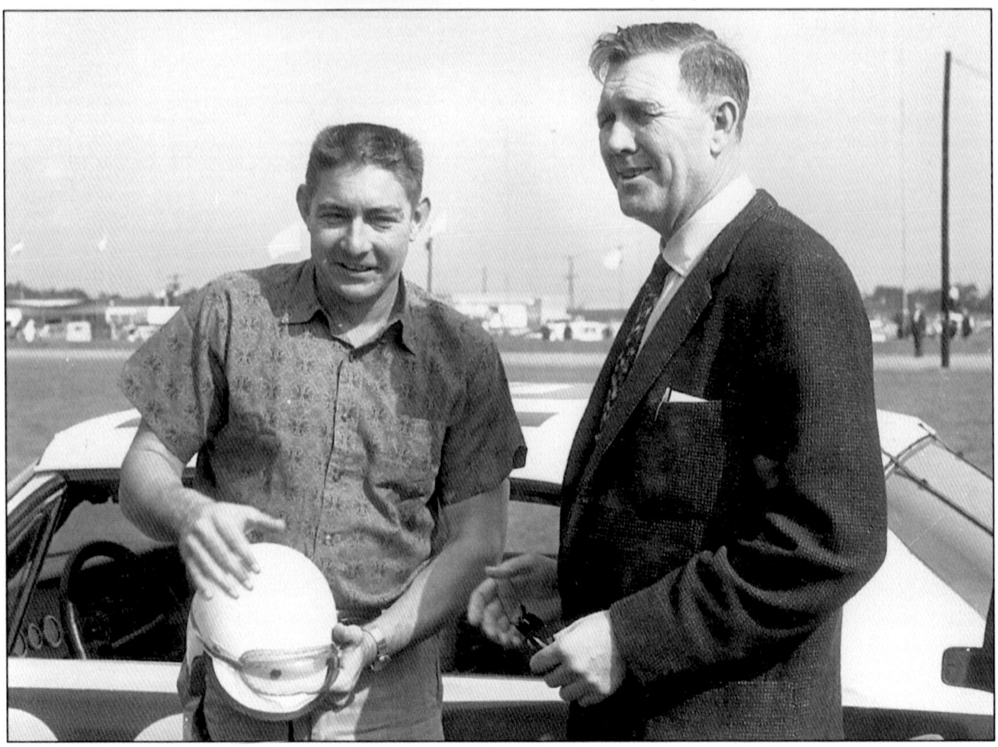

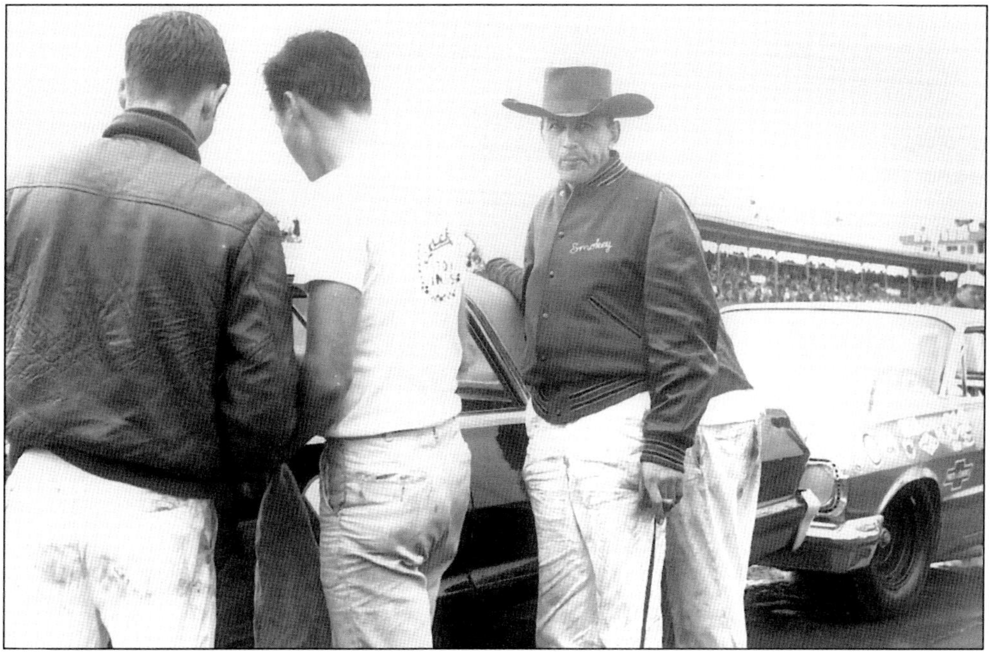

SPEED WEEKS, FEBRUARY 24, 1963. Henry "Smokey" Yunick, who was always recognized by his trademarks—a cowboy hat and a special cigar—was a Daytona garage owner. He engineered and prepared many race cars for different drivers. He was controversial and outspoken in his beliefs about auto racing. He died on May 9, 2001, and has left a legacy that will long be remembered. (Courtesy of John Gontner.)

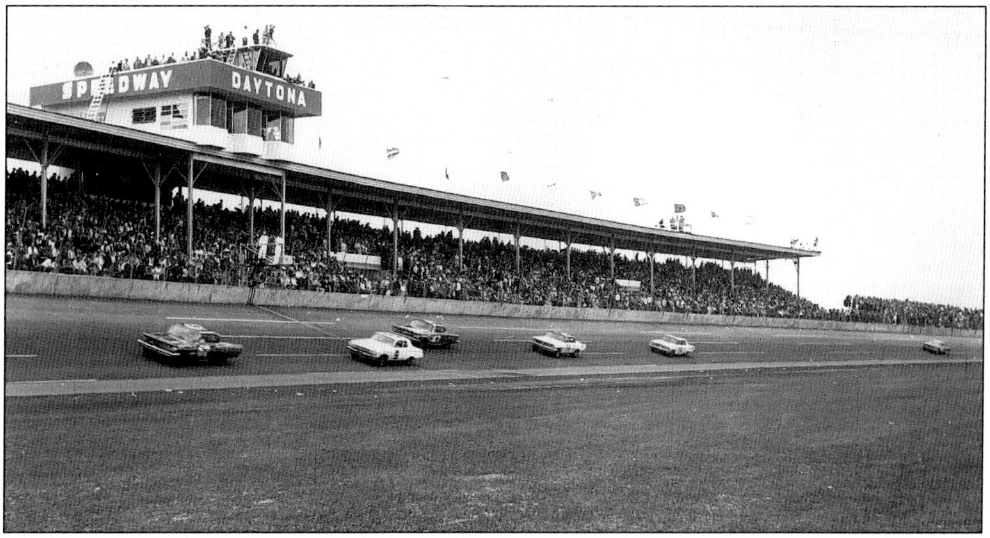

DAYTONA 500 RACE, FEBRUARY 24, 1963. Dewayne "Tiny" Lund won the race in the Wood Brothers Ford 200, with Fred Lorenzen coming in second and Ned Jarrett in third. Lund was a relief driver for Marvin "Pancho" Panch, who was injured 11 days earlier in a test car run. Lund is credited with saving Panch's life after pulling him from his race car after the fiery crash. "Tiny" stood 6 feet and 5 inches tall and weighed 270 pounds. His illustrious career ended on August 17, 1975, when he died in a crash at Talladega, Alabama. A grandstand is named in his honor at the Daytona Beach International Speedway. (Courtesy of John Gontner.)

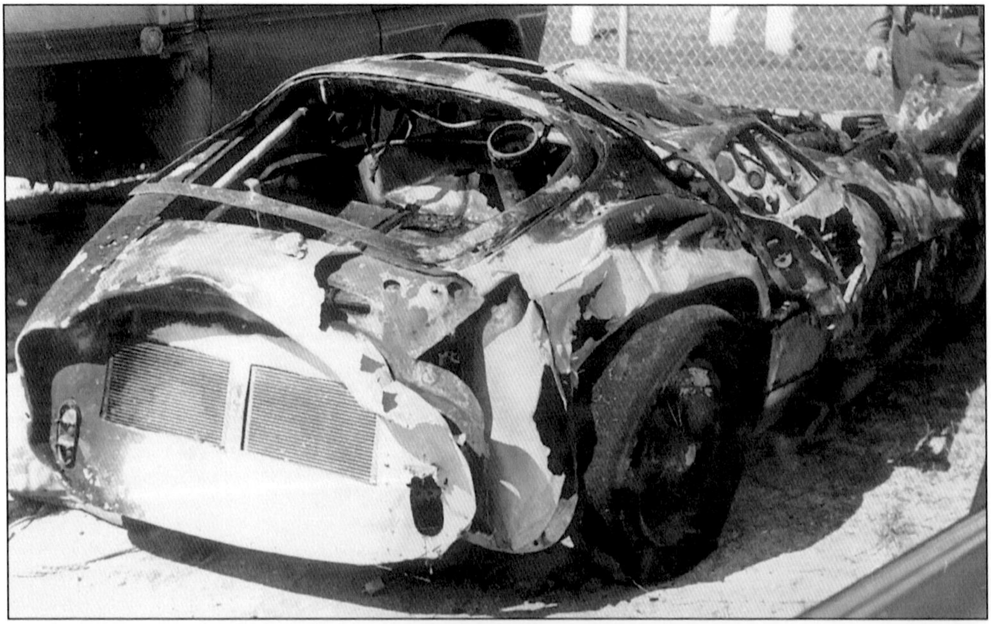

THE WRECKAGE OF A FIERY CRASH AT DAYTONA BEACH INTERNATIONAL SPEEDWAY, FEBRUARY 1963. Marvin "Pancho" Panch, driver of the Maserati-Ford experimental car, was injured in this crash and was pulled from the wreckage by "Tiny" Lund. This test car was owned by Brigs Cunningham of New York. Apparently, this crash was caused by high speed, which raised the car off the track causing Panch to lose control. There were no spoilers on this high-performance vehicle at the time of the crash. Today, much has been learned about spoilers through research and current race cars always have these attachments. A spoiler is an adjustable fin-like attachment to the rear of a race car that helps control the air stream and stability, which prevents the vehicle from lifting off the pavement. (Courtesy of John Gontner.)

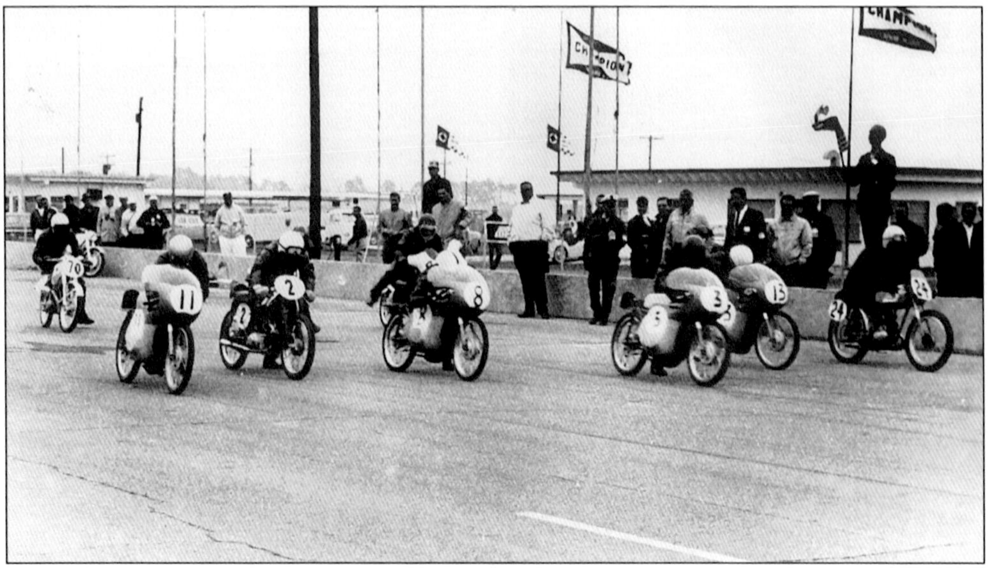

AMA EXPERT RACES, FEBRUARY, 1963. The signal to start the race is given as the official waves the flag. The riders are pushing off to start the Daytona 200 Motorcycle Races. (Courtesy of John Gontner.)

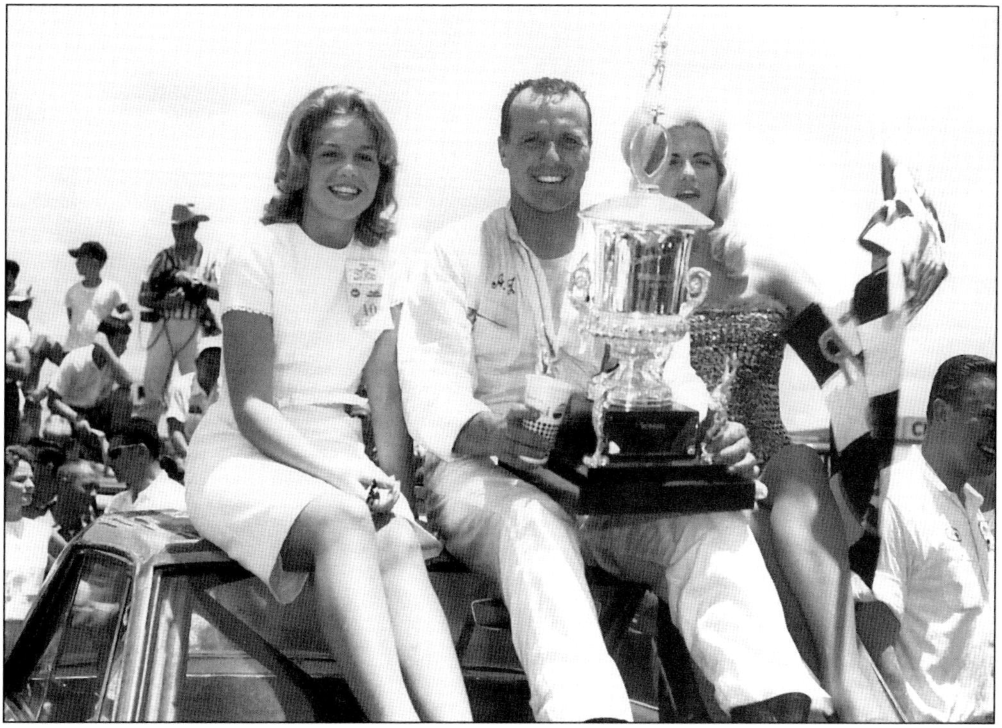

Firecracker 400 Race, July 4, 1964. A.J. Foyt was the winner in Victory Circle. He is pictured here receiving accolades while holding his trophy. (Courtesy of John Gontner.)

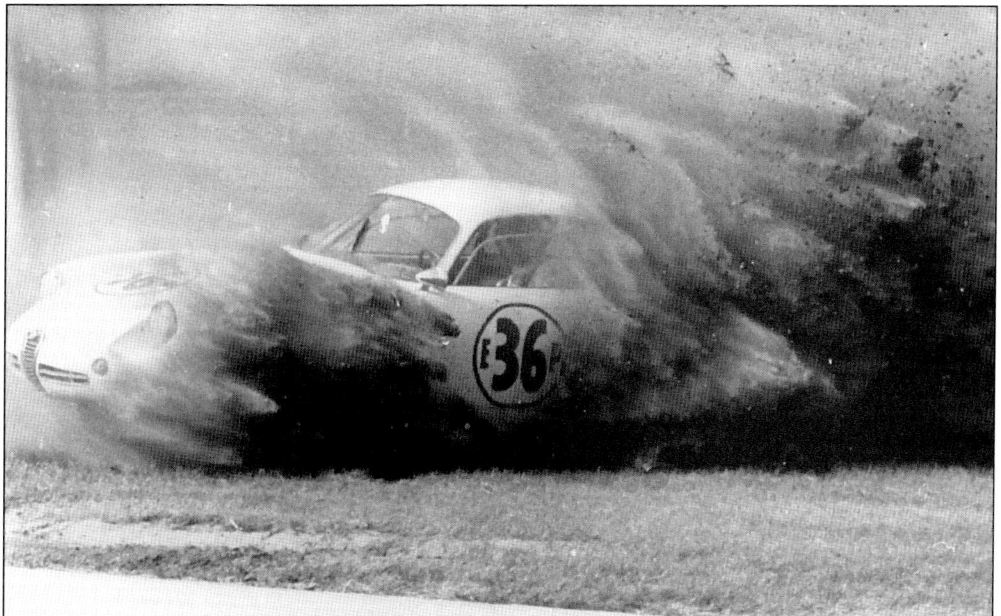

Sports Car Club of America (SCCA) Races, September, 1966. Dr. Wilbur Pickett was always a fast contender in these sports car events. He spun out at this turn during several races and drivers began to call the turn "Pickett's Corner." Pickett was a local neurologist and was later killed in a plane crash. (Courtesy of John Gontner.)

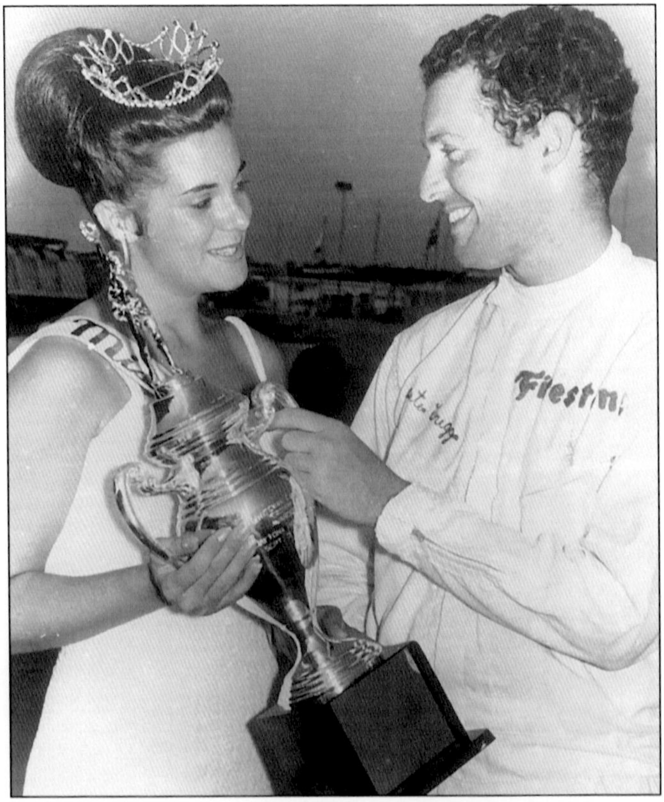

Paul Whiteman Trophy Race, September 1966. Peter Gregg, International Sports Car driving star, receives the trophy from "Miss Southland," Martha Joy Bowen, at the Daytona International Speedway. He averaged a speed of 100.54 mph on the special sports car track. (Courtesy of John Gontner.)

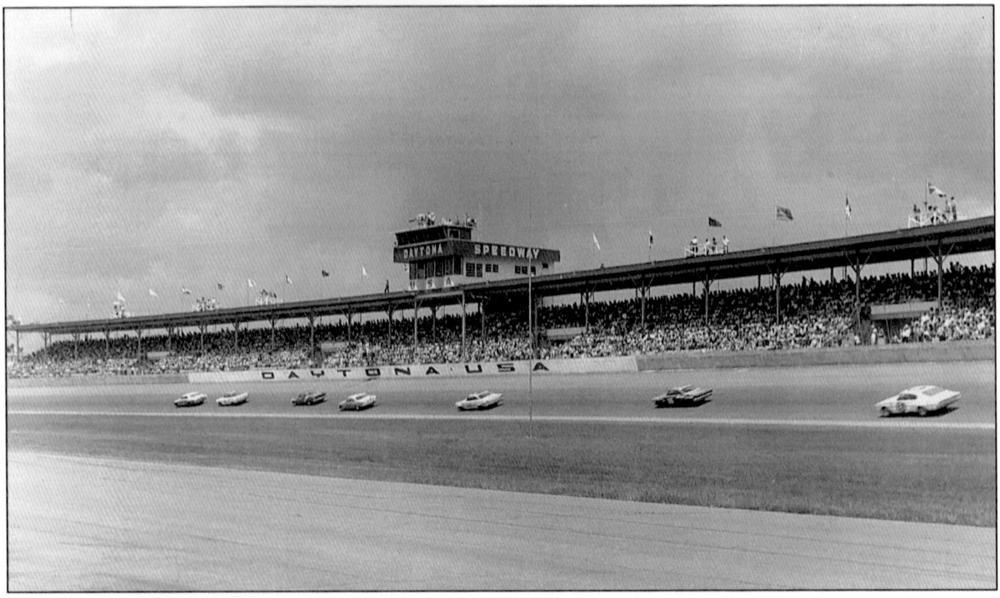

Firecracker 400, 1967. This is a photo of Bobby Isaac (#71) leading in front of the old grandstand. He won the 1964 Firecracker 400 in a Ray Nichels factory Dodge, and again in 1971 in the K and K Insurance Dodge. The Firecracker 400 was named in honor of Independence Day, and was held each year as close to this holiday as possible. In later years, the Pepsi 400 took over the name. (Courtesy of ISC Archives.)

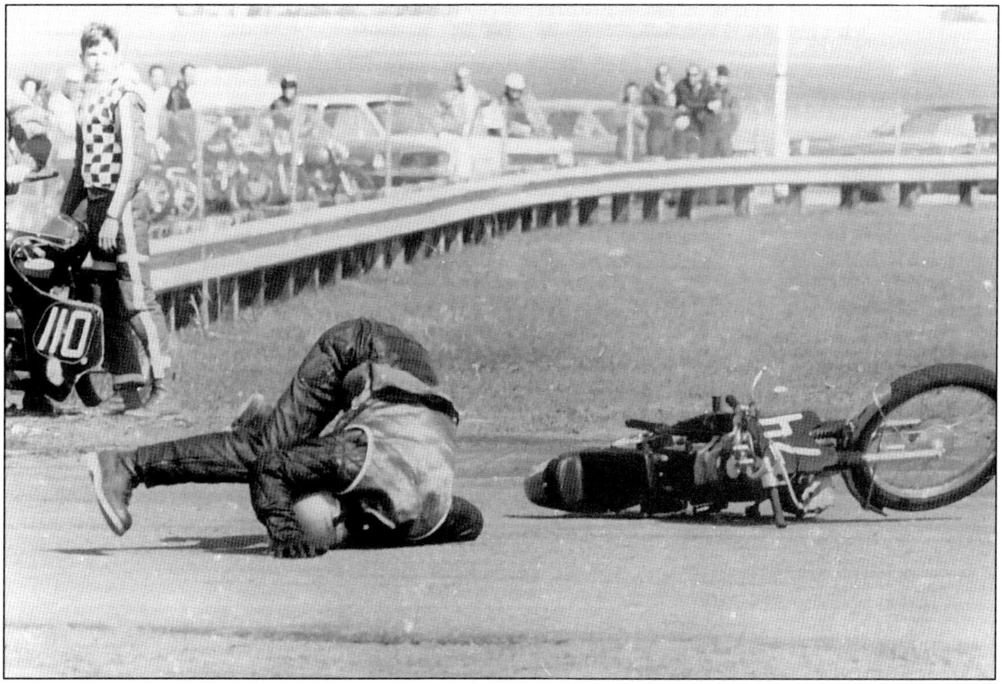

Daytona International Speedway and Corporation (DISC) Races, March 13, 1968. Ralph Swegar is caught on film in the final stages of his spill, completing his rollover, before laying flat on the track. Most cyclists are not seriously injured during crashes usually suffering only scrapes and burns. They often continue in the race. (Courtesy of John Gontner.)

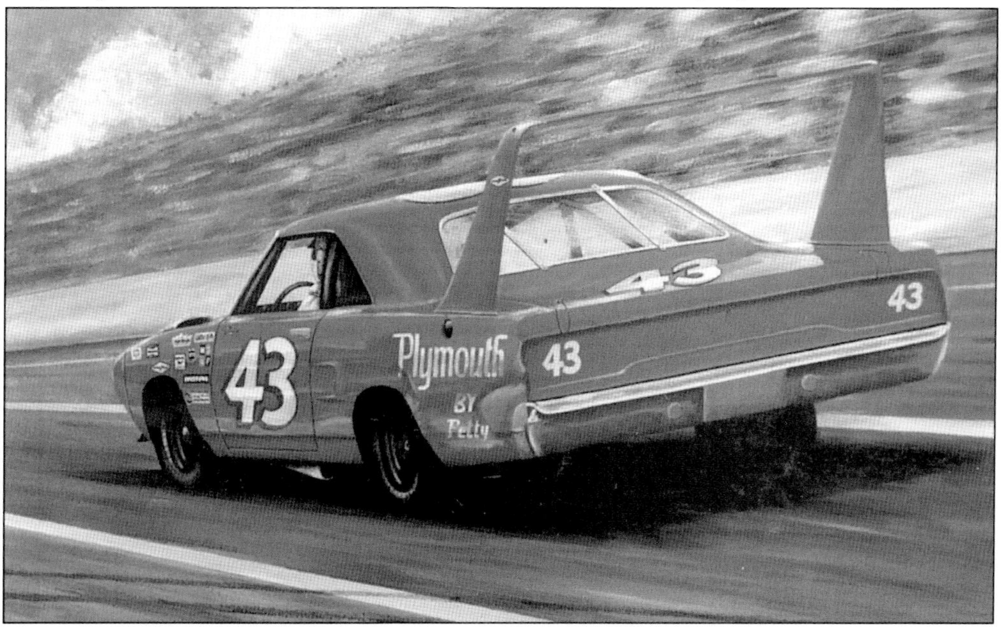

Richard Petty in his #43 Plymouth, 1970. Although Petty did not win the Daytona 500 or the Firecracker 400, Pete Hamilton won the 1970 Daytona 500 in a Petty Plymouth *Superbird* while Donnie Allison won the Firecracker 400 in a Ford. The above image is an artist's rendering of Richard Petty at full speed. (Courtesy of Buz McKim.)

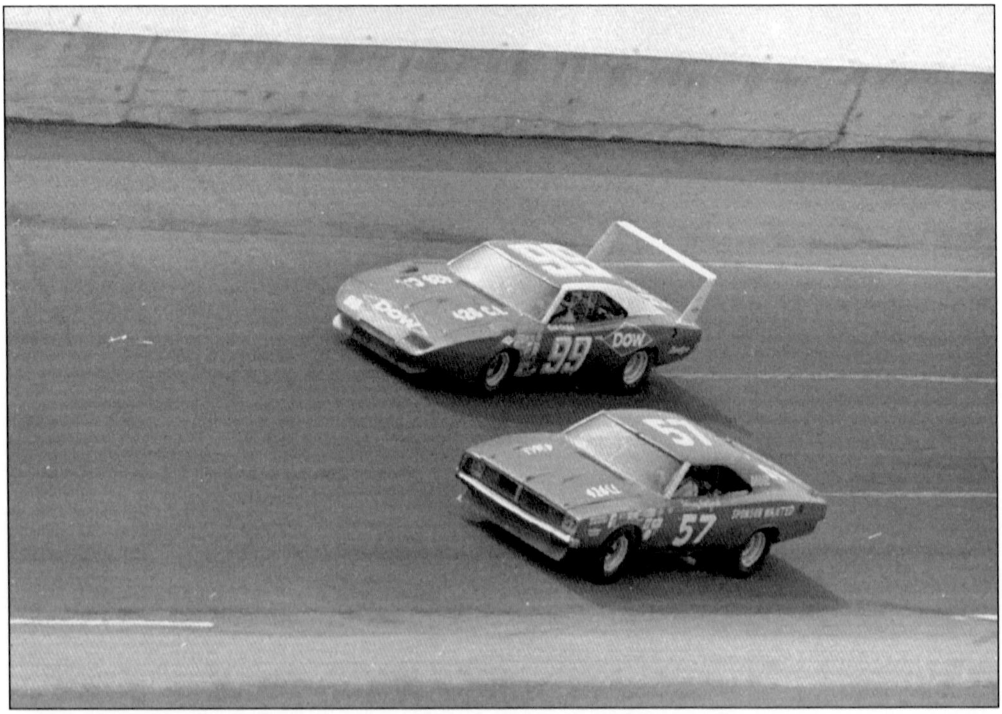

DAYTONA 500, SPEED WEEKS, 1970. Here is Johnny Halford (#57) running neck and neck with Charlie Goltzbach (#99) on the steep grade of the Speedway turn. Peter Hamilton won this race in his winged *Superbird* Plymouth. Hamilton drove in only four Daytona 500s and was injured and recovered in the 1970s. (Courtesy of ISC Archives.)

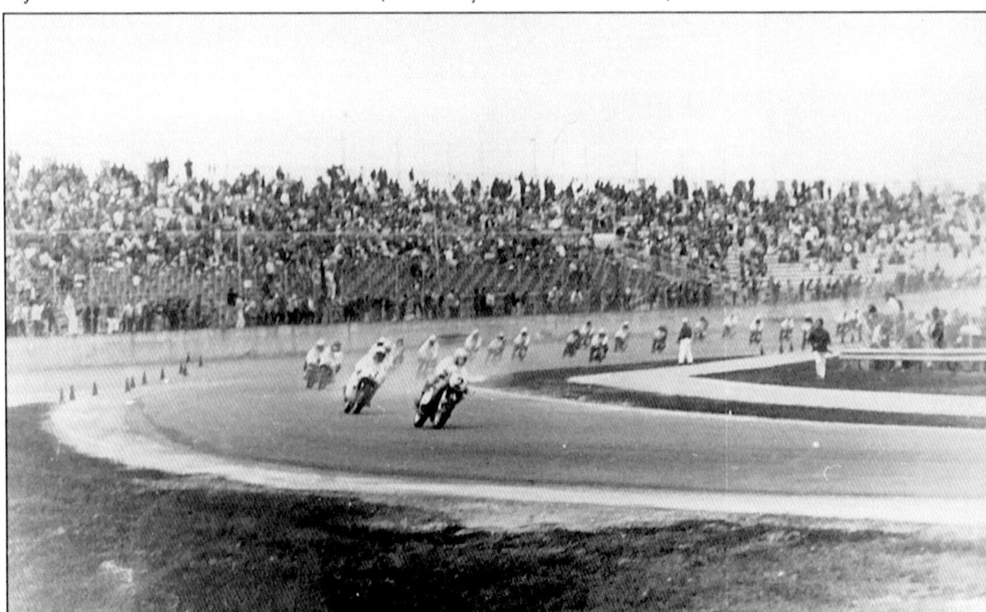

DAYTONA BIKE WEEK, DAYTONA 200 MOTORCYCLE RACES, MARCH 1970. Fans come from all over the United States and abroad to take part in Bike Week and Biketoberfest. These events are held annually. (Courtesy of John Gontner.)

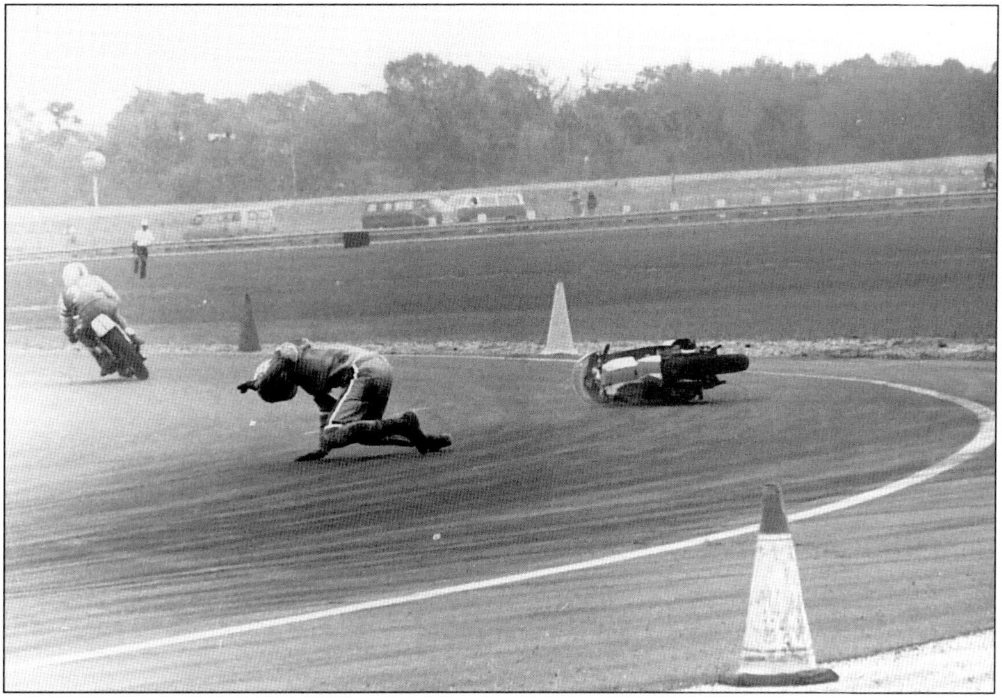

Bike Racer Thrown from his Machine on March 11, 1971. This was a 76-mile race included in the competition events. Most riders walk away from their spills and continue the race. (Courtesy of John Gontner.)

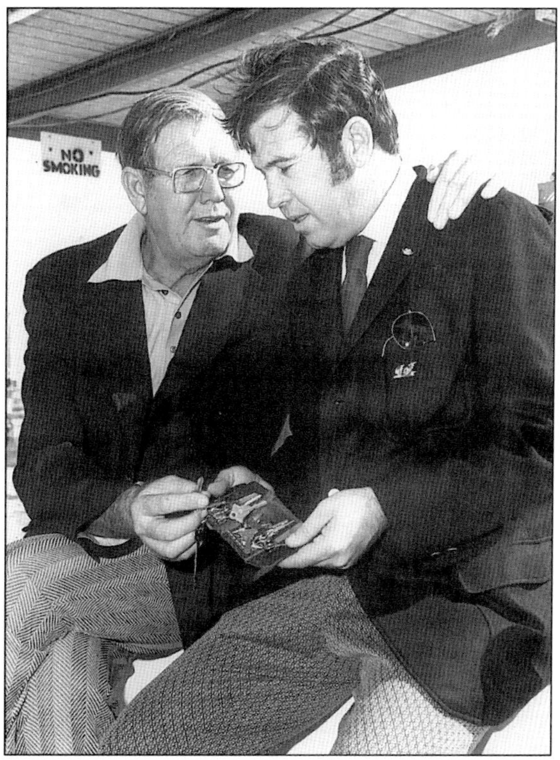

Bill France Sr. (left) and son, Bill Jr., 1972. Bill Sr. gives Bill Jr. instructions about their busy itinerary for the following weeks of racing activities and, to everyone's surprise, he hands over the keys to the International Speedway Corporation (ISC). Bill France Jr. became chairman of the board and chief executive officer of ISC, and his brother, Jim, became president of ISC and executive vice-president and secretary of the National Association of Stock Car Auto Racing (NASCAR). (Courtesy of Halifax Historical Society.)

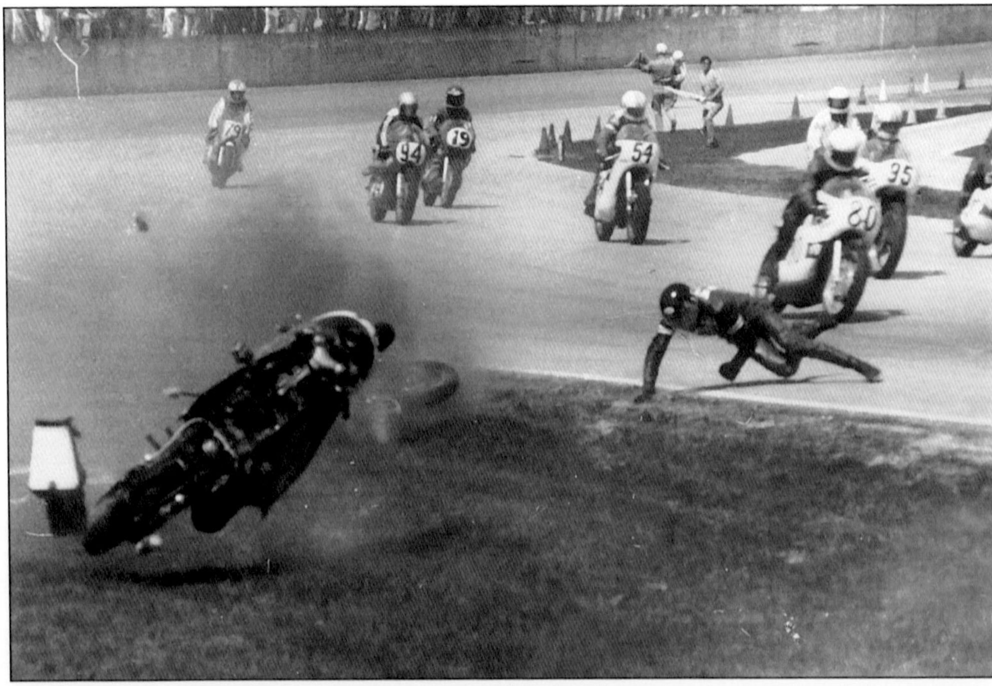

BIKE WEEK AMATEUR RACES, MARCH 1972. These mishaps are always a dreaded occurrence. These collisions happen in a chain reaction form and a race can be won, or lost, when this occurs. (Courtesy of John Gontner.)

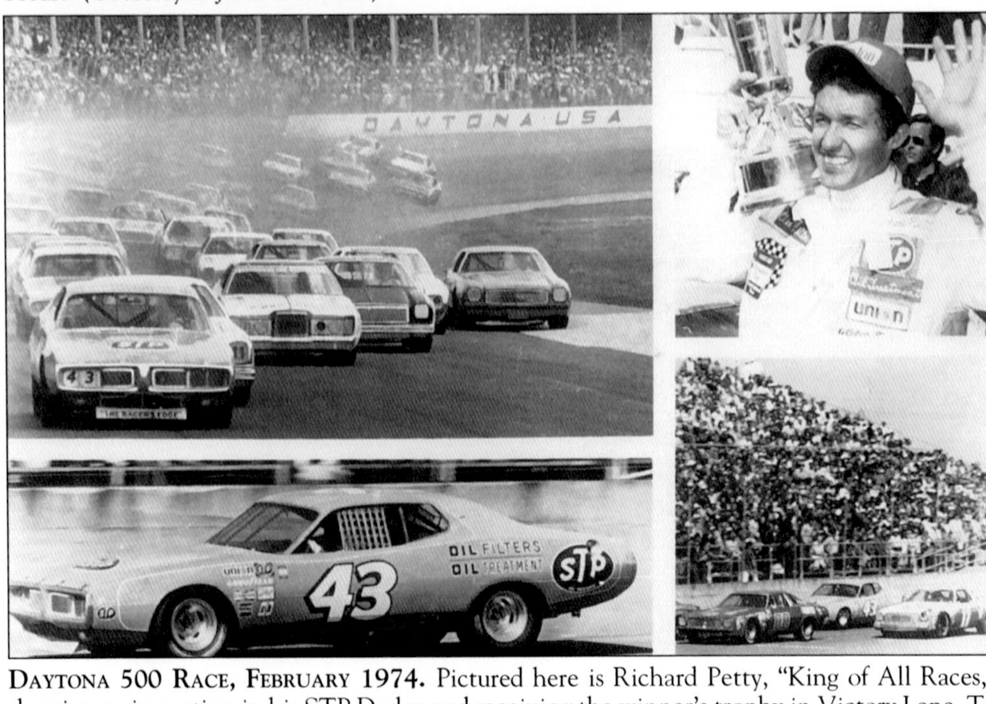

DAYTONA 500 RACE, FEBRUARY 1974. Pictured here is Richard Petty, "King of All Races," showing racing action in his STP Dodge and receiving the winner's trophy in Victory Lane. To honor Petty, the City of Daytona Beach named a street after him near the racetrack. (Courtesy of John Gontner.)

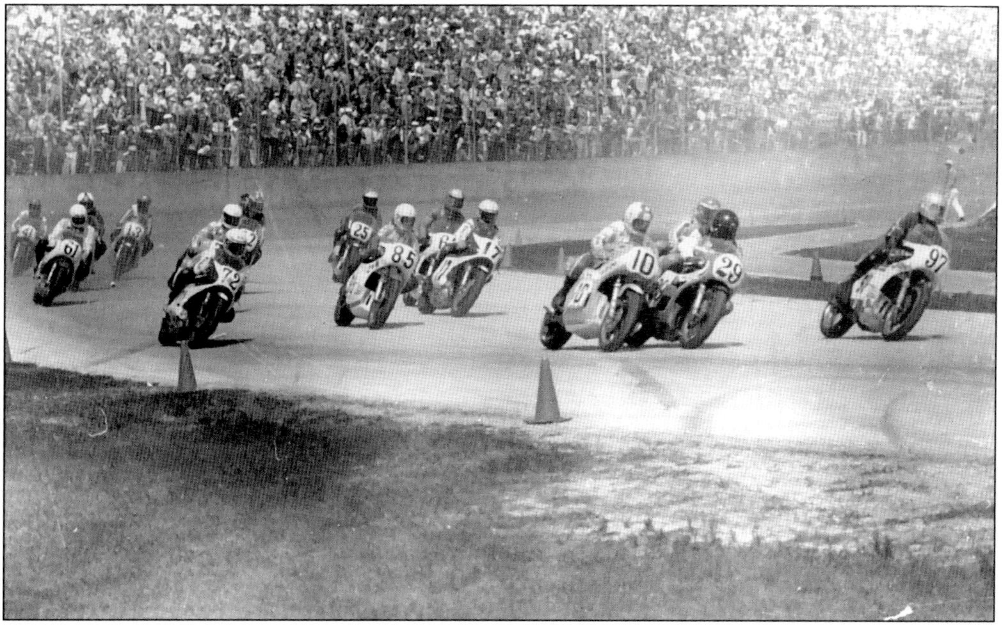

Bike Week Motorcycle Races, March 1975. Who is going to lead the pack from this tight start in turn one? The most skilled rider with the fastest machine, if he has good luck and can avoid an accident. That's what determines the winner! This is true with all of the competitive events during Bike Week at Daytona, which is held annually. (Courtesy of John Gontner.)

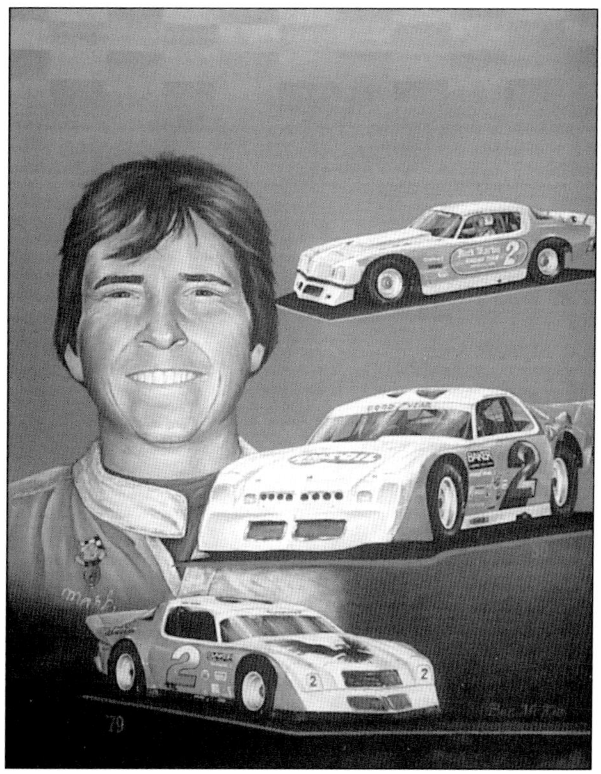

Mark Martin with his Race Cars from 1978, 1979, and 1980. A native of Batesville, Arkansas, now residing in Daytona Beach, he has finished high in the Winston Cup points standing since 1989. Martin is probably the most professional, levelheaded driver on the NASCAR circuit and is well liked by the fans. The above image is a painting of Martin and his race cars. (Courtesy of Buz McKim.)

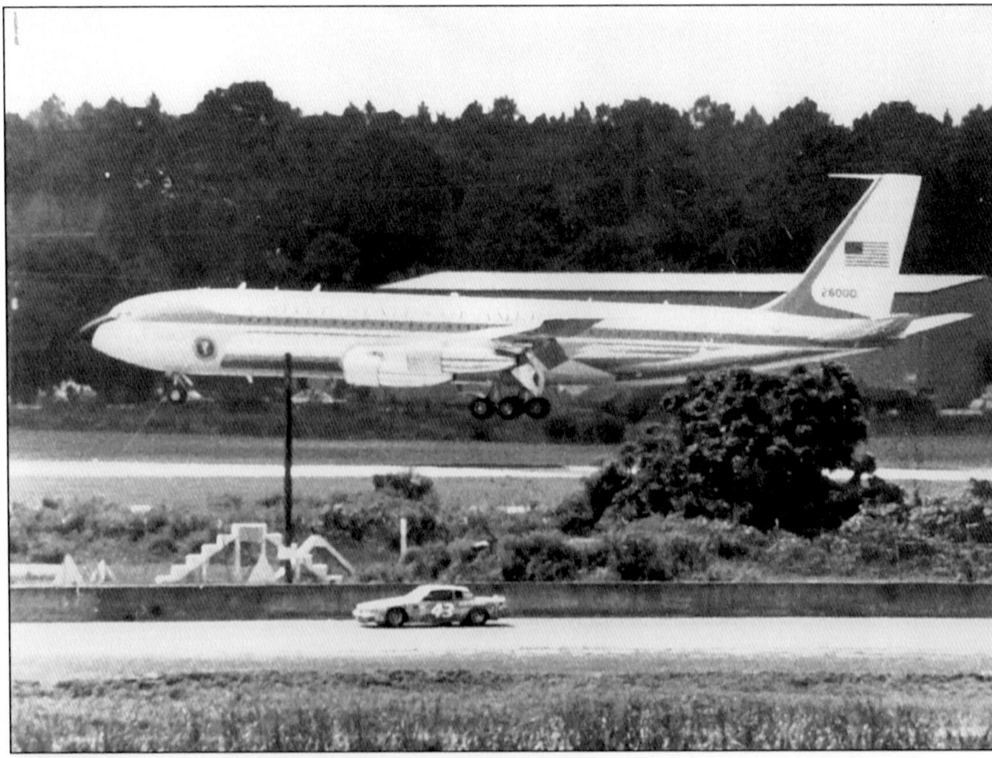

RICHARD PETTY (#43) ON THE BACKSTRETCH, JULY 4, 1984. Petty is pictured with Air Force One, which is landing with President Ronald Reagan on board. (Courtesy of John Gontner.)

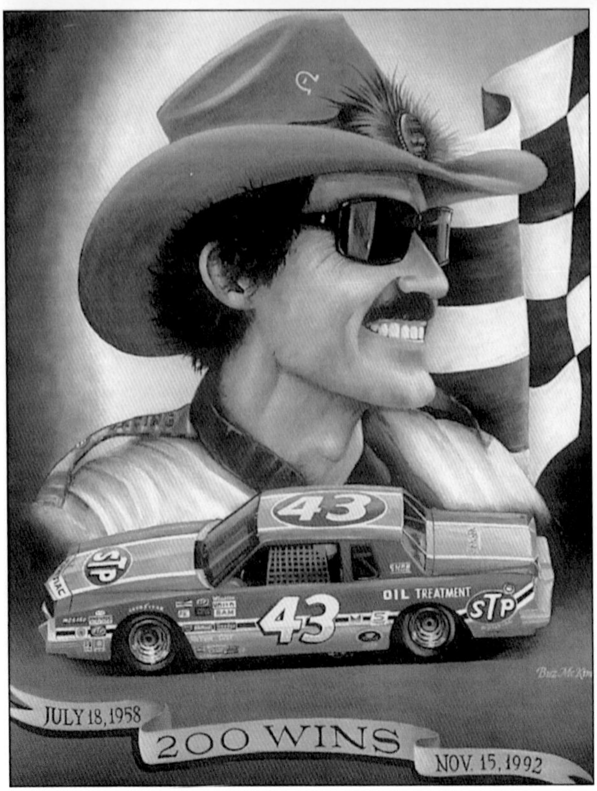

RICHARD PETTY, "THE KING," 1992. The City of Daytona Beach honored Petty for his contributions to auto racing by naming a street for him, which leads to the speedway. Petty is recognized as one of the most outstanding race drivers of all time. The above image is a painting of Richard Petty and his car. (Courtesy of Buz McKim.)

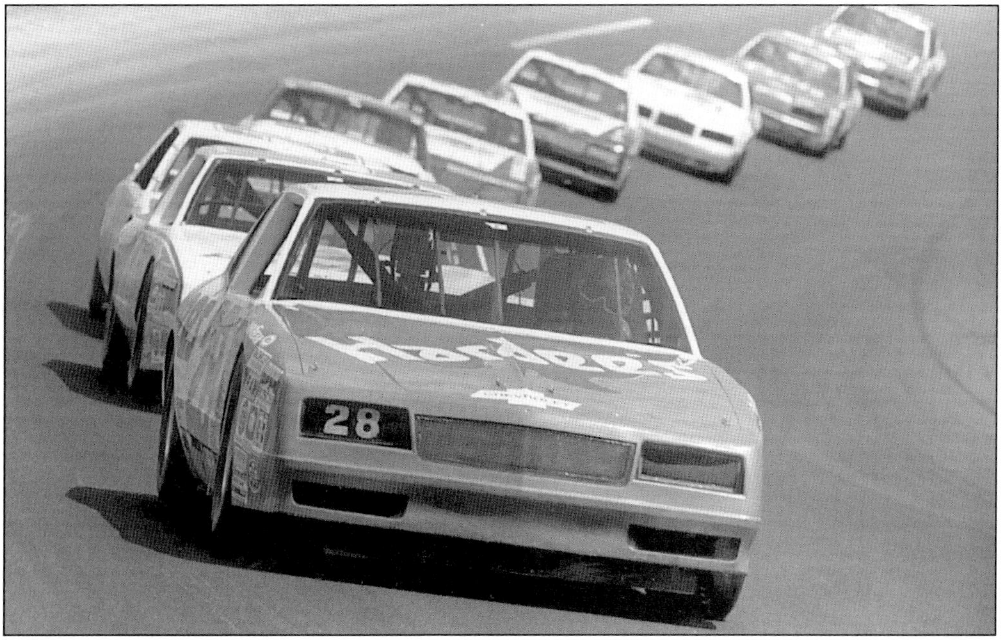

DAYTONA 500, SPEED WEEKS, 1994. Cale Yarborough (#28) speeds through turn four. A longtime favorite of the fans, he won the Daytona 500 in 1968, 1977, 1983, and 1984. Sterling Marlin won this 1994 race. (Courtesy of ISC Archives.)

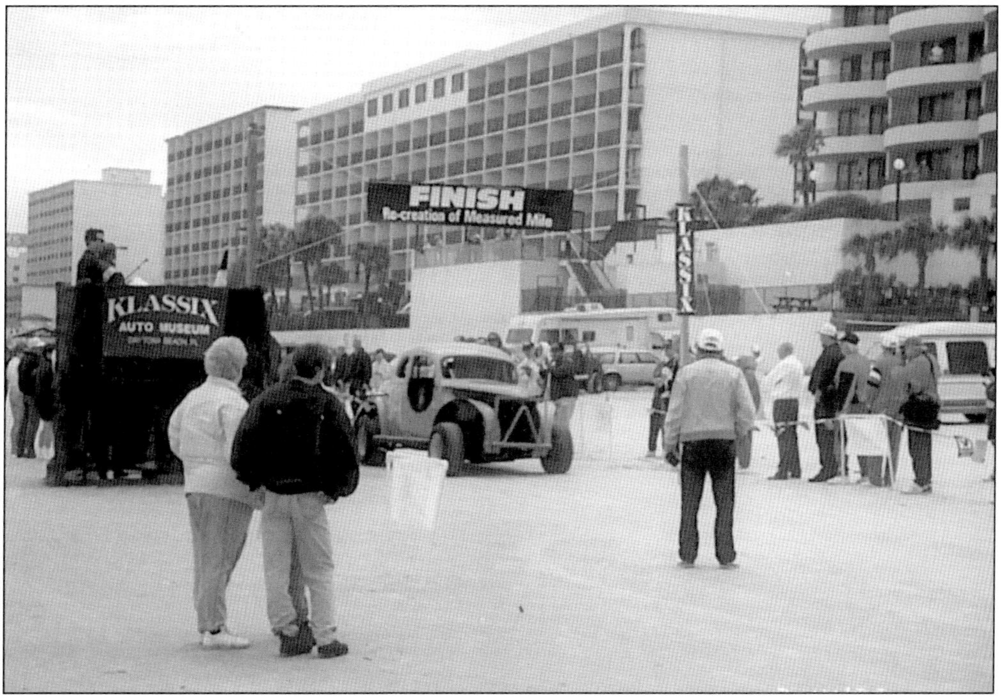

THE BANNER INDICATING THE FORMER SITE OF THE FINISH LINE FOR THE MEASURED MILE, 1995. Officials can be seen preparing for a fast finish of the old classic cars. This event gave classic car enthusiasts a chance to bring their cars back to the beach for the feel of racing on the sand. (Courtesy of Port Orange Historical Trust.)

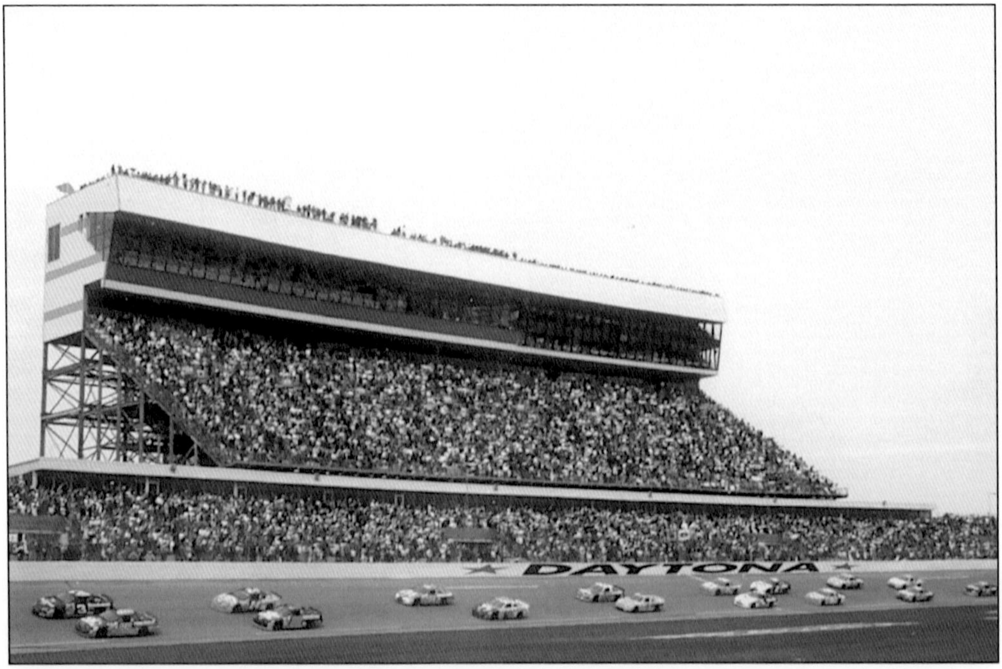

DAYTONA 500, SPEED WEEKS, 1996. Dale Jarrett (#88) and Dale Earnhardt Sr. (#3) are both pushing with all their might to cross the finish line first. Jarrett nosed out Earnhardt for the win and rode into Victory Circle. (Courtesy of ISC Archives.)

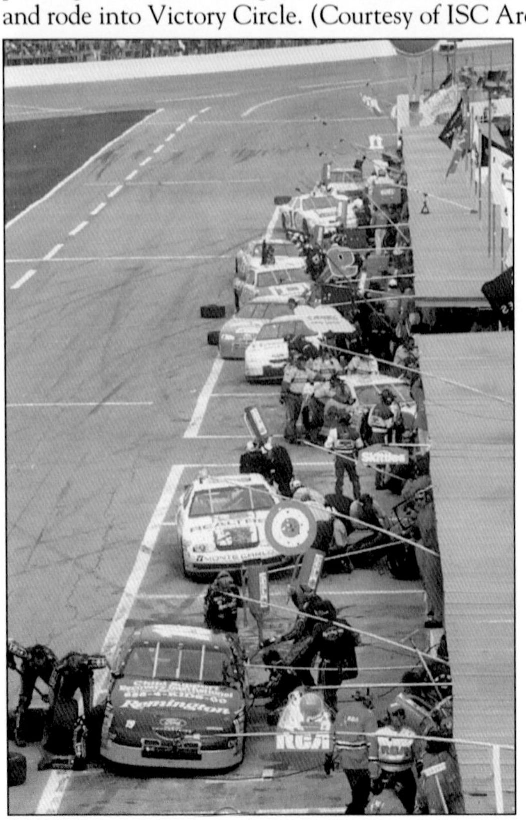

DAYTONA 500, SPEED WEEKS, ACTION IN THE PIT AREA, 1996. A car comes in during the race for a quick tire change, fuel, and repairs. These are tense moments when every second counts. The race could be won, or lost, in the pits! (Courtesy of ISC Archives.)

Mark Martin, International Race of Champions (IROC). Martin is seen here with his 1994, 1996, and 1997 race cars. Martin makes his home in Daytona Beach, Florida and races in many of the NASCAR events throughout the United States. He is an outstanding professional racer who is respected by his associates and fans. The above image is an artist's rendering of Martin and his race cars. (Courtesy of Buz McKim.)

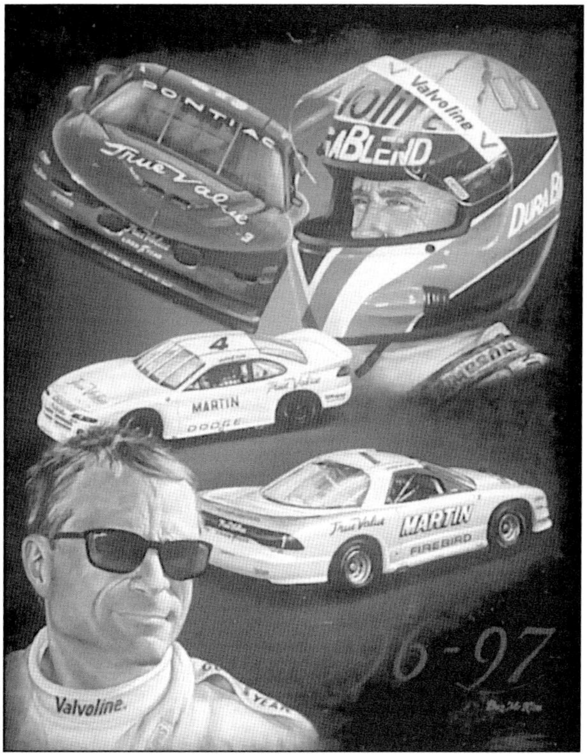

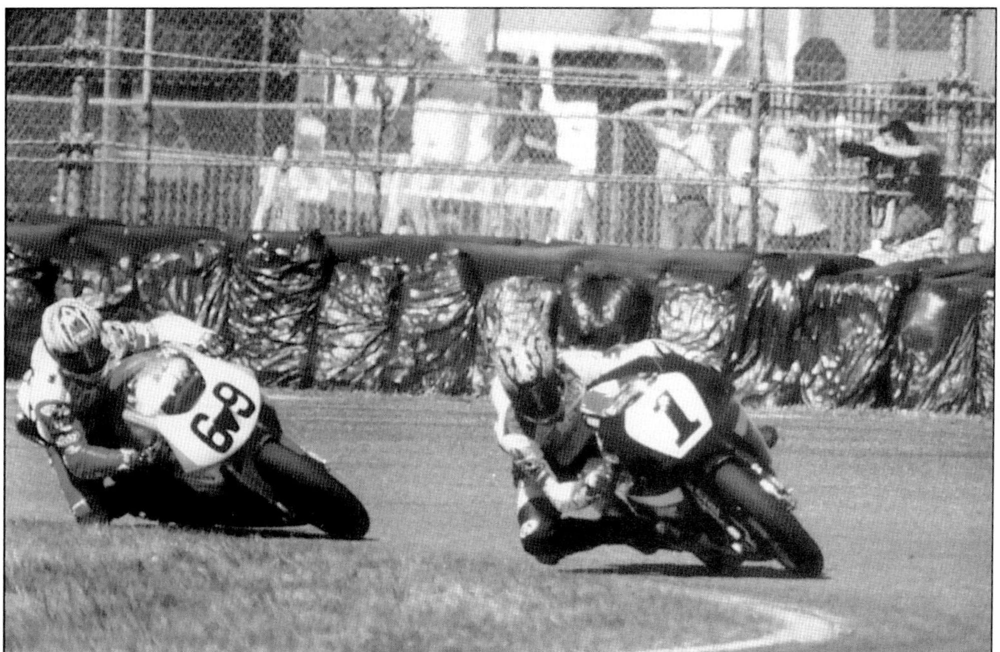

Qualifying Races for Bike Week, 1998. Motorcycle races have been held in Daytona Beach since 1937, sanctioned by the American Motorcycle Association (AMA). Several different divisions of bike races are held during Bike Week, which allows for a variety of competitions. (Courtesy of Russ Atwell.)

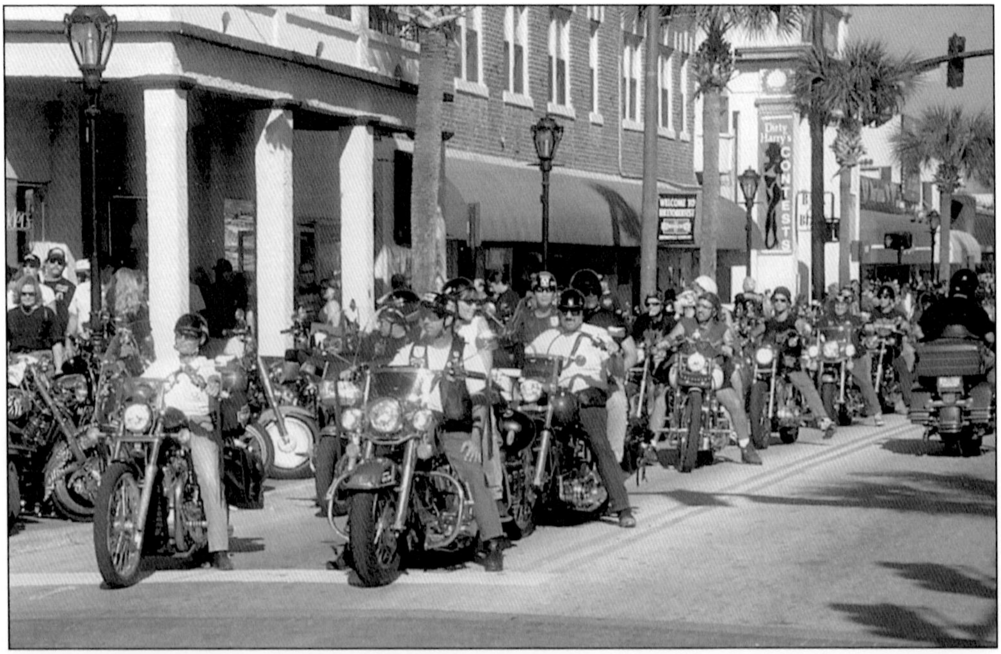

Biketoberfest, Main Street, 1998. Each October, motorcyclists gather in Daytona for the Biketoberfest events. Many bikers like to ride the 30-mile loop to their favorite taverns to socialize with other bike enthusiasts. Some of the more popular places are The Last Resort, Sopotnick's Cabbage Patch Inn (where coleslaw wrestling events take place with two women in a ring throwing coleslaw), The Boothill Saloon, and The Iron Horse Saloon. Many of the visitors prefer this type of entertainment over the actual speed events. (Courtesy of Russ Atwell.)

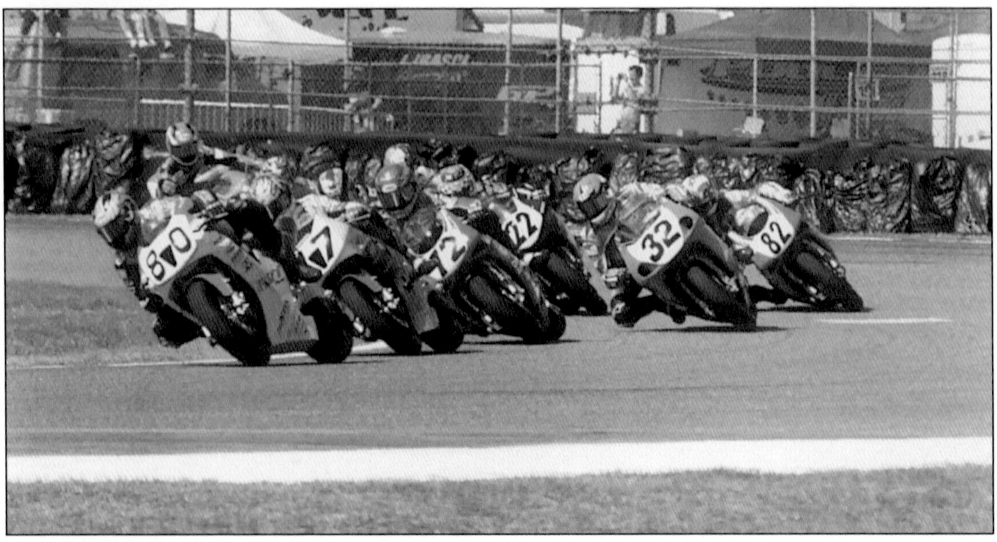

Bike Week Qualifying Event, 1999. Motorcycle racers come to Daytona from all over the world to compete in the Daytona 200 and other special racing events. Beach racing is a thing of the past and races are now held annually at the Daytona Beach International Speedway. This modern facility provides a safe, controlled environment for the riders as well as the fans. (Courtesy of Russ Atwell.)

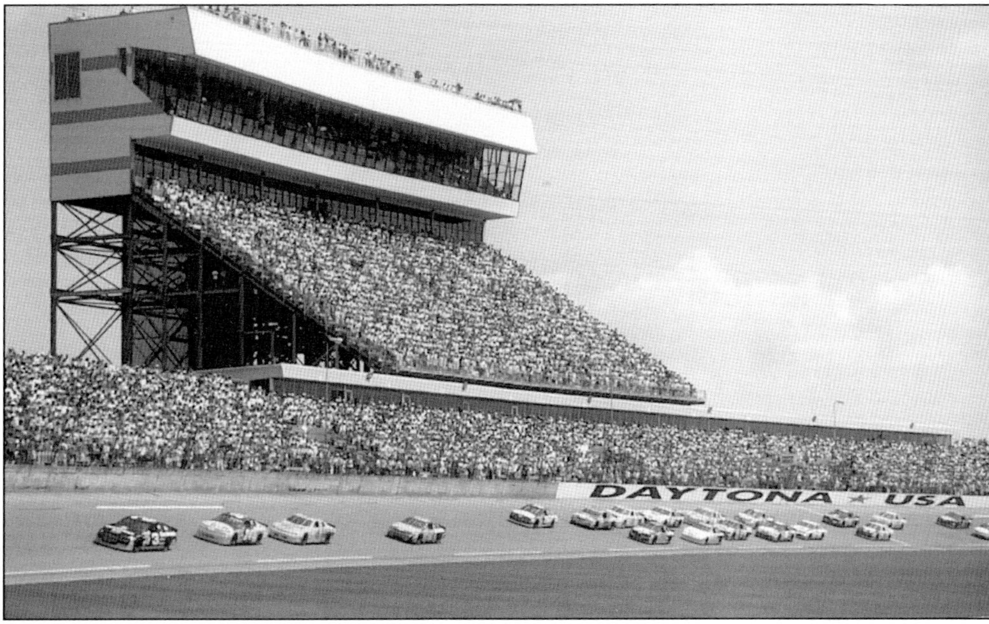

WINSTON TOWER, DAYTONA INTERNATIONAL SPEEDWAY, 2000. One of the main features of the speedway is the Winston Tower where VIPs and the press gather for the Daytona 500 in February and the Pepsi 400 in July. (Courtesy of ISC Archives.)

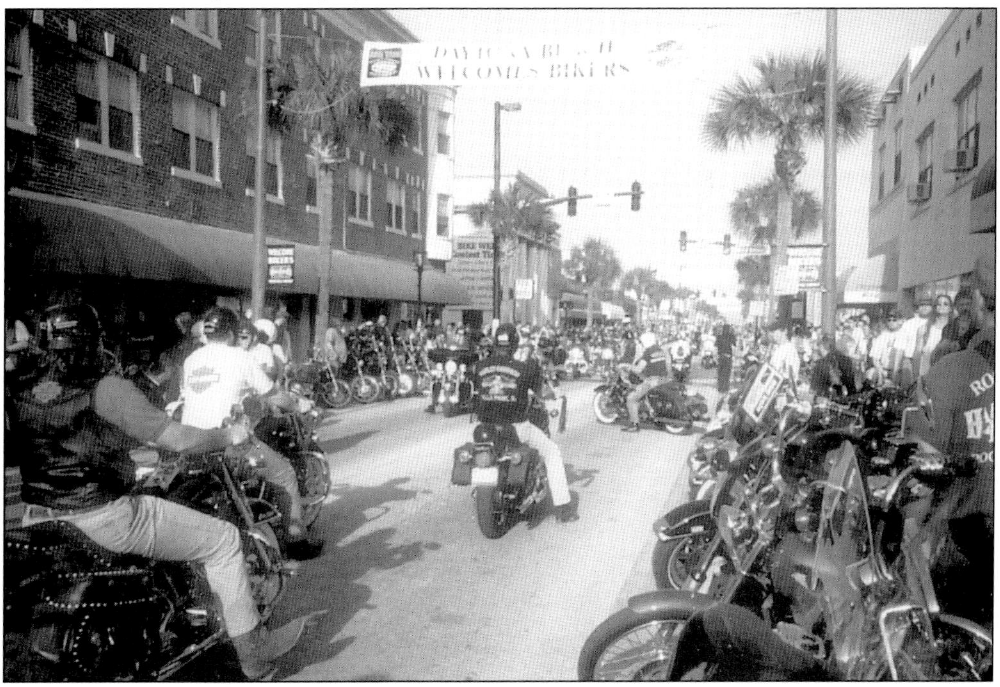

BIKE WEEK, DAYTONA BEACH, 2000. Thousands come here each year to see the events and the Daytona 200 Motorcycle Race at the speedway. The most highly sought after parking places are on Main Street where spectators stroll the sidewalks to look over these magnificent machines. Many bike riders are very creative and innovative in adding accessories to their motorcycles. (Courtesy of Russ Atwell.)

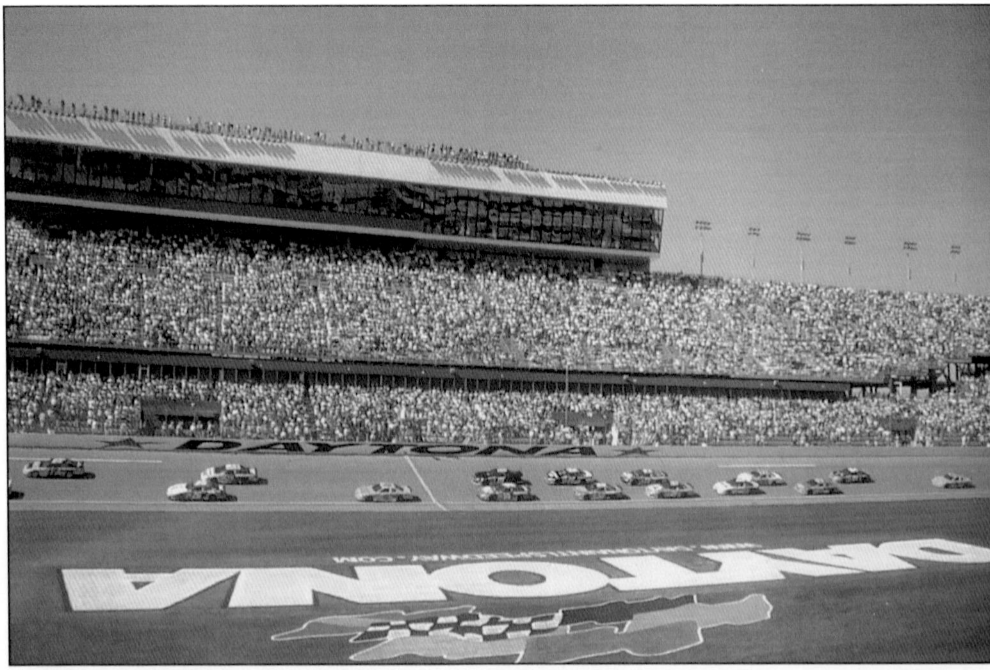

International Speedway, 2000. The START/FINISH Line is visible, as are spotters on the roof of the Winston Tower, and the press suites can be seen in the upper level. Among the many drivers in this race are Jeff Gordon, the late Dale Earnhardt Sr., Dale Jarrett, Rusty Wallace, and Mark Martin. Dale Earnhardt Sr. was killed in a crash on February 18, 2001, during the Daytona 500 Race. (Courtesy of ISC Archives.)

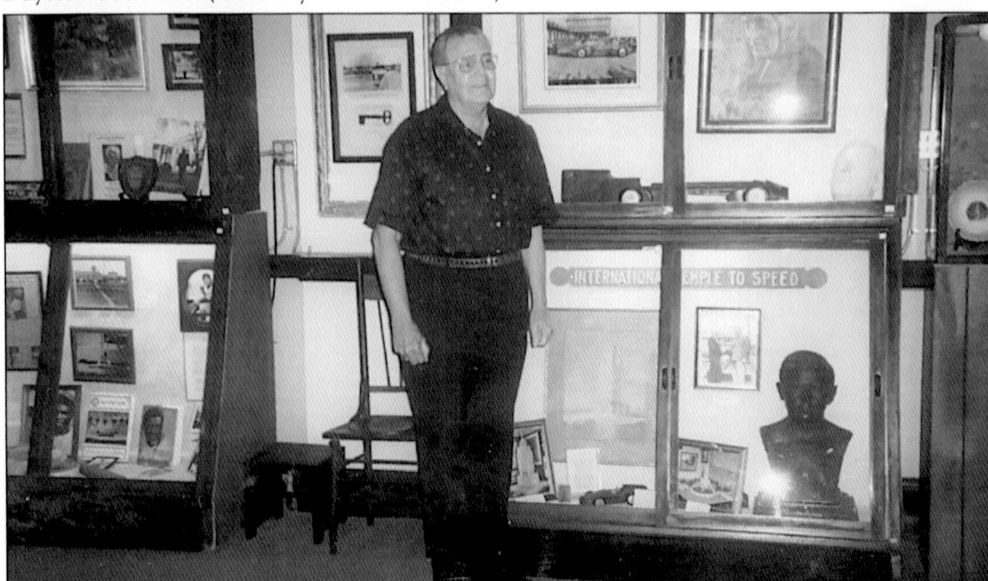

Halifax Historical Society Museum, 2002. This photo is of a special racing exhibit displayed at the museum for the February Speed Weeks. The display includes a portrait of Sir Malcolm Campbell and a model of his famous *Bluebird V*. The author of this book is standing in front of the outstanding display. (Courtesy of Halifax Historical Society.)

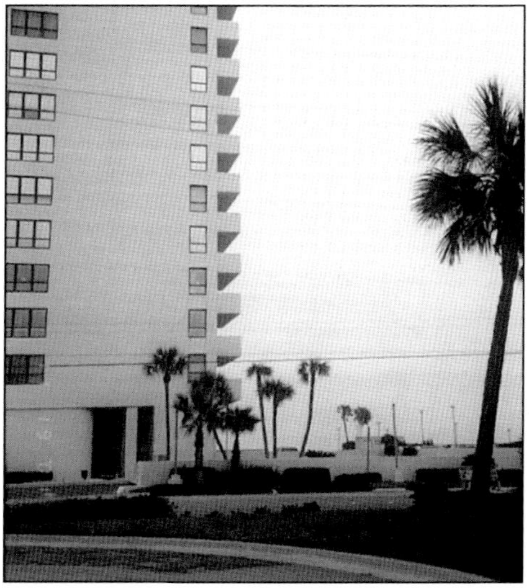

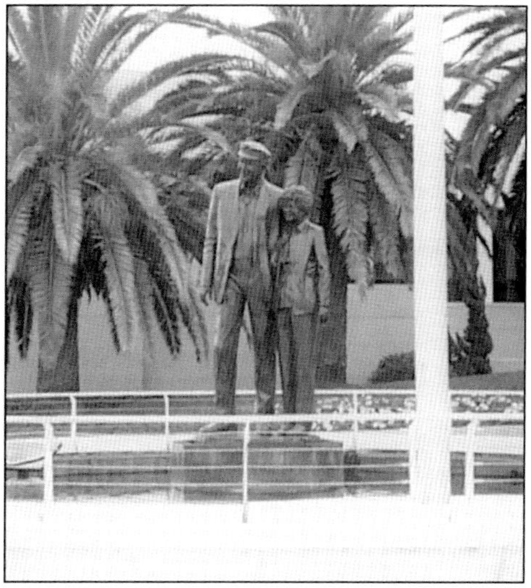

(LEFT) SITE OF THE FORMER 3.2-MILE ROAD/BEACH COURSE, NORTH TURN. The course was here from 1936 to 1947; this is how it looks today. The luxurious Oceans Five condominium, at 2987 South Atlantic Avenue, Daytona Beach Shores, stands near the site of the former North Turn. It is also near the site of the north entrance for the historic Measured Mile. The bleachers from the speed trials, which stood on the beach, were moved to accommodate the North Turn in 1936. Among the first drivers to race on this course was the young Bill France Sr., placing fifth in the March 8, 1936 race. (Courtesy of Cardwell Family Collection.)

(RIGHT) WILLIAM "BIG BILL" FRANCE SR. AND ANNE "ANNIE B" FRANCE MEMORIAL, 2002. From a garage and filling station to the mammoth International Speedway at Daytona, France's vision became a reality. His leadership and organization of NASCAR with national speedway events each year is a testament of the American Dream. The legacy lives on with their family, who continue the tradition and growth of the International Speedway Corporation, Daytona USA, and NASCAR. (Courtesy of Cardwell Family Collection.)

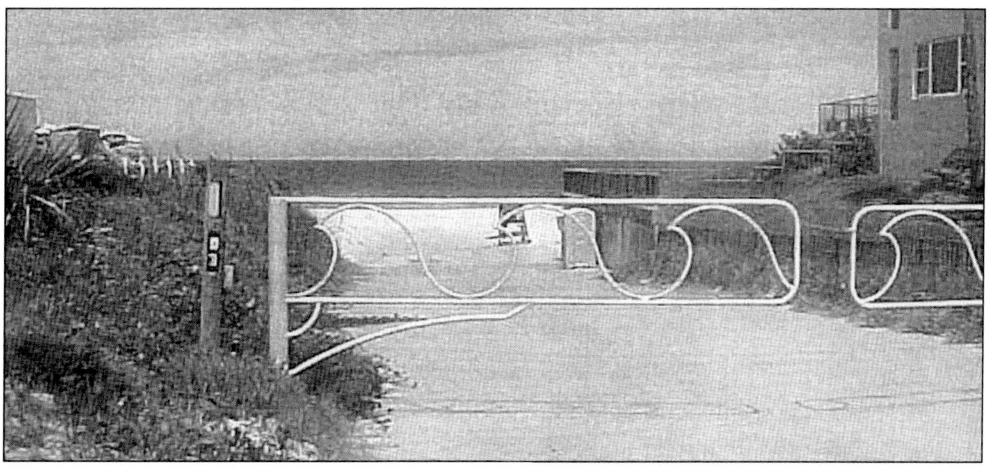

SITE OF THE FORMER 4.1-MILE ROAD/BEACH COURSE, NORTH TURN. It is hard to believe that from 1948 to 1958 thousands of race fans gathered here, in the grandstands, to view Modified, Stock, Motorcycle, and Grand National Races. Cars came into the turn, sliding sideways, slinging dust, sand, shell, and marl into the stands. Motorcycles made the turns with the rider's left leg extended at an angle to stabilize the bike and prevent them from losing control, as these banked turns were unpaved at the time. (Courtesy of Paul Sexton.)

At the time of the new International Speedway opening in 1959, distinct differences in provisions for health and safety were evident. On the old courses, spectators were expected to treat themselves for scratches, sunburns, etc. Today, at the new racetrack, there are 8 doctors and 125 emergency workers. The fans get expert help for any condition.

The medical staff does everything possible to protect the drivers. A strict physical examination of all racers is required. Today, the medical facility present at the speedway can handle the most challenging crises, whereas at the old beach races, all that was required was a Red Cross First Aid card for the emergency worker. The equipment is also quite different. At the beach events, the ambulance was really a converted hearse. Today, modern vehicles with trained paramedics handle all urgent cases.

On the beach, volunteer fire departments were utilized, as well as Daytona Beach firemen. Back then, these men were trained to fight fires, but were not trained for treating human casualties. Today, fire and rescue teams are posted at the speedway and are specially trained to handle all accidents, including extricating drivers from burning cars. Modern tow trucks handle disabled vehicles by quickly removing them from the track and severely injured drivers can be airlifted to Halifax Hospital. In the old days, victims were driven, sometimes 10 to 12 bumpy miles, from the beach to the hospital.

Racing evolved on the beach to the point where the beach courses had to be changed. The lack of secondary access roads for removing drivers and cars, the inadequate methods of dispersing and controlling crowds, the lack of restroom facilities and running water, the inadequate parking facilities, the increasing number of new homes and businesses, and the danger of brush fires were all factors indicating that a new raceway needed to be built. The timing was right, and Bill France Sr. and NASCAR promoted and built a modern speedway equaled by none other in the world.

Today, racing is a highly technical business, with finely tuned cars, highly trained drivers, and wealthy backers. This industry proves that with enthusiasm, dedication, and community involvement, the seemingly impossible can be achieved.

Bibliography

Fielden, Greg. *High Speed at Low Tide*. Surfside Beach, South Carolina: The Garfield Press, 1993.

Fitzgerald, T.E. *Volusia County: Past and Present*. Daytona Beach: The Observer Press, 1937.

Florida State Library and Archives.

Halifax Historical Museum and Archives. Halifax Historical Society, Inc.

Hebel, Ianthe Bond. *Centennial History of Volusia County, Florida, 1854–1954*. Daytona Beach: College Publishing Company, 1955.

International Speedway Corporation Archives.

Neely, William. *Daytona U.S.A.* Tucson, Arizona: Aztex Corporation, 1979.

Punnett, Dick. *Racing On The Rim*. Ormond Beach, Florida: Tomoka Press, 1997.

Schene, Michael G. *Hopes, Dreams, and Promises: A History of Volusia County, Florida*. Daytona Beach: The News Journal Corporation, 1976.

Tucker, Tom and Jim Tiller. *Daytona: The Quest for Speed*. Daytona Beach: The News-Journal Corporation, 1994.

Tuthill, William R. *Speed On The Sand*. Daytona Beach: The Museum of Speed, 1969.

United States Library of Congress.